THE
UNLIMITED
SPARKS
OF A
BONFIRE

Molly McCord

D1706549

The Unlimited Sparks of a Bonfire
by Molly McCord
Copyright © 2015 Spirituality University Press
All rights reserved.

Kindle eISBN 978-0-9896045-9-8

Paperback ISBN 978-0-9965680-1-2

Cover design and interior formatting by Starfield Press
www.StarfieldPress.com

Discover more of Molly McCord's books
and offerings at her website:
www.ConsciousCoolChic.com

THE
UNLIMITED
SPARKS
OF A
BONFIRE

Molly McCord

DEDICATION

To J and Oliver,
who have each provided
more blessings
than stars in the sky.

OTHER BOOKS BY MOLLY McCORD

PAPERBACK AND DIGITAL:
The Art of Trapeze: One Woman's Journey of Soaring, Surrendering, and Awakening

The Modern Heroine's Journey of Consciousness

The Thought That Changed My Life Forever

DIGITAL ONLY:
Conscious Messages: Spiritual Wisdom and Inspirations for Awakening

Conscious Thoughts: Powerful Affirmations to Connect with Your Soul's Wisdom

Your Awakening Self: Connect Deeply With Your True Evolving Soul

DIGITAL TRAVEL GUIDE:
Caché Paris: A Guidebook to Discover New Places, Hidden Spaces, and a Favorite Oasis

FREE DIGITAL DOWNLOAD:
Free download at www.ConsciousSoulGrowth.com:
Guided By Your Light: Ridiculously Loving and Celebrating Yourself

CONTENTS

INTRODUCTION

Your LIFE IS NOT random. Nothing is happening to you *just because,* or simply out of the blue, or due to unexplained phenomenon that happened to magically land in front of you because you wore a certain color of shirt on a Tuesday. The Universe is a highly intelligent and dynamic life force that is alive and pulsing with supreme wisdom. And this is where you come in.

You are an intentional existence of energy. You are composed of layers of energies that are constantly *on* as you interact with life and move through your journey. You are a mass of atoms, molecules, DNA, and physical particles that have convalesced in beautiful form to contribute to the experience of humanness. Not only do you exist in physical form, you also exist in energetic form beyond what our limited eyesight can see. Your physicality is actually tiny in comparison to your full energy state. And it is within the vastness of your energy that you tap into the depths of your soul journey.

Your current life is only a fraction of the energies you have experienced as a soul. When viewed from higher consciousness, you open up to the fullness of your soul story and a broader understanding about who you are as a soul, as well as the energies you are experiencing in this incarnation.

You as a soul are composed of many stories, and through your life, the energies of those stories are activated with the intention of guiding you to higher levels of consciousness.

Surely somewhere along your path you have asked yourself: *Why has my life unfolded in this way? Why do I experience certain themes, or repeating patterns, or ongoing relationship dynamics and lessons? Why are some emotions bigger for me, and yet not as prevalent for other people? Why do I carry specific dominant needs that other people in my family do not relate to?*

And on and on the questions can go because once we voyage down the rabbit hole of soul questioning, we often find more areas to seek out and explore.

It is my guiding intention that The Awakening Consciousness Series brings you to more of these answers for yourself. The first book, *The Art of Trapeze* was The Opening to how soul energies are experienced in the present which ultimately create exactly the life experiences we need to ascend to higher levels of consciousness. The second book, *The Modern Heroine's Journey of Consciousness* is The Deepening, which shows how in every lifetime we are guided to embark on a journey that takes us into all aspects of our energies for greater power, knowledge, and soul growth. Now, in this third book, we embark on The Renewal by understanding the multiple layers of soul energies that we are experiencing by going into the heart of their origination.

For example, if you have experienced a theme of betrayal or abandonment in your life, where did that energy begin? If you have felt deep fears around your emotional expression, how did that originate for you as a soul? If you have found yourself locked into many ego battles with others, what is being triggered within you that can be released now? Or perhaps you have noticed a theme in your life around lower female or Masculine relationships that you wish to inject greater consciousness into because you want more authentic connections with other people. Whatever energies and themes may be prevalent for you, you will find greater understanding to them in healing your soul imprints.

What are soul imprints?

Think of your body as being embossed with a stamp. An imprint is left on your skin by the stamp and creates a new design on you. Similar to a tattoo or a permanent marking, soul imprints are energies in your energy field that have been imprinted on you from your soul experiences. Because your energy is so vast and huge, it is likely that you are not consciously aware of all of your soul imprints and the stories connected to them. Part of our free will is in deciding to explore and work with these energies with higher levels of consciousness in order to heal all imprints back to their original expression of love, which comes from God, the Universe, Spirit, and The All That Is.

Soul imprints exist across the full energetic spectrum, from deep fear to grand love. We have lifetimes composed of all types of energies, and therefore, we have multiple types of imprints in our energy fields.

Energy never dies; it simply changes form. When your soul is imprinted with energetic experiences, those energies continue to exist until you consciously transmute them to another expression. As you learn more about your soul's story, you discover themes in your soul imprints to work with and elevate to another expression.

However, what is also fascinating about soul imprints is that you are actually none of these imprints in a permanent sense. You are simply the vessel who is experiencing those energies. They do not ultimately define your essence nor describe your I AM presence. Rather, they are each temporary expressions from soul stories that are available for you to energetically work with and heal to their fullest expression of Love.

Before incarnating, a soul can choose the number of imprints they wish to work with and heal. But what will be the catalyst for this healing? How will you be sure you won't miss those opportunities or "forget" to do the work you intended? The answers to these questions can show up in any number of ways, and it will always be the most perfect catalyst for you.

The Unlimited Sparks of a Bonfire is going to take you on a journey of soul stories and healing soul imprints with the intention of guiding you into more of the power and beauty of your soul's light. As you read these chapters, you may intuitively feel and connect with the energies as part of your own experiences in other incarnations. The themes, situations, and emotions may feel incredibly familiar. Or they may not resonate with you on a personal level, and that's perfect, too. Seven themes are described through each chapter, which you may recognize if you read *The Art of Trapeze*. Then the last chapter connects the full journey of the three books in The Awakening Consciousness Series to provide you with a modern-day understanding of how all of your soul's energy is here now, which is why this is your most powerful lifetime ever.

Ready to go? Our first soul story begins in the French countryside. No passport required to experience this adventure.

FRANCE
{Endurance}

"**N**O! PLEASE, MY DARLING!" She whispered feverishly into the cold night air, grasping onto his dry, hard hand. "Please don't go yet!"

Layers of darkness filled the barren bedroom.

"Stay a bit longer for the children, for us...*s'il vous plait*..."

Her last plea faded down into the soft blanket. Her wide eyes searched eagerly for his in the blackness, struggling to find his gaze, but she only heard his labored breathing. She stretched her body outside of the protective blankets and attempted to reach for his familiar chest, to pull him close, but he turned away as her desperate hand fell down to their bed quilt. The one her mother gave them for their tenth wedding anniversary. The one they made love on nightly. The one place she could always find him after another long day of plowing, milking, and sweating on the farm.

He finally cleared his throat. "I have no choice, Marie. This is my duty and I am needed with the other men."

"But you are needed here just as much, if not more, my love. The children need you. Who will teach Paul about operating this farm? Who will guide Josephine in her studies? Who will support us?"

She withheld mentioning herself, her own needs. She could not reveal how much she needed him if he was set on leaving. She could not add her own layer of vulnerability to this most vulnerable time in the night.

Claude stepped up from the bed and walked firmly out of the bedroom, his rough boots hitting the worn wood planks, forcing them to sink deeper into the earth. As he passed in front of the cold moonlight, his sturdy shadow was broadcast down the hallway.

She knew there had been a growing possibility of Claude actually leaving this time. Talk in the village of the ongoing wars always stirred up the men's desire to fight for their religion. This time, however, the local recruitment rumors had grown louder after the massacre in Paris on St. Bartholomew's Day. Terror spread like relentless vines as villagers gathered in the square to yell about the king's assassination. Claude had gathered his countrymen in their kitchen, the roaring fire no match for their passionate responses, and they shared information they had heard from other villages and messengers. The need to protect their homes and farms was continually threatened as violence from Paris spread to the countryside; they could not stand by and watch the destruction continue. Claude had banged his fist on the wood table regularly as their voices rose with anger, fear, plans.

Even in the countryside where they were poor and simple and the harvest was declining, Marie always felt they were lucky and blessed as a family. Claude's father had gifted them with the livestock and land when he died four years ago, so she always believed they must be looked over by God. Surely they would always be provided for no matter what came their way. As she tossed corn to the chickens every morning, her fingers scraping the near emptiness inside the feed bag, Marie silently spoke to God about their predicament and asked for His guidance and protection. She deeply feared her husband would be taken from her. She deeply feared the irreversible changes that were flooding her beloved country. Their son, Paul, returned home daily from school with new questions about Calvinists and why they were destroying the country. Young Josephine wanted to know why the king was a bad man. The children did not even understand their own questions; they simply repeated what their teacher said.

Marie grabbed her favorite wool shawl, covering her thin shoulders, and followed Claude's shadow out of the bedroom. He was stubborn, defiant, and proud; she already knew his decision was made. Claude had always desired to be a soldier since the ending of the First War nearly ten years ago, especially when his school mates shared victorious stories they had heard from their fathers. He silently yearned for the pride, the honor, the fierceness of fighting for France's religion, and to be known as a strong man for his beliefs.

She watched helplessly as Claude moved around the kitchen briskly, grabbing a few essentials for his pack. He was too preoccupied to look up to her eyes.

"We are meeting at Monsieur Bernard's home and leaving before the sun rises. We must get on the road under the guise of night." His words whispered through the main room, yet Marie heard a stir in the children's room; Paul had always been a light sleeper.

"I will be back as soon as I can, of course, but I do not know when that will be."

He stopped moving and finally conjured up the courage to look at her. Finally saw the terror in her eyes, yet the strength in her posture. Noticed the tightness in her mouth, but the upward tilt of her chin. Observed the shaking in her shoulders, but the sturdiness in her legs. Marie, his Marie, was always the strongest woman he had ever met. Since she had moved to the village with her mother after her father died, she had always challenged him to be better, to do more. She was the only girl who raced him to the fence line, her dress gusting behind her. The only girl who mischievously told him he was not good enough for her so he would understand her value. The only girl who questioned his thoughts when other women had no idea what their husbands were thinking. Marie had always told him "*non*" before she ever answered "*oui*."

As teenagers, Claude would stop by her house on the far side of the village, even after long hours of grueling farm work, just to see her blue eyes squint when she smiled. He would knock on the door and ask if she was available, to which she would respond "*non.*" Then, after laughing loudly, she would throw the door open widely and run down to the river bank, tossing her shoes into the grass. She would disappear along the curves of the water's edge. Claude followed her tiny footprints through the mud as the gushing waves rolled by, the late summer sun blinding his eyes, until he finally arrived at a hidden inlet. The river curved to the right, but a quiet lagoon appeared to the left. When Marie saw him, she smiled and pointed to a nearby tree: a swing dangled on a strong branch extending above the water. They played and kissed and fished and dreamed and laughed in this secret location, their secret location, until long after Paul was born.

Marie was the only woman he had ever desired. Their wedding day was simple; they exchanged vows on the riverbank in front of a small group of people, a pure white daisy behind her left ear and a steady gaze in his eyes. Little Paul arrived eight months later. Whenever villagers raised an eyebrow about the baby, Claude explained how it was a premature birth, knowing no one else would understand their passion for each other or what they experienced on the quilt, their only wedding gift. The bed quilt captured their panting and whispers as they made love, and became their safe haven as the waves of life came through. They curled under it when the winter winds picked up and the wood stove's fire unexpectedly blew out. They held each other under it when the second pregnancy abruptly ended. They promised to love each other until eternity in the comforts of its domain. The bed quilt wrapped them up in a life bound together and returned them to each other nightly.

But now he must stay focused on his duty. The country needed him to be strong and he knew this was his calling. Ever since he was a young boy, Claude knew he must fight for what he believed in. He felt his pack growing heavier as Marie stared back at him with one final silent plea, her eyes steady and desperate. Claude moved towards her, standing in front of his wife in two broad steps, and yet maintaining a restrained distance.

"*S'il vous plait,*" she whispered intently into the hollow space between them. "Choose us over the country." She closed her eyes as she received his kiss on her cheek and inhaled his familiar musk.

Claude then stepped back, as if reminding himself he could not get too close to love when war was on the horizon. He threw his bag, loaded down with a knife, beans, tomatoes, and his coat over his left shoulder, and gazed back at his Marie.

"It is time." He reached for the door, and upon opening it, a sliver of light slipped into the bleak room. Then a wild gust of wind moved into the empty space and Marie felt her breath catch on the cold air, her throat clamping tight. He moved quickly through the opening, and in a silent moment, his shadow disappeared with the evaporating moonlight.

"*Maman?*" Two small hands arrived on her paralyzed hips.

"*Oui, mon cherie?*" She moved her right hand down to touch the small fingers, her left hand still clutching the shawl directly over her heart.

"Where did Papa go?" The sweet voice was high-pitched with curiosity, knowing his father was typically a hard sleeper who could never be disturbed in the middle of the night.

"He has made an important choice for our country, so he is being brave tonight. But you must go back to sleep now, *mon cherie.* Isn't it someone's birthday in the morning?"

The small hands tugged at her nightgown with excitement. "*Oui!* We will celebrate with my favorite pastries. I hope Papa will be back in time to celebrate my birthday with us. *Bon nuit, Maman!*"

His feet shuffled like angel's wings back to the top bunk bed; the complete opposite sound of his father's steps that always echoed throughout the whole farm.

As Claude's boots hit the end of their gravel driveway, he reached into the depths of his front pocket. A soft square of fabric was nestled into the bottom corner; its texture familiar and warm as if he still heard their whispers, laughter, and love under its protective covering. He silently committed to carrying this part of their life together with him everywhere.

Marie stared at the door for awhile longer, silent with shock, trying to feel her heart as it beat soft and slow in her chest. She could not return to the bed, to the quilt, to the passionless darkness. Her small frame sunk into the small chair by the wood stove as she allowed the night to carry her away to anywhere else.

She awoke with confusion as the rooster crowed before sunrise. Her shawl had slipped off one shoulder; her legs were stiff from being tightly wound together. Marie steeled herself for the morning routine by refusing to think about the previous night. It was the first time she had ever slept in the house without her husband.

She stood up slowly, allowing her legs to fully circulate blood, and grabbed her long wool coat, the one with the worn lapel and rugged edges. Marie headed outside to complete the morning chores: feed the chickens, rotate hay for the cows, check on water for the horses. Paul and Josephine would tend to the dogs, cats, and pigs when they awoke. Then she put a kettle on the stove for the morning meal and began preparing Paul's favorite pastry, knowing he would devour three instead of his normal two. Her heart panged as she looked at the worn stool that Claude occupied for every meal. She kept her wool coat on all morning, allowing it to cover up her shawl and nightgown so the children couldn't see that she was still in her bed clothes, nor observe the aching in her heart. She couldn't return to the bedroom yet.

As the days extended into weeks, and the weeks turned into months, Marie heard updates and stories from neighbors about the many wars. Political changes were supposedly sweeping through the country, and many people were highly suspicious of one another in town. Religion was a passionate topic, with men arguing over "*la liberte*" in cafes and on the street. As she went about her daily needs, she realized no one looked her in the eyes when she went into town for supplies or brought the cow's milk to trade at market. She felt a hushed silence, as if they knew something about Claude and the other men, but she kept her head high and her thoughts strong. Claude loved her, Paul, and Josephine deeply, and would return in time; of this, she was certain. In the meantime, she focused on the farm, supported the children with school work, and tended to her small life with pride. She wanted their home to be normal for Claude when he came home. At least that was under her control.

As Paul became a man with a deep voice and Josephine blossomed into a ripe young woman, a mounting grief slowly crept into Marie's heart. Her posture became less erect; her chin tilted down; her shoulders hunched over. The sadness of losing her husband was a constant silent weight in her heart. Her chest heaved with deeper inhales and slower exhales with each passing year. The silent fears came in during the middle of the night when she was softer and more vulnerable, enveloping her with despair. She cried deep into the pillows, releasing her anguish and pain and loss. The cherished bed quilt had long ago been stored in the closet, as it was now only a representation of all she had lost. On the hardest nights, she would fall asleep exhausted and wake up with a start, calling his name in the dark, believing she saw his shadow move through the house. By the morning, she was once again fortified with strength to face the day ahead and put on a brave front for those who needed her. The war was making them both soldiers.

Then one day at market, while Marie was trying desperately to trade anything she had for bread, a neighbor rushed up to her with alarm.

"*Excusez-moi, Madame Baron*?"

"*Oui, Madame.*" Marie hoped this was a purchaser for her milk. The July sunshine had brought intense heat early in the day and the market day was painfully slow.

The woman spoke in a hushed manner, her head spinning to watch if anyone was approaching. "There are visitors asking for you in town, and I have not seen them before. Perhaps they know about Monsieur Baron?"

Marie stood up straight and looked the woman directly in the eye, trying to discern if this was a cruel joke. Marie glanced down the road, following the woman's feverish gaze with anticipation.

"The person inquiring about you is a young lady, tall -" the woman raised both her hands to describe height "- and carrying a basket." She stepped away from Marie and looked down the street again.

"Ah, here she comes, Madame!" Then she ran away from Marie, her curls bouncing high, and the neighbor walked up to the tall woman to point towards Marie.

Marie inhaled sharply with slight dread. The stranger wore a simple blue top and a long flowing red skirt that appeared to be custom made for her size. She approached Marie with calm hesitation.

"*Bonjour, Madame.* I believe you are the person I have been looking for."

Marie nodded curtly in reply. This stranger was a foot taller than Marie, slender, with long raven hair and deep blue eyes. She only became pretty after looking at her face for a moment, her build too wide and her height a distraction to her kind mannerisms.

"Madame, do you have a moment to speak with me?" Her eyes were silently begging for attention, asking to be heard.

"How can I assist you, Madame? Why are you looking for me?" Marie held the stranger's gaze with strength.

"My name is Naomi, and I was sent here to give you a message. A message from Claude."

Marie's legs wobbled slightly and her eyes blinked faster, but she maintained her posture. Warmth escaped her body as the sun quietly slid behind the clouds. What could this woman possibly know about her husband?

"Where is he? Where is my husband?" Marie's voice was

demanding and proud. If anyone was going to tell her something about her Claude, she wanted the information quickly. She would not be anybody's fool, nor play any games.

"Madame, I believe it is best that we speak in private." Naomi eyes gazed at her steadily, suggesting she knew important things.

"Very well. You may come to the house with me. The market is slow today due to the heat, anyways."

Marie turned and called to Josephine who was sitting in the shade.

"Yes, Mama?"

"We are closing up early today, Josephine. Please help me gather up our supplies." Josephine began packing up their unsold milk, looking curiously at the tall woman who silently watched their every movement.

And then, as Marie slowly raised her head to look around the market before heading back to the farm, she saw him. Walking down the road towards her. She recognized his gait, the swing of his arms. She recognized the coat in his arms, the one he wore nearly every winter as he tended to the cows and chopped wood and plowed snow from the entry way. She saw the outline of his shoulders and the stomp of his feet in the gravel. She watched as he approached her, the sun hitting the top of his head and her weary eyes squinting as if it were a mirage. Then this miniature replica of Claude ran up to the tall woman, his dark eyes laughing, as he proudly showed her a little kitten he had found in the village and wrapped in his coat.

Marie could only stare in silent shock at this young boy in front of her, no older than eight, and his striking resemblance to the man who had left her years ago. Then she collapsed to the ground. All of her strength melted into the gravel; her heart no longer able to sustain any courage. She felt the air move out of her lungs.

"Mama! Mama!" Josephine ran over, her long brown hair swinging wildly. "Are you okay? What is it?"

Josephine had been too young to know her father's

physique or to even recognize him in a crowd. She had no idea what had triggered her mother's physical meltdown. Naomi and the boy rushed over to assist as well, but Marie pushed them away. She pushed them all away as the sun crept back behind another set of passing clouds and a new type of intense heat bore down on Marie's face. She watched as the young boy held the small black cat in the nook of his arm, tenderly stroking its head. An unaware smile sat on his precious face.

"It must have been a heat stroke. I am fine, please excuse me. I probably need some water."

Marie stood up slowly, Josephine assisting with her left arm, and made her way to a shady spot under a tree. A cool breeze ran across her face as she sat down again and her hand gripped at the earth, looking for support and grounding.

"Mama, what can I do? Should I return our supplies to the house by myself?" Josephine's blue eyes were searching her face for answers, looking to understand if her mother was going to be okay.

"Yes, please take what you can back to the house, my dear. Let me rest for a moment, and then I will join you."

Naomi and the young boy stood awkwardly in front of them, unsure of what to do next. Marie took a deep breath, then said to Naomi, "What is the boy's name, please?"

"His name is Luis, Madame." She looked at the boy when she spoke, not at Marie.

"Luis, please help my daughter Josephine move these supplies to our farm." She paused to look at Naomi. "Is this okay with you? It is not far and the job is better for two people."

"Yes, Madame, that is fine."

Naomi leaned over and directed Luis with the tasks that needed to be done. He tenderly held the kitten the whole time, then placed it inside a box to carry to the farm. In a few moments, both children were on their way back to the farm as if they had walked the road together a hundred times before.

"He is seven years old, Madame." Naomi sat down on the grass, hesitant to be too close.

Marie simply stared at a speck on the horizon.

Naomi continued. "We live in a city in the French Alps called Lyon. I am a seamstress and this is the furthest from home I've ever been." Naomi played with a loose thread on her top, then her hands dropped down to the cold grass. Silent discomfort surrounded them.

Finally, after another full breeze passed over her face, and a distant bird finished its song, Marie whispered loudly, "Where is Claude, Madame?" Her voice caught in her throat as she said his name out loud for the first time in years.

Naomi looked at Marie, trying to catch her eyes, but Marie stared straight ahead with pride.

"Claude was seriously injured in one of the wars, Madame. He lost the use of his left leg." Marie bit her inner lip as Naomi continued. "He also suffered amnesia, and while he was in the hospital in Lyon, he did not remember his previous life. I met him through my brother who was in the same hospital; their beds were across from each other."

She glanced down at the grass again, twirling a blade in her hand. "They were considered to be the lucky ones because they were alive."

Marie blinked back tears as she imagined her strong, noble husband lying wounded in a stale hospital bed, unable to move or stretch as he had done all of his life. She flashed back to watching him lead the stubborn cows down the field, and how he rode and trained his favorite horse, Fierté, for hours before twilight. It was not possible for him to be stationary.

"He left the hospital after nine months, and by then we had fallen in love. I tried to discover more about his previous life throughout the months, but he could not even recall his own name. I tried to guess his name and help him remember it. When I offered Paul as a possibility, he said that sounded familiar."

Marie flinched. A tightness took over her heart.

"We built a life together in Lyon, Madame." Naomi spoke with distance, like it was a lifetime ago. They sat in silence, allowing the sun to appear on the dirt in front of them.

Marie asked, "But what could he do if he was injured in the war?"

"We lived in the city after Luis was born, but then we moved out to the countryside because Paul - I mean, Claude - said he needed more fresh air and quiet. My father owned a small vineyard that provided us with a place to stay. Claude had space to practice walking again with crutches. I drove into the city for work a few times a week."

Marie felt an inner smile. Claude always detested going into a big town for anything. He never wanted to sell milk, or get supplies for the farm, or gather in the town square. He would rush back to the farm, insisting once again on self-reliance, and this was why he wanted the men to gather in their kitchen when planning to be soldiers. He believed everything they needed could be found or grown on their own property.

"But then, his leg became infected and he developed pneumonia. The fever got to his head in only a few weeks." Naomi paused. "And that's when he started calling me Marie and asking about Paul and Josephine."

Marie's eyes filled with tears and her chest inhaled deeply. He did remember her; he did remember their life together. A slow heaving began to move from her stomach, to her lungs, to her heart.

"It was as if the fever returned him to his previous life, finally, and he started talking all the time about a farm, and a young woman, and a river bank, and a rope swing hanging from a tree... He was off in this other world."

Marie turned her head away and wiped silent tears from her cheek. Everything around her became blurred with a soft rain.

"And that is when I finally heard his real name - Claude - and he remembered the name of this village. He kept calling me Marie, and I stopped correcting him because he became angry when I said my name was Naomi. It was like he was rejecting me to my face, as if I could only be Marie to him..." Naomi's voice trailed off.

Both women were lost in her pasts, in a life that no longer existed with this man. Naomi's heart was heavy with her own grief. She reached into her wicker basket and rested her hand inside, feeling the stiff construction.

"He passed away two years ago, Madame, in his sleep. The fever took over his body and he was gone by the morning. Luis and I were devastated, even though we knew it was coming. He kept calling Luis "Paul," which always confused him."

Naomi paused to wipe away a tear. It was devastating to lose the man she loved even though he never really loved her in return because his heart was always with another. She kept trying to forgive him for that. She gathered her next words together warily.

"Claude left a note with this piece of fabric, Madame. That is why I am here. I came to give you both." She never understood why he would hold this square fabric for hours at a time.

From within the wicker basket, Naomi handed Marie a cream and green swatch as the sunlight hit their hands. Marie instinctively raised the fabric up to her nose, desperately trying to inhale his musk, his smile, their life together. Then the bed quilt began to catch her falling tears. She could no longer maintain her posture as the scent of his strength overwhelmed her being.

Naomi placed the note next to Marie on the grass and stood up to give the woman her privacy. She whispered down to her, "I will go find Luis at your farm, Madame." Naomi turned away, and walked alongside the children's footsteps in the dirt, her head down, long skirt swinging with each forthright movement.

The market was nearly empty now as the heat had chased everyone inside. Marie knew curious onlookers had witnessed her exchange with the tall unknown woman, and they were surely the topic of all mid-day conversations. She closed her hands around the bed quilt and looked up to the sky. She always believed God would protect her, but He had not. He had failed her and her family. Her optimism had seeped out of her life over the years, and this was the ultimate affirmation that she had been abandoned. She was completely separate from Him.

After watching a nearby tree branch rise and sink in the sky, she glanced over at the crumbled note. She was both terrified and desperate to read it. After years of not hearing anything at all, this piece of paper held so much power.

She inhaled deeply and reached to open it. Claude always had terrible handwriting. He believed his hands were meant for more important things than pen and paper, so he never practiced his letters in school. But perhaps being bed-ridden had provided him with a revived interest because it was still his unmistakable writing, yet slightly more refined.

My Marie,

My body has failed me but my heart is strong. I lay here hopeless until I think of you. I finally remember you, precious you, after years of forgetting our life together. I thought of you, our family, and our life every day while I was away from home. You kept me strong.

I must confess fighting in the war was a highlight of my rather insignificant life. I stood shoulder to shoulder with other strong men, and we experienced a few victories before a terrible turn of events occurred. I witnessed horrible acts and even worse attributes in men that I will spare you from hearing. Thousands died and I was blessed by God to be alive, even though He took my leg and spared my breath. I was a true soldier, Marie. A true man of honor, pride, and strength with my countrymen. But when I awoke afterwards, I was none of those qualities.

It was through vivid dreams that I recalled my previous life with you. Years have passed now and I do not know if you will ever see these words, but it brings me periods of hope to believe that you will read this. I have practiced writing this letter for a few months now.

As I lay here in this bed, a woman who loves me cares for my body and does her best to tend to my needs. The young boy is strong and smart. Paul would be an excellent older brother for him. I hope both he and Josephine have matured well over the years. They are surely perfect in your care. Both of them remained in my heart and mind as I stood on the battlefields. I hope they can see me as a father with honor and dignity; a man they can be proud of even though I left them behind years ago. I never forgave myself for that, yet I could not think of anything else to do at the time. I hope you can forgive me for my selfishness, yet grant me grace for my mistakes.

My dear Marie, I am sorry I failed you in the end as a husband and father. My time on this earth is not long, and as I return to God to be in His grace, please know that I will still forever meet you at our place by the blessed river.

Always,
Your Claude

Marie read the letter three more times, attempting to stretch every word and every sentence into a deeper connection with him, as tears gently fell down both sides of her face. A silent wind danced around her, lifting her hair and skirt slightly into the air. The village was still completely empty as if she and Claude were the only ones in town.

After all of these years, she finally knew her husband's true story and where life had taken him after he had left her, left them. These insights brought up every emotion possible from the depths of her being as if what she had thought were dormant parts of herself were now alive and burning within her. With a deep inhale, she tucked the quilt swatch into her skirt pocket and stood up to walk home, trusting her feet to somehow carry her forward.

But instead of going back to the house, Marie headed down to the river bank. The path was overgrown, but she knew the way intuitively and traced the familiar curves. She eventually removed her shoes and let her toes sink into the cool chocolate mud. She followed the river to their private lagoon, and saw the tree swing swaying gently over the water, back and forth with a carelessness she hadn't felt in years.

Claude had always grabbed the tree swing with a branch he kept behind the oak tree, pulling it to the shore with ease and a giant smile on his face each time. He loved the adrenaline rush of pushing away from the shore, his strong limbs somehow supported by a single braided rope as he flew over the waves, laughing up into the sky. She had watched him do this so many times that she knew the pace of each jump; by the time she counted to four, he would release his hold on the swing and be soaring through the air for a brief moment before hitting the lagoon's calm surface with a crashing splash. His head would bob up seconds later and he was instantly cleansed every time; the hard days on the farm sank to the bottom and his renewed spirit would guide him back to the shore for the next splash.

Marie stared at the quiet lagoon for a few moments, holding the beloved quilt in her hand, and then started unbuttoning her blouse. She set her top, followed by her skirt, on a cool patch of grass. She went to the oak tree to find the branch that would reel the swing to shore, and her stomach turned with anxiety as she stared out over the glassy landscape. She had never been on the tree swing before. It had always been Claude's favorite thing, and never her preference to try it, no matter how much he pushed her to give it a single jump, just once, just to be free for a few moments in time. She would shake her head "*non*" every time, then yell "*Allez! Allez!*" to his beaming face as he began another attempt.

But now she was a different woman who had been finely shaped and sculpted by life and war; tossed and turned by love and loyalty; pushed and pulled by loss and courage and faith and heart. She already knew what it would be like to feel the crashing splash of shivering water encapsulate her small frame because she had already lived through the roughest possible waves. She had already survived the worst.

In her soft cotton undergarments, with the beaming afternoon sun and distant clouds and hovering oak tree as her only witnesses, she pulled the rough rope to her chest with both hands. The soft piece of quilt was tucked inside the grasp of her right hand. She felt her toes curl down into the softened mud; she intentionally spread each toe apart as far as possible to focus on her feet before the initial jump. The river moved silently out beyond the seclusion of the lagoon, carrying her mind away to memories of other summers and soft kisses and babies and wine and fresh white cheese and quiet evenings of escape. Then a crow cawed inches above her, startling her concentration, and she burst into laughter at her own nerves.

The sunlight glistened off the top of the water, requiring her eyes to squint in retraction, and at just the right second - for one escaping blink in time - she could see Claude on the bank cheering her on, prodding her to go for it. And in her usual defiant tone, she yelled "*non!*" with loud laughter ringing through her throat. She saw him leap up from the mud and rush towards her, his mischievous smile racing at her with both of his arms ready to push her forward.

And that was when she took a running jump out towards the lagoon.

With small hands holding on tight, she ran, ran, ran, and leaped up right before the water could tickle her muddy toes. She instinctively curled her legs around the swing as it soared out above the slow-moving surface, her weight nothing for the oak tree's massive branch as it carried her further over the lagoon. She felt the air swirl through her hair and a rush of wind surrounded her back, her arms, her knees. Marie looked back at the shore for a split second and swore she saw him standing there with one hand shading his eyes, his teeth shining in the sun, his broad shoulders sturdy and strong.

By the count of four, she let go of the braided rope with both hands, and gallantly, wildly, freely tossed the quilt swatch into the air. And in that split second of time, as the wind carried their life away and the water cradled her fall, she let him go.

She let him be all he needed to be. She let him be at peace with his decisions and choices. She let him be the very best husband and father he could have been to them. She allowed him all of the grace and forgiveness and redemption that she knew he deserved to receive. She chose to see how God had always been present in their lives because Claude had been guided to fulfill his dream of being a noble soldier; he had always been that man. He had to do that for himself, and she would choose to allow the wholeness of his life to be perfect for her, too. She would choose to love him even more. She would choose to finally experience the freedom of love.

She felt the immediate surge of water take over her body and soul, the coldness jolting her alive in a whole new way. She had never been fully immersed like this before. She had never felt so connected and surrounded and free all at the same time. She released into the river's embrace.

Her head finally bobbed up to the surface like a cork. She instinctively started the slow paddle back to shore, the water pushing her forward with each stroke. The tree swing was once again moving carelessly in the wind, waiting for the next invitation, almost taunting her with anticipation.

Marie approached the shore and stood up as the water level hit her soft exposed thighs. She turned and looked out towards the river for a final glimpse of the quilt square; any hint of where their old life may have landed, or sailed, or travelled.

She saw nothing.

With a tilt up of her chin, and a renewed sturdiness in her feet, and a deep inhale in her lungs, Marie walked the shore with an awakening of lightness in her heart. She felt an awakening of a higher energy within her being; a cleansing of what she had been carrying and what she was ready to release.

She finally claimed the fullness and perfection of their love story.

She felt a renewal in her spirit that had escaped her for years.

She began to settle into a fresh experience of her newly-cleansed skin.

In that moment when her heart was at peace, and her mind was free, and her being was full, and her soul was newly awakened, she finally sensed how very much she had always been loved and seen in her life.

And as she stood silently in the waning sunlight, Marie whispered a blessed "*merci beaucoup, mon cherie*" to Claude for teaching her what it meant to love unconditionally.

Soul Imprint Healing

Relationships as Connections with God

Since we are all aspects of God (or Spirit, or the Universe, or the All That Is; whichever term you prefer), every relationship we experience is part of our connection to God energy. Every person holds a piece of God and we interact with that part of them to heal deeper parts of ourselves.

When we experience abandonment, rejection or betrayal, for example, it triggers our deepest fears and feelings of separation. On an unconscious level, we feel abandoned, rejected, or betrayed by God because love was removed, or taken away, or lost on some level. These situations then show us where we are working something out with God through another person. Our deepest fears of separation can be carried over between lifetimes, build up, and become quite massive issues in the present moment. Separation from God is the true fear, and we unconsciously bring this energy into relationships as a way to ultimately heal the perceived disconnection.

Separation Consciousness is based on the illusion of powerlessness. It is believing that your opportunities, your choices, and your circumstances are outside of yourself. Separation Consciousness includes Poverty Consciousness and Victim Consciousness, as well as other terms that support how we may limit ourselves and deny our innate power. This is the most unconscious of all energies, and as such, can create a vicious circle of unconscious life actions including thoughts, words, direction, and emotions that perpetuate feeling like a victim in one's own life.

Separation Consciousness is energized by the Ego-Mind's fears - all of them! Pick a fear, any fear, and you are tapping into the m.o. of unconscious energy that keeps you the furthest from your innate power. Unconscious emotional and mental loops may include blame, rejection, abandonment, shame, guilt, and lack of any kind, including financial, emotional, creative, mental, or energetic.

Separation Consciousness is also where we may unconsciously give our power away to something outside of ourselves, from exaggerated importance on money and professional status, to blindly following and trusting politicians, kings, and authorities. We are giving our power to what we perceive as being more powerful than ourselves.

When we look at relationships and Separation Consciousness, we see that the origination of this fear is when we left Spirit to incarnate in physical form. We left God to become separate. We left home to begin a grand human journey, but then we had more fears come up: *Will I be seen? Will I be valued? Will I be loved as a separate entity from God?* Our human selves question all of these points.

We are deeply encoded with this soul memory of leaving God, and any time we experience a form of separation, it triggers us on this level. This is why betrayal, rejection, and abandonment are such pervasive themes on the human journey. Ultimately, on a deeper unconscious level, every act of betrayal triggers our relationship with God.

When seen from this perspective, every relationship is then a beginning point to greater inner healing around separation, rejection, betrayal, and feeling unloved. You are working this out with God who has shown up in another form as your partner, boss, family member, parent, or whomever is triggering this part of you.

The ongoing human work - which is not to say it is easy, nor quick, nor simple - is in continually coming back to the understanding of Awakening Consciousness, which is that you are powerful in all ways regardless of anything that anyone else chooses. You are loved and respected and valued just for being here at this crazy human party. You are deeply loved for having the courage and strength to become a separate entity who still holds a special piece of the God mosaic. The separation is the illusion.

But we forget this. We doubt it. We don't feel it is true. We feel powerless at times. We feel that somehow we are wrong, bad, less than perfect, or not lovable. And as a result, we carry emotions, reactions, opinions and viewpoints that continue to limit our connection to our most powerful Selves and God. It is actually normal for our human selves to feel these separation fears because we are complex and multifaceted. It is absolutely okay to have all of these temporary experiences and feelings around separation. But your power is in what you do next with those emotions, opinions, and viewpoints.

If you can choose to see the experience of abandonment, rejection, or betrayal as the beginning point to healing a connection with God, then your core healing occurs because you got to the source of the issue: the relationship is helping you heal separation from God. When you work through that authentically and honestly, you get to the heart of a fear and heal the deepest pain, which is ultimately the gift of that relationship in the first place.

And that is also how you tune into the truth of unconditional love. When you connect with the understanding that every relationship comes from a God connection, you can let go of human imperfections, choices, and expectations easier. You see the God energy in another and that is enough.

So how do we ensure we learn to move through separation and find deeper love in ourselves and others?

Soul contracts are one such tool.

Soul Contracts

We are alive to know the full spectrum of human experiences, from deep fear to intense Love. But how can we "stay on task" and be guided to learn, grow, and evolve?

Soul contracts are binding contractual energies made at a soul level to ensure your soul's growth in this lifetime. The contract is often around an integral life theme (such as owning your power, trusting Self, recognizing self-worth, etc.) and the theme probably starts with early childhood experiences. Parents can be connected to this theme, as can other family members, childhood friends, and pivotal life events.

In order to grow through the soul contract lesson, you need someone (or multiple people) to be "the other" in the scenario. If your dominant lesson is greater Self-trust, someone needs to point out the theme by betraying you. If your lesson is self-worth, you need opportunities to stand on your own and believe in yourself. If you are here to be more powerful, you may have many experiences of feeling powerless and being disrespected in order to build a stronger core of inner strength. All of these themes, and more, can concurrently exist and overlap in a lifetime; the potential combinations are limitless. A soul contract is meant to empower you, but it may bring you to your knees first and be the source of extreme emotional reactions, deep fears, and life-defining experiences. Soul contracts often have a lot of emotional energy around them, and those feelings are meant to propel you forward because they will probably become too uncomfortable to bear. Quite a brilliant catalyst.

Many people have similar soul contract themes in this lifetime around self-love and self-trust, which is why betrayal, power struggles, disrespect, and other related situations are so prominent on earth at this time. It is also why spiritual awakenings are so significant on the planet because people have had *enough* of the circular themes and are willing to ask deeper, self-probing questions which lead to Awakening Consciousness.

A soul contract includes other souls, but it is also a commitment you made to yourself in this lifetime. After being identified, soul contract themes continue and will reappear throughout a lifetime, but you begin to recognize the theme sooner (say, within ten minutes instead of ten years), and then you can consciously make different choices around your actions. This allows you to move through the experience faster (say, in one week instead of twenty years), and you can experience greater detachment, grace, and peace because you know *what it's really about*. For example, if your main soul contract is self-trust and you find yourself betrayed by another person because you didn't trust yourself *yet again*, you will probably move through the emotional reactions and understanding faster because you understand the theme and your responsibility in this situation. Ideally, you arrive at self-forgiveness faster than in previous scenarios and with hindsight, know what to do next time to change your experience.

Knowing that every relationship represents your connection to God allows you to open up to the growth that presents itself in each experience. It is not to say that this is easy, or fast, or your first inclination! In fact, there could be some people that you are working out God energy with for your whole life. There could be some people that really push you to the brink in some way, as they test you at the deepest level and trigger your Shadow Self energies and reactions.

That's okay. Love yourself for how you are consciously aware of this energy dynamic and that you are willing to grow from it. Soul contracts are not always neat, pretty, or simple situations. They can be highly complex, messy and complicated. That's okay, too. Don't be too hard on yourself at times. Just continue to set the intention for Love, and you'll eventually move through the dynamic in the most perfect way for you.

Our soul contracts often exist through many lifetimes. Have you ever felt that you've just met someone that you already know deeply?

Meeting an Unfinished Soul Mate Energy in This Lifetime

In this lifetime, we are connecting with unfinished stories that are asking us for an energetic resolution. You will recognize these fellow soul travelers through your deep emotional reactions to them. Familiarity, instant sensations, unexplainable knowingness, feelings of connection, and/or a profound desire to be with them are often indicators of unfinished soul contracts between soul mates. You may have a hard time letting go of them for reasons you don't understand or can't figure out. Or you may have certain expectations of them to treat you a certain way or to fulfill an obligation of some sort.

Ultimately, it is because your soul story with them is much bigger than this lifetime, or perhaps any one lifetime. You have multiple stories and storylines with them that could be currently active in other timelines. You could feel that in another lifetime you did not work something out with them, but in this lifetime you really feel a pressure or need to resolve a situation, experience, or emotion.

When you meet one of these unfinished soul contracts in another, it is a feeling you cannot quite describe. It is remembering and recognition; comfort and connection. You want to stay with them, speak, share, and reconnect that previous lifetime. Confusion may set in when you are not aware of where this energy stems from and why you feel it with a "stranger." It is as if you can't help but stare at them because of the desire to reconnect that seems to come out of nowhere.

This is especially difficult if you are the only one who remembers the previous lifetime and the experiences shared between the two of you. It may be that the other person is not at a level of consciousness to remember, and so they are also confused but more likely to dismiss it. The remembering of these previous connections may ignite many emotions within you, everything from deep love and joy to extreme confusion and grief. At a soul level you are recalling the original energy shared between you and you are looking for a re-experience of that energetic connection. But chances are, you have found this other person so you can ignite that energy within yourself without needing their participation this time around. They are serving as a reminder of the joy you are able to experience without relying on them; an energy that is naturally a part of your imprint.

For example, consider the story of Marie and Claude. There could very well be unresolved energies there when they meet in another lifetime. There could be the urge to marry and have a family, yet also a deep fear of abandonment for Marie and an unexplained guilt for Claude. Those energies would be active in their relationship in the current lifetime so they could work through them consciously and ideally arrive at a new understanding and deeper healing between themselves and God energy.

The purpose of meeting an unfinished soul mate in this lifetime is to resolve the energy by making choices that support your current needs and who you are now. There is often a pattern that is being repeated so you can create a new outcome or choice for yourself. The relationship may work if both people have the same level of consciousness and are willing to participate in the same energy dynamic together. But when one person has evolved more than the other person, chances are higher that the relationship will not continue because there is no longer an energetic match. This can also lead to difficult and confusing break-ups because chances are you do not have the full soul story that brought the two of you together in the first place. Deep emotions are there, yet they are rooted in another lifetime or energy that is no longer a fit for one, or both, of you.

The best intention to hold while experiencing an unfinished soul mate energy is to focus on the highest and best outcome for all involved. This is easier said than done as your heart is involved; your ego may have expectations; and your mind may know what to do next. But your soul story with this person is bigger than here and now, and it may be that going your separate ways is the best choice for your individual soul paths. Or it could be that both of you are ready to make the same choice and continue ahead together. There are many other options that can unfold, too.

Since you are ultimately healing something in your relationship with God, keep in mind that your true power is found in healing within yourself, no matter how sexy or amazing that soul mate may be to you.

Healing Within Yourself

If you remember a certain less-than-desirable part of your soul's story it is because you are ready to heal it. And not only are you truly ready to heal it, on a deeper level, you will feel a responsibility to yourself to heal it. There will be an ongoing theme, or regular part of your life experiences, that you keep coming into contact with to assist you on your healing path.

You are not meant to live your life in a state of ongoing struggle, or emotional turmoil, or deep fear. No one here is meant to be in constant pain. But it is a choice some people unconsciously make because they do not know how to move through their inner turbulence; or more accurately, they do not know how powerful they are in their abilities to heal and complete parts of their soul story.

Healing is a choice. Marie made the choice to heal herself by claiming all of the wonderful aspects of her relationship with Claude, and then allowing the less-desirable parts to be smaller ingredients in their love story. She accepted all parts of Claude - the fullness of who he is - and this set her free from the past and how she was living with unfulfilled expectations. But she had to make the conscious choice to heal herself. That choice was in her power.

Healing comes through forgiveness, acceptance, trust in a bigger picture, and loving yourself. Realistically speaking, this is ongoing work. It is a continual commitment to yourself to allow a story or relationship to be complete because you know it is for your highest and best good, as well as for everyone else's, too. As you heal more within yourself, you discover new ways to sustain the ongoing commitment to let something go, or forgive, or truly feel over it. It is very rarely a "one and done" situation; you continually massage and fine-tune the energy in order to soften and release it.

At a soul level, no one truly means to hurt you or cause you pain. People make choices that reflect their needs and priorities at that time, and this is why we are told "it is never personal." We can know that statement is true even if the behavior feels personal; we can feel a hurt deeply even though our intelligence can rationalize it in some way. When a hurt lingers, it is because it resides deeper in our psyche and heart energy, and it is requiring more healing in order to truly let it go and be done.

We can continually practice deeper healing within ourselves through Heart Consciousness.

Heart Consciousness

Heart Consciousness is connected to Universal love-based feelings: compassion, forgiveness, joy, gratitude, abundance, success, and happiness. Heart Consciousness is a voice that speaks above the noise of the Ego-Mind and guides you to do what is best for everyone. It is energized by inclusion, similarities and connection. We see how we are each doing the best we can based on who we are in the present, and we can offer this compassion to others, too. If we can see that every person is following what they perceive is best for them, we can practice detaching from our expectations and needs, and focus on allowing them their choices. We remove ourselves from the equation and fill up that void with unconditional love instead. And wouldn't you like to receive the same infusion of unconditional love from another, as well?

Heart Consciousness supports true healing within yourself by accepting everyone for where they are at on their journey. Not where you want them to be, or where you think they should be, or where you need them to be; rather, a pure and calm acceptance of What Is. This frees you, and it frees them. It allows you to call in unconditional love to surround everything. And this unconditional love is a strengthening of your relationship with God.

In this lifetime, you will experience the most-perfect relationships that will advance your connection with God. Each person will be a direct link to your soul's ability to love more and trust your bigger soul story. All have the potential to support healing your own heart by consciously choosing forgiveness, compassion, and acceptance regularly, every time your mind wanders to that relationship or experience. This will be easier to exercise when you also connect to the vastness and strength of your energy and how you are able to endure anything.

The Endurance of Your Soul

You are made to carry on. You are energetically limitless. Nothing temporary is more powerful than your eternalness. Your soul knows this, yet your Ego-Mind looks for control. Your soul is filled with unlimited reservoirs of strength, fortitude, and perseverance, yet your Ego-Mind wants details, a timeline, and to be in charge of a particular outcome that meets its needs. But when you tap into the vastness of your soul, you see how trivial the human perspective can be at times. You then open up to how wise and full all of You truly is in your natural state.

Your energy will wax and wane at a human level because you are picking up on the continually changing energies of the collective, yet your soul's ability to endure is always within you even in the darkest moments and quietest periods of doubt. This is why we don't die so easily (well, all things considered). Humans are stronger and more resilient than ever before because we are now more tapped into the strength of our limitless energy and the soul's plan for growth.

You have more support than you may know at times. Your human responsibility is to just keep showing up in this minute, this hour, this day. Just as Marie tended to the basics of life while she had no answers about Claude, all you have to do at times is keep life simple. Focus on the essentials and let the Universe take care of the bigger picture. Come back to center and start with what you need now, and allow those intentions to carry you forward.

More than anything, remember that you will persevere.

You will carry on. You will keep going and witness another sunrise because you are more connected to your soul's endurance than ever before and it moves you forward in the best possible ways.

As you continue to deepen your connection to God energy in yourself and through others, your life will deepen in meaning and love. You will be more love that the world needs now and see others as the same vessel of love, regardless of their human actions. Together, we will raise the ability to unconditionally love each other as unique sources of light.

ST. PETERSBURG
{Flexibility}

A MEDLEY OF HIGH voices burst out in unison laughter, shaking the glass on the coffee table, their petite feet swinging and moving freely, soft chins in the air.

"And it's not like she knows where to put it properly!"

"Oh, I believe she definitely knows what to do with it!"

Another round of laughter swept through the room, picking up the debris of stale thoughts and insecure feelings. The fire's jagged heat added more blush to their faces; a few loose curls hung down with unnoticed freedom from tight buns. It was the hour before dinner, an hour to themselves, when each of the eight ladies-in-waiting retired briefly from the rigors of court etiquette to enjoy the pleasures of gossip. Two women sat on a velvet lounge sewing dresses in need of ignored repair, their fingers working easily with the fabrics, needles, laughter. One lady silently prepared the Queen's toiletries to bring in after dinner, and yet another brushed the always-smooth coat of a little prized dog. Mindless activities carried on with mindless remarks. A sweet jasmine perfume floated around the room; the only space in the Palace where rich scents could be gloriously inhaled into loosened skirts, lockets of hair, and small patches of exposed skin.

Each of the eight ladies had been appointed by the Queen to take care of her personal and private affairs, but it would be more accurate to say that all affairs became public within the hen house. Their cream corsets attempted to hold in their envy and jealousy, but secretly, each woman yearned for the Queen's attention, approval, and time. To privately wear just one piece from her exquisite jewelry collection would be enough to satisfy their need for a personal royal connection.

Gwendolyn, the most senior female in the group, moved from standing near the fireplace into the center of the room, and the women quickly reined in their lingering giggles. Some had wondered if Gwendolyn reported their remarks back to the Queen since their longstanding loyalty to each other was known for being stronger than the flag's weave.

"Ladies, we must now turn our attention to the evening's entertainment. As you know, we are receiving foreign guests who are quite important to her Majesty. Please select three of her finest ensembles for consideration. I will go ask her now what she is in the mood for wearing during tonight's unusual celebration."

The women regained their formal composure by tucking their smart quips back into their corsets, and sped up their routine of preparing for the evening. Sophie brought out three suitable selections from one of Her Majesty's deep closets: a dark green silk dress with long thin sleeves, a blush pink ensemble with a fashionably high waist, and a deep ruby red gown overflowing with luxurious folds and gold hems. Anna inspected each selection for loose threads or tears, and Elizabeth carefully gathered together the appropriate shoes and undergarments. Her Majesty was often decisive, but her preferences could be unpredictable. The women knew to have three more dress options ready and waiting in the closet.

Gwendolyn finished sipping her ice water, gazing with a keen eye at the room's motions, and placed the glass on the tray that would be returned to the kitchen, then she moved to the door. Liza lowered the pampered dog to the floor, his bronze coat shining gorgeously, and the pooch instinctively ran to the door for release, tailing wagging with glee. Gwendolyn pushed him away with her dark brown slipper, not allowing her disdain for the animal to show on her tight lips. She opened the heavy door as quickly as her thin frame allowed and slipped into the hallway just as an ice cold gust blew through the Palace's interior. A window was cracked open a few feet away, but she didn't rush to close it from the aggressive November storm. Instead, she exhaled slowly and allowed this brief moment of silence to envelope her. *Only a few more years until I will be free from these childish conversations.*

Gwendolyn's worn chocolate soles tapped briskly on the polished floors as she sauntered to her Majesty's office, moving quickly only to stay warm and not to arrive soon. As was typical in the Palace, she heard muffled voices while passing nearly every room. Anticipation was always high before big dinner events as the Court and their visiting guests prepared for the festivities. No one ever publicly admitted how much time they put into choosing their evening attire, especially the Lords and Generals who are far away from their wives and open to anything the evening may bring their way.

Gwendolyn arrived in front of her Majesty's office, and as the five wrinkles on her hand grasped the icy brass knob, voices rose in octave behind the door. She paused and leaned in, her heart pounding against the solid panel.

"I will NOT be told what to do in this situation!"

"But Madame, you must understand that I am providing you with serious counsel that is in the best interest of the state."

"You have not been asked for your counsel, Sir. You do not have authority over my decisions. You are dismissed."

Gwendolyn slid to the side just as the large ornate door swung open. A short gentleman, his belly protruding with excess, wobbled away from the chamber, never noticing the Queen's highest-ranking lady-in-waiting. His grumbling was silenced as every Palace hall clock chimed that a new hour had arrived. The ringing echoed down the walkway as his heavy legs under mumbling lips disappeared around a corner.

Gwendolyn pulled her posture up, just as she was trained to do since her first dance class decades ago, then entered the grand office with grace.

"Your Majesty, I am here to inquire about your dress preference for the evening."

As she spoke, she instinctively looked for what was different in the opulent space: a new foreign gift from a diplomat or a fresh pen from the Queen's legal counselor. Everything the Queen acquired had a story, and as her most loyal ally, Gwendolyn loved hearing the latest cultural news and alliance changes that often accompanied each gift.

The Queen sat at her desk glaring at the roaring fire, oblivious to the question she was just posed. Her face was hard with concentration; her dark eyes narrow with resolve and dignity.

"How dare he challenge what I know is best! No one has any idea the responsibilities I bear for this country. If I could do what was easy, I surely would. Unsolicited recommendations from fools are a waste of my time."

She stood up and walked with fierce pride to the window facing an inner garden. Her office was private, hidden behind another apartment, and allowed her to see the world without the world seeing her. She cherished the freedom of watching her flowers bloom every spring, knowing exactly what blossoms each bushel will offer. The intertwining medley of soft pink petals, lavender stems, dark red curves, bright yellow blossoms, and golden nectarine waves were her sacred canvas; a sweet cocktail of softness, femininity, and escape. As the white blankets of winter approached, those same flower buds now suffered under the weight of seasonal transitions. Temporary decay was needed for evolution; losing a few leaves never destroyed the whole tree. She gladly welcomed guidance from wise nature over the recommendations of fat fools.

"Your Majesty, with all due respect, I must inquire about your decision for the evening's dress. The ladies will have everything ready for your grand entrance based on your preferences, of course." Gwendolyn tilted her head down with respect as the back of the Queen's bun still faced her.

"Dark blue silk with the gold ribbons. That is all, Gwendolyn."

"Thank you, your Majesty."

Gwendolyn then turned swiftly to exit, making an elegant *pas de bourrée* movement while the Queen still gazed at her secret garden. Gwendolyn often performed brief ballet movements in order to remember her years of dance training, and to remember the long hours she had devoted to her passion since she was a young girl. It was never realistic for her to be a professional dancer, with her slower steps and wider middle, but she vowed never to forget how to dance, even now as an old maid in her late forties. The quiet movements gave her a deep, silent joy. Her mother would have loved knowing those disciplined years were still put to use; in a grand palace, no less.

The Queen listened for the hard door to close, allowing her dear friend Gwen the privacy to practice her gliding dance moves once more. Gwen was always an exquisite dancer, moving with exuberant joy and quiet strength in every limb, but she had abandoned her dream too easily due to self-created false excuses. *Too many are afraid to fail at their dreams.*

Her slow exhale pressed against the window pane. A long knotted tree branch was whipped around violently, the wind sparing no mercy and allowing no moments of peace, but hanging on to the strength of its trunk, core, roots. She would be that tree branch regardless of any Palace weather conditions.

By the time she turned away from the mesmerizing view, the room had diminished in light as November's night had quickly, eagerly, moved in to take over the Palace. The fire's flames slowly sank into the dark cave. The Queen still enjoyed tending to the fire herself whenever possible, a reminder of her self-reliance and independence. Years on the throne had turned her into a dependent child at times, and if it didn't always insult her staff, she would insist on doing more things for herself. Adding wood to the dark cave reminded her of her own inner fire; her own desires to take care of her people and tend to their survival by any means necessary. But sometimes being a leader meant doing what was unpopular in the moment in order to maintain what the country needed in the long-term. She would not give up what was hers or weaken the State in any way.

"Your Majesty? A word, please?" Her Legal Counselor opened the door and peered inside, then strode into the room without waiting for a reply. His assistant bustled in behind him, stacks of papers piled up against his wide chest. Both men stood in front of her as the fire roared back to life.

"Madame, I apologize in advance for the inconvenience, but we should review your financial commitments and business agreements before the evening's events."

"Why, sir? Why is it important to do this tonight instead of during our standing appointment tomorrow morning?" The blazing fire flamed up behind her as she spoke.

"Because, with all due respect, Your Majesty, when we have many foreign guests in attendance you have a tendency to make commitments when everyone is jolly and enjoying themselves. It is favorable for you to understand the State's situation sooner rather than later, so you can make the best possible decisions this evening." Pause. "If that is fine with you, Your Majesty."

His chest was confident but his eyes waited anxiously for her agreement. In truth, he would rather review the current state of affairs now so he did not have to rise early the following morning and leave his lover.

"Very well then. I do prefer to do this now so I do not have to meet you early tomorrow morning." She also wanted the luxury of spending a lazy morning with her lover.

The assistant took this remark as his cue to distribute the necessary documents while the Queen returned to her grand chair. She shuffled into place, lining up her petite arms with the worn leather armrests. The front half of the chair had been softened over the years under the daily presence of her arms and plump seat, but there were many parts of the chair's upholstery that still appeared brand new; her tiny frame had never touched them.

After thirty minutes of providing the typical and necessary updates, the Legal Counselor glanced at his watch.

"Your Majesty, if it is agreeable with you, I believe we have covered the most important aspects of the State's financial situation. And it sounds like we are in agreement about what needs to happen tonight?"

"Yes, sir, that is correct. You may let the others know my decision. Thank you. Please enjoy yourself this evening."

"That, I will definitely do, Your Majesty." He again looked at his watch as the Queen carefully eyed his hurried behavior. She had been in this office long enough to know why an ambitious man suddenly rushed away from his favorite business matters.

The duo exited her office, the assistant again piled high with papers, and in the hallway, each man turned in opposite directions to tend to different priorities. The assistant turned left to return to the business office and share the evening's developments with his staff; then he would take another sip from the flask resting under his coat and retire early.

The Legal Counselor turned right and walked quickly to the end of the hall, pulling on his coat with nervousness. He eventually glanced back to ensure no one else was around, and instead of going down to his apartment to prepare for dinner, he eagerly climbed the nearest stairs up to the third floor, the heels of his black shoes not touching a single step.

At the top of the staircase, he again glanced around nervously, aware that he had no explanation for being in the children's wing, and made his way to the third door on the left. Voices echoed into the hallway behind him as fervor for the evening's event picked up around the Palace. He tapped anxiously on the door, employing their secret knock, and just as he started to fear that she had forgotten about their rendezvous sessions during big events - for it had been many months since they had been able to meet - the door swung open and he smelled her sweet vanilla scent, the flavor he dreamed about when he had to make love to his wife.

"Good evening, Counselor." She stood in front of him in a tight black corset, her red hair pulled up high to reveal a pale smooth neck. "The children are already in bed. Perhaps I'm next?"

He pushed her back into the room, eagerly taking off his coat and sinking his mouth into her bare neck and shoulder. The potential scandal of sleeping with the young nanny evaporated from his mind as he pulled her corset down and put a soft nipple into his mouth. Their backgrounds, class differences, and Palace rankings would always keep them apart, but Catherine was the only woman who stirred up an uncontrollable passion in his pants. From the moment she glanced at him at the New Year's Eve Ball, her brown eyes daring him to approach, to their first kiss in a private pantry during the last dance, to the passionate exchange in his office after midnight, they had vowed to meet in her apartment whenever the Palace was too distracted by celebrations. His hands formed around her cool buttocks as she reached into his tight knickers and giggled. Then a knock on the door jolted them into stillness.

"I must answer it," she whispered into his ear with deep breathing, tugging up her top, tossing back her loose hair, stumbling away from him.

"Yes?" She inquired calmly behind the closed door.

"Catherine, the children are awake, and young George is claiming a fever again. What do I do?"

Catherine exhaled slowly. "It is best to take the request to the kitchen, Hannah. We had this issue last week, too, and they solved it perfectly with warm milk. He is fine, just adjusting to the winter chills."

"Yes, Madame. I will do that. Thank you." Hannah waited in silence for a beat, her ear pressed to the door. Then she heard the soft moans start again and she smiled to herself, her chubby hand covering her mouth to keep the secret inside.

Catherine was rumored to have many lovers due to her

beauty, charm, and access to the Queen. Strolling with the children allowed her to innocently enter nearly any chamber in the Palace under the guise of the children's needs. But Hannah knew the value of a secret rendezvous, and more importantly, knew who she needed to seduce next. If Catherine could have him, why couldn't she?

For the next hour, Hannah moved down the third floor and listened to conversations; knocked with false inquiries; and collected updates on ladies' love affairs and gentlemen's intentions. She purred with innocence and nodded with obedience as necessary, with no one aware of how she traded in secrets and harbored gossip with greed. A plump girl who easily blended into the ornate curtains, Hannah's dreary brown hair and bland dark eyes rarely made a lasting impression, but when she did get attention for a witty comment, she was remembered for her innocent demeanor and kind touch with the children. Secretly, she felt entitled to claim anything anyone else possessed. The earrings she wore were from a maid's drawer; the locket that sunk into her heavy bosom was taken from a visiting guest. Her distinguished uncle had always said Hannah was just as good as everyone else, so why couldn't she have all the things they enjoyed, too?

After collecting the Palace's freshest gossip, Hannah slipped away to the private staircase that led down to the serving kitchen. Her wide feet moved quickly down the spiraling stone steps, and the air grew warmer as she arrived in the chaotic kitchen, out of breath and pink with glee. A mingling of delicious smells invaded every corner of the space. Giant pots bubbled with bright vegetable stews; four types of bread baked in the ovens; ham and meat were being carved by two male servants.

Aunt Anna, as she was called by the staff, was shorter than every large pot, wider than the oldest oven, and commanded the kitchen like a general; her loud voice ran all of the cooking activities, and before important events she was especially frazzled. The pressure to prepare and cook and bake and serve for over two hundred people at once kept her awake for three nights before every gathering. She just found out this morning that there were not enough eggs to prepare all of the desserts, and meat was scarce everywhere in the country. She still did not know how to feed everyone, but she must or the Queen would be furious. The reputation of the country was on the line.

"Move!" Aunt Anna yelled at Hannah who was standing perfectly in the way, as she pulled a tray of hot bread rolls out of the oven. "Or put yourself to work!"

Anna then grabbed baskets and started filling them with the soft rounds, her fingertips immune to burning heat. Hannah, paralyzed next to the seductive smells, reached for a hot roll to stuff in her skirt pocket. She hadn't really come to the kitchen for warm milk as Catherine had instructed over an hour ago because there really wasn't anything wrong with George. She simply lied to get attention and to go anywhere she pleased. The children were still sleeping peacefully, and she was bored, and everyone was busy, so there was no harm in checking out the menu and discovering tonight's celebration. The guests sounded fascinating.

Aunt Anna shoved three bottles at her. "Here, take more wine out to the tables! But be invisible. No one wants to see you, they want to see the Queen."

Hannah carried the red wine tight against her bosom, the bread roll still warm in her pocket against her meaty thigh, and prepared to hand the three bottles to one of the official servers standing on the outskirts of the large dining hall. But as she peered through the doorway, she froze in wonder as her eyes moved upwards. Men were swinging wildly from the ceiling in the dining hall. Back and forth they flew, disappearing out of sight for a moment, only to return with big smiles and dark moustaches the following minute. Her mouth dropped open at the sight. Loud music filled the room; men spoke passionately as they bit into bones; the Queen's head shook with laughter; and candles blazed against every wall. A man swung above on a small bar across the room again, his toes pointed like arrows.

Hannah was mesmerized by the whole spectacle. Suddenly, a loud crash hit the floor beneath her.

"You fool!" A server hissed at her, his moustache sharp and stern. He grabbed the remaining bottles from her hand, shoving her out of the way. "Get this cleaned up now! You're a disgrace!"

Thankfully, no guests heard the crash as the room was blissfully absorbed in all of the other amazing distractions. The server regained his public composure; tucked one bottle in his arm, the other in his serving hand; and made his way to the main table, keeping his back to the wall as he had been trained to do by his mentor. To be of service meant he must keep his eyes on the room at all times and not miss a request. The Queen's visiting guests were exceptionally rude, always demanding more wine to be poured every fifteen minutes. His dark overcoat expertly hid the red stains and meat juice that splattered on him from all of the ravenous table animals.

The server refilled the Queen's glass first, then poured in order of seniority, starting with the diplomat on her right. Thankfully, they were now all distracted by the crazy fools flying above the tables in ridiculous outfits. He never made eye contact with the guests, obviously, but as they were looking up towards the jokers in the sky, he glanced at their expressions and lingered longer to hear their conversations.

The Queen spoke loudly to be heard by most of her table guests, "Oh, what a joy it must be to experience that type of freedom! I do believe it would be an exceptional experience to fly above the worries of the world like that. Don't you agree, sir?" She turned to her right as her guest of honor, a handsome foreign diplomat, nodded in agreement.

"Yes, Your Majesty, it is certainly a revolutionary demonstration of great skill and talent. I would call it an art, actually, similar to ballet or the practice of any dance. Does that please you?"

"Yes, indeed it does. What a wild invention this is, this trapeze! The art of trapeze, as you call it. If only we could all experience the sensations of leaping and flying."

"With all due respect, Your Majesty, I do not think it is for me. The risks, the unknowns, being out of control. Surely falling from such heights would be quite damaging."

"Oh, but one cannot let fear stop them from taking a risk, sir! We take risks every day for our countries, so surely you understand that risk is what also makes life so rewarding. I believe we are far grander than we know, and we must not hold ourselves back due to silly false self-perceptions. Of course, one must be wise enough to know that there are risks with anything in life."

His finely sculpted hair nodded again in agreement. "You are quite right, as always, Your Majesty." He completely disagreed but didn't dare risk expressing his true opinion. He was here to make an ally for his nation, not to indulge in personal perspectives.

She took another sip. "We mustn't be afraid of life, sir. These men show us anything can happen, even what we thought would be ridiculous. I also believe there is a natural cycle to everything, which nature brilliantly teaches us throughout the year. Would you agree with that statement?"

Just then, the trapeze artist released his grip on the bar and performed a flip. The whole room applauded with glee and erupted with cheers. Every candle flame swooned sideways from the room's energy.

The server returned to his stance in the hallway, his dark eyes staring straight ahead as the dining room continued to roar with "bravo, bravo!" Another round of excited clapping swept through the tables. Just as his shoulders started to carelessly slouch from another long day on his feet, the servant's mentor stepped in front of him and cleared his throat abruptly.

"Sir, please follow me to the pantry." The server nodded and followed his mentor to the side room stocked with linens, water, silverware, and stuffy air. The tile floor was covered with crumbs and stains.

His mentor cleared his throat and then looked him in the eye. "Sir, it is with great regret that I must inform you that your services are no longer needed after this evening. The Queen has made budget cuts and regretfully, will no longer be able to employ many of her staff members. I am deeply sorry, but you are now free to leave the Palace."

The servant blinked suddenly, quickly, completely caught off-guard by the announcement splattering on his face. An image of his petite wife reclining in bed, her body sore and exhausted, flashed through his mind; their third child would be arriving within a month. He stifled a response about his personal affairs knowing they did not matter to the Court.

"Yes, sir. Thank you for the honor of serving Your Majesty and the State." He nodded in servitude, then proudly walked to the private staff room to remove his Palace attire.

The fear of being able to provide for his family crept up his spine, his neck, his hairline, and stalled in his head. If there was only one paycheck left, and the country was rebelling against the monarch, and there was a shortage of harvest and food, how would he find a stable job? How would he care for five open mouths in these conditions? He slowly exhaled, and recalled that he always landed on his feet, no matter what hardships life brought his way. Perhaps he could teach those flying fools in the dining room how to do the same.

He slowly removed his stained overcoat and grabbed his light winter coat which was never a match for the harsh St. Petersburg blizzards. Then in a moment of desperation, his survival instincts kicked in, and he emptied a sodden laundry bag by dumping the worn garments in the corner. There was more than enough food in this Palace for his family, and as these fools decadently enjoyed their pleasures, he would take what he could to ensure his family's survival over the coming weeks. It was the least the Queen could provide after ten years of his loyal service during seasonal celebrations, grand balls, holiday festivities, childbirth announcements, garden parties, and daily dinner service. Ten years of service and his family was left with nothing in a single night.

He followed a back hallway into the kitchen and walked confidently into a side pantry stocked with dried goods, breakfast breads, and canned vegetables. His shaking hands quickly stuffed the laundry bag until it sunk down to the stone ground. He could see Aunt Anna out of the corner of his right eye preparing desserts, but she was known for swiftly appearing out of nowhere, a seemingly impossible feat for a woman made of flour and sugar and heavy cream.

Adrenaline pulsed wildly through his arms and legs as he surveyed his collection. Only a few shelves of food remained now, but it was not surprising with the country's food shortage. Just as he was about to throw the heavy bag over a shoulder, Aunt Anna appeared in the door with red cheeks.

"What are you doing in here!" she barked and glanced around the barren room. "I need more sugar, where is it!"

He felt his racing heart vibrate through the room. "I'm restocking, Madame. A new shipment arrived late this afternoon."

"Brilliant!" She reached a pudgy, sticky hand into his bag, her heavy breathing spilling over everything, and pulled out a container. "Bring more if you can find them, please! I can't believe how empty this closet is now. We are really feeding a village tonight." She shook her head in disbelief.

"Yes, Madame. And please, ask Hannah about the whereabouts of some provisions. She is known for taking what is not bolted down."

Aunt Anna stared in wide-eyed wonder at this news. "Well, I'll be damned. That sly wench." She shuffled back to her baking station, still shaking her head.

The server exhaled deeply, and hoisted the sack on his back. A kitchen delivery, if anyone asked.

As he exited the kitchen, Sara, a timid maid, brushed by his left arm with a tray of tea, biscuits, and chocolates. She continued to avoid eye contact with every staff member as rumors spread about people being fired this evening. She hoped to continue her duties unnoticed, not wanting her name to come up in any official conversation or gossip or side chatter. And if it did come up, she was prepared with a retort. *Oh, I believe you meant Hannah, not myself. Sometimes people confuse us because of our age.*

With tray in hand, Sara stole a glance inside the dining room to witness what everyone had been talking about all night: men hanging from ropes on the ceiling and flying across the room! She couldn't believe it until she saw it with her own eyes. And as she stared up at them in amazement, their muscles strong and their smiles permanent, she wondered what other silly things people do out in the world. Perhaps there was a bigger life for her beyond the Palace walls if she was fired. But she wasn't ready to dream bigger yet. Sara knew how lucky she was to be a maid for the Queen.

She expertly carried the polished silver tray up the staff stairs, passing three servants in whispers, and decided to go the long way back to the Queen's bed chamber as a form of quiet rebellion. She knew it took exactly forty-four minutes to prepare everything for the Queen's evening bed routine, but because the entertainment was capturing the crowd, she had a few extra quiet moments to herself tonight. The Queen would most likely retire late this evening, anyhow, and Sara always made sure to disappear before one of her male visitors knocked.

Sara continued on to the third floor, careful not to spill the hot water, and was about to step outside of the staircase when she heard voices in the hallway. She cracked open the secret entrance and peered out to see her crush emerging from an apartment. They had a standing agreement to meet after the Queen retired on Saturdays, after the Palace was asleep, after another day of service was complete. Her crush closed the door and sauntered down the hall, the wood floor creaking as the cold air constricted it. Sara knew who lived behind that door, and would be sure to let the woman's other suitors know about this latest dalliance.

A window was slightly ajar further down the hall; the incoming winter winds hallowed wildly through the crack. In the silence of this side of the Palace, Sara could hear the faint yells of the uprising through the open window. She had worked for the Queen for over three years now and had never heard chanting and shouting like this before; the intensity, the consistency, the rage in the air had chased away innocent passing clouds and winter birds. The Queen had tough decisions to make, and she was a fierce woman, but it appeared the crowds continued to grow more unruly each night. And yet she managed to entertain despite the harsh realities of the country and rumors of another war.

Sara turned to go back down to the Queen's quarters on the second floor, her arms tired of the now-heavy tray, and her moments of freedom gone. If the Queen could carry on during turbulent times, she knew she could follow suit and do the same without question right now. *I must be strong.*

The Queen's private apartments were grand and luxurious, covered with gold and rich fabrics and dark wood and endless artwork and ornate decor Sara never knew existed in the world. She came from a poor farm hundreds of miles from here, and yet fate had chosen her to be special. She happened to meet the right woman in town one day who was desperately searching for a simple maid. Sara was only fourteen with short blonde hair that made her look even younger, but she had the eagerness to be part of something bigger in the world and she wanted to work. The woman selected Sara because of her strong posture and confident words. She moved to St. Petersburg without a second thought, and promised to write letters home to her family regularly. Then she became swept away by Palace life.

The first time she saw the Queen in person she stumbled and mumbled and felt like an absolute fool; a silly girl who was desperately out of place in a privileged world. But she managed to maintain her strong posture even when her eyes could not focus in the grand room. Her Majesty said she liked Sara's innocence and common ways, so from that day forth, she became her youngest lady-in-waiting. Most women were fired, or pregnant, or sent away unexpectedly in the night within two years of their employment, so Sara learned quickly that it was best to say nothing, but to hear everything. She believed this approach was how she had lasted as long as she did at Court.

After setting down the tray, the tea water no longer hot and the biscuits now touching each other, Sara peeked through the heavy brocade curtains to see the crowd outside growing more unruly and louder. It was rumored that Pugachev's Rebellion was determined and strong because the serfs were more organized than ever before; ready to fight for their freedom as warriors. Faint glimmers of their torches danced in the distance as if the flames were flying alone in the night sky, just like those amazing men performing tonight.

Sara closed the curtains and turned back to the Queen's bed chamber. If she were Queen, she would call in the army to maintain the peace and to protect her sovereign rule. She took a bite of the extra biscuit she always saved for herself on the tray, and used the Queen's brush to comb her long blonde hair in preparation for her meeting with her secret lover in a few hours.

Life in the Palace meant always being ready for the next development, to constantly be on one's feet with flexibility. Survival required adapting and moving with change. Sara had become an expert at such ways. No matter what happened next she would be okay. She would do what needed to be done in her situation. Her shoulders then sank under the silent secret she carried. Yet the heaviness of fear was not a feeling she could entertain right now.

She glanced at the clock and saw it was just about to chime midnight. Sara put everything back into place just as the Queen had left it and pulled her blonde hair strands out of the brush. She spritzed the Queen's custom perfume into the air - an intoxicating blend of jasmine and vanilla - and then glided to the door without disturbing the lingering scents, allowing them to coast and soften and romance the room with pleasure.

The Palace hallway was buzzing with energy as the dinner party broke up into groups and couples for the evening's next round of activities. Sara returned to her small bedroom, still avoiding eye contact with everyone, and prepared for her lover to arrive within the hour. She would not reveal to him yet that she was with child because she knew it would be the end of her time at the Palace, especially since there was no way a diplomat's son could be officially acknowledged as the father of a maid's baby.

After throwing up every morning for three weeks, Sara had crafted a plan to travel back to his home country under the guise of being the Queen's messenger. Upon arriving in the country, she would make arrangements for the baby to stay behind and be cared for, and then she would return to Court. With the harsh winter approaching, she feared the worst about travelling far distances, and knew there was great risk with this plan, but just like the Queen, she had to make a tough decision that would be beneficial in the long run. She would be strong and flexible like the Queen.

Sara reclined on the worn green lounge chair with one hand resting on her belly, the other palm sitting on her forehead. A small window allowed her to stare up at the indigo sky dazzling with stars. *I will do what is best for my baby's future and for myself.*

All of the clocks in the hallway chimed loudly.

Soul Imprint Healing

Soul Groups as Healing Connections

Soul groups are clusters of people you've had many lifetimes with for the purpose of mutual growth and support. This almost always includes your immediate family and/or parents who require you to learn something significant for soul growth, mastery, and personal power. You may meet multiple Soul groups from various past life scenarios throughout your life, or you may have one significant Soul group that you stay connected with from birth to death.

There is usually a dominant theme within the group, and there can be complex overlaps in soul contracts, soul agreements, and karmic relationships. Examples of soul groups may include childhood friends; co-workers and colleagues; classmates; social circles; immediate and extended families; spiritual groups; sports teams; political allies and rivals; and/or any collection of individuals connected by strong emotions, Ego-Mind energies, and/or mutual growing experiences.

Soul groups incarnate together to learn, grow, and heal, and to do this, they typically reenact the same themes throughout different lifetimes by changing roles (such as rotating parent/child roles; murderer/victim; political rivals and combat enemies; master/slave; best friends and support systems; plus countless other combinations). Soul groups are "working something out" together, often like a tangled knot of energy.

Another example is how everyone in a soul group may contribute to an overarching message to benefit others. For example, some soul groups choose to die together in horrific circumstances to open humanity up to Love, Forgiveness, and Peace. Souls volunteer for these roles and offer their energy for the good of Heart Consciousness and Awakening Consciousness. Other soul groups choose to expand society's definition of Love by challenging norms, protesting laws, and requiring legal changes, such as civil rights, women's rights, and gay rights campaigns. Another Soul group may live in a small remote community and agree to learn lessons together that they couldn't, or didn't, complete in previous lifetimes.

You can be connected to multiple soul groups based on multiple lifetimes of experiences. The combinations are unlimited. Ultimately, Soul groups remind us we are all connected to each other.

A soul group is connected through shared experiences. All of the people in the Palace are connected to energy of that time and place, as well as to the undercurrent of lessons that are being experienced and animated there: betrayal, lust, entitlement, power, gossip, fear, and survival are some of the lower energies that are being shared and passed around.

Every participant in a scenario is connected to the same healing opportunities. Like picking at one thread in a quilt, all of the other threads pick up on the 'pull' to heal that same energy within themselves, which is often at an unconscious level. One person, or many people, within the group will be the trigger that activates healing potential for others. This can be through destructive means, such as exposing a scandal, or healthy means, like sitting down to communicate feelings from the heart.

Soul groups meet up through various incarnations to help each other with healing and growth opportunities. Professional settings are a common modern area for these re-connections to occur because they allow people from separate paths to meet each other again for the purpose of completing energies. The professional world also allows the full expression of all free will choices, from sabotage, betrayal, and power games, to leadership, abundance, and integrity. Soul groups can (literally) work together to move through a plethora of energies and roles from other incarnations while also activating new choices and higher ways to connecting with each other that promotes healing. For example, the person who fired you may have killed you in another lifetime, so how do you allow the 'death' of the job to catapult you into a better opportunity? Or maybe the one person you despise in the office stole your partner in a previous incarnation and that is why you never trust them. There are many, many possibilities, of course, but the greatest healing will come from the power of your choices based on who you are now.

But heads up: these connections can also trigger the most intense lessons you are here to master. Soul groups activate energies from all incarnations which is why these situations can be complex and complicated. They may feel messy and emotional. With higher consciousness, you can see how the most difficult and trying situations are helping you to grow forward. You are only responsible for your own energy and choices. As you raise and heal within yourself, it affects the soul group and provides a new outlet for their healing, too. In this way, you are always contributing to the whole and offering healing potential to everyone when you honor your own healing and what is best for you.

Every person in the Palace is part of the same soul group that agreed to participate in these shared energies. As they re-connect through other incarnations, they will be given opportunities to experience the same energies, but also to make new choices about them. The same themes of betrayal, lust, power, and gossip may show up in a work place, and one or two individuals may be the triggers who activate new dynamics and outcomes that ultimately benefit everyone in the group. One of the main themes of the Palace was the dominant experience of Earth Consciousness.

Earth Consciousness

Earth Consciousness is our default starting point for understanding life because it is based on what is around us. Earth Consciousness is energized by the five senses including looking for proof, validation, data, stimuli, what is visible, and what is verifiable.

Earth Consciousness is everything we see, touch, hear, taste, and smell, which is why it is the most dominant energy in our lives. From science and medicine, to nature and social media, Earth Consciousness is the basis for our existence as human beings, including the croissants we eat, the wine we drink, and the high heels we flaunt. It is density, form, all materials and music and perfumes and paddle boards and landmasses. Look around your surroundings now and there are probably numerous examples of Earth Consciousness everywhere. And by the way, Earth Consciousness is one of the JOYS of being alive in a physical body!

However, when the energy of Earth Consciousness becomes out of balance, there is an overemphasis on power, proof, validation, stimuli, and an excessive Ego-Mind drive. This can show up as extreme power through domination and submissive roles; obsession with fame and celebrity; sensationalism, materialism and accumulation of possessions; extreme emotional reactions; competition and war; unconscious judgments; polarity and duality; hierarchy, status, rank, and external authorities. And the list goes on.

There are great gifts and opportunities with Earth Consciousness, too. Ultimately, we learn what we value in our surroundings, relationships, and daily needs. What job brings you joy? Where do you want to live and spend your days? What food choices are best for you? How do you want to invest your time? What relationships do you want in your life that support, respect, and love you? Essentially, what reality are you creating for yourself on the planet?

We all have lifetimes that focused on responsibility, obligations, duty, public needs, status, and finances. These are themes that truly brought us into our human experiences. There was little spiritual focus and an overall lack of curiosity for spiritual growth in those incarnations. It was easier to "follow the leader" and do what everyone else was doing, especially in the areas of religion, politics, and government. Earth Consciousness brings our attention to practical concerns that support survival and livelihood.

All experiences of consciousness have value. We learn and grow in multiple ways as we experience ourselves through these various dynamics and energies. With Earth Consciousness, we learn how to appreciate and value money; the responsibility to serve others; the importance of duties and obligations; and the discipline that goes into achieving a goal. Earth Consciousness connects us with the energy of the masses and where the collective is currently learning (or not). Our priorities revolve around "earthly concerns" with little or no connection to anything that is potentially deemed unusual, odd, or weird.

As consciousness rises on the planet, we continually open up to new choices and potentials that support what we want to create next, including our soul's growth through lifetimes. It is common to take these Earth Consciousness experiences from previous lifetimes and choose to create a whole new life beyond them. You may have no interest in status, or finances, or achievement. You may not be that wrapped up in what everyone else is doing or the latest reports on the evening news. You may be "off the grid", so to speak, and interested in more spiritual, esoteric, or metaphysical matters that feel like your true home. Many people volunteered to move away from Earth Consciousness in this lifetime in order to help humanity move forward into different interests and knowledge. You may feel a 'been there, done that' mindset around areas of life that you previously explored and experienced in other lifetimes.

Yet it is not to say that Earth Consciousness areas are bad or lesser than; we all need financial energy in our lives, after all! And we are in bodies that have physical requirements, such as shelter, food, relationships, and daily comforts. We incarnated to have these sensations and experiences, but we are also here to move beyond them and to bring in our soul's light to daily life.

Awakening to higher levels of earth-based experiences can occur in any number of ways and is very personal to each of us. As you progress on your journey, you will have more opportunities to connect with the flexibility of your soul.

The Flexibility of Your Soul

Before you incarnate, you choose themes and areas of growth that will support your soul's intentions. Yet after you arrive here in your fancy-dancy human suit, you may change direction and follow a new path. Your soul supports your free will through its ability to be endlessly flexible based on where you wish to direct your intentions and energy. Your soul accommodates, remains nimble, and adapts as needed to your choice because when you are in physicality free will dominates. Being human is the game of free will, and your soul knows this because it is choosing to support your growth in this world of unlimited choices.

Your soul honors your free will because there is no timeline or deadline from the soul's perspective. Whatever intentions or lessons you "forget" to work on or master can be returned to in another lifetime. Unlimited do-overs! No worries, mate! It is yet another way you are loved and valued simply for being alive and being here at this time.

So go easy on yourself if you feel you're not doing enough or have been in a lesson longer than you'd like to admit. We each learn and grow in the ways that are perfect for us, and this is the true validation you seek. The validation is not in a timeline or particular outcome; it is in loving yourself along the way and honoring what you need now.

This flexibility of your soul also supports loving and accepting yourself throughout your life, knowing you are seen regardless of what growth you choose or what experiences of consciousness you participate in. Do not put any grand expectations on yourself; watch where the "shoulds" pop up or that darn inner critic yells loudly about whether or not something is perfect. You are enough as you are. And as your path continues, you will expand into an even newer experience of enough-ness.

AN AFRICAN SAVANNAH
{Grace}

THE ONE BLESSING IN situation was the glorious sinking sunset being consumed by the endless horizon. Bright streaks of yellow, orange, pink and red wallpapered the sky. He inhaled his last evening on earth with gratitude for the view that was distracting him from what was surely to come soon. He knew all too well how the vicious savannah was composed of all of life's extremes, and even more so at night.

The approaching hunters would be drawing closer to him as the sun grew further away. Distant yips and longer howls would continue to scroll through the open desert plains. He knew the hunting skills of these ravenous beasts, and from a young age, his father had taught him how to out maneuver their unsuspecting wit. Although they may appear to be laughing in their uncontrollable manner, they were actually circling with frustration and will, determined to find the right time to strike. Spotted hyenas roamed this territory without fear of serious consequences. Many men in his tribe had returned from lengthy hunts with stories of hyenas circling their camps, resulting in sleepless nights and hours of tightly gripped knives. Tales of those not returning after a night on the savannah had become legend in all of the villages.

The tree bark started to now itch his muscled back as ants came out to scavenge for their nightly food. He could feel them moving between his skin and the patched bark, some mistaking one for the other as they crawled fast and lightly between both surfaces. His long dark arms were wrapped behind him around the tree trunk, tied tightly with a harsh rope, and this binding only allowed him to step inches away from the dancing bark. But the ants were actually a nice distraction from the other sensations taking over his body.

The spear mark in his left side was slowly draining his remaining energy as bright crimson blood created a flowing river down to his feet. He knew this scent was how the hunters would find him in only a matter of hours. He knew, for the first time in his life, he was tethered to a destiny he could not fight.

He slowly moved his aching skull back to rest on the bark, and gazed up through the lean branches of the acacia tree. The acacia tree had been his life for years: supplying seeds for soups; creating delicious honey from the small yellow flowers; and offering a beautiful smell that adorned his beloved wife. Now this well-known friend that had brought life to his tribe would be the site of his death.

Rarely had he ever been the prey in life. He grew up training under his wise father and had become a fierce fighter during years of battling his older brother. Eventually they had each inherited one of the family's villages and were given territory to farm and raise cattle in under the intense African sun. His older brother had chosen the bigger village and land, but he was given the better located property along a seasonal river. His people had easier access to water even though they took care of fewer animals and had less to trade. When their father died more than four seasons ago, his brother had become more aggressive about expanding his village's resources and demanded control over both villages. In response, he reassured his tribe this would never happen; they would always have their own place to live. Over time, he had learned to protect his property and not allow a coup or midnight takeover to occur by establishing nighttime security patrols.

There had rarely been a serious problem between him and his brother until today. Most of his men were on a seasonal hunt for more meat and would be gone for at least a week. Typically, this was a secretive venture to ensure the village was not vulnerable or left unprotected for long. But his brother had sent a young messenger yesterday inviting his tribe to an upcoming feast, and the young boy must have relayed that the village was unusually empty. Within the day, five men from his brother's village had arrived to speak to him about a truce.

They stood around him in an intimidating semicircle with this unexpected request. He felt an odd sensation move through his gut. A silent pause that created an initial hesitation in his mind. He was compelled to decline their invitation, but then his diplomatic skills told him he owed it to his tribe to enhance peaceful relations. He ignored this soft whisper of doubt and decided to say yes. Then he followed the five men out to this opening by the acacia tree to discuss how peace would work between the two villages.

As he now stood against that tree, his body dehydrated and worn out from the relentless heat, the last glimmers of the sun disappeared into the earth. The vision was so gorgeous that it brought a small tear to his eye. This was his final sunset; his last sensations of color and warmth and buzzing insects and hard dirt and whiffs of fragrant air. The harsh land had never looked more beautiful than it did right now.

The sounds of yips and howling circled closer as the winds picked up the scent of his blood and carried it out into the night. The wind would return with his predators within the hour.

After he had followed the other tribe's men to this spot, he saw his brother emerge from the tall grasses with a spear. His dark eyes held no soul; only a viciousness that declared his real intentions.

"I see you followed my men here to speak with me about a truce, brother. Surely you are no fool."

The warning message from his gut came through again, only this time it twisted itself into a knot.

"What do you mean? I am hear to speak of peace with you and your tribe. It is time for us to put down the spears and support each other."

His brother walked closer to him as the other men slowly formed a circle. "There will be no supporting one another because I do not care about your people. They are worthless and small. Your tribe is undeserving of your land and I am here to rightfully take it."

A huge fear now grew inside of him as the reality of the situation set in. This had been a trap; he had been a fool. He glanced around quickly and saw there was no way to turn and run; he was blocked in on all sides.

"You cannot and will not take over my village or people, brother. We will defend it fiercely!"

His brother laughed wildly into the sky. "It is too late! Right now, my other men are in your village taking your food and tying up your people. We are leading them to our village to be our slaves. When your hunters return, we will be waiting for them with our spears." He smiled cruelly, loving all of the deception and betrayal and dominance that demonstrated his superior wit.

Then all six men started stomping the bottom of their long spear sticks into the hard dirt, pounding loudly into the desert floor. The unexpected noise distracted him from his thoughts about how to escape. He felt the striking vibration reverberate along the bottom of his feet and up his spine as they pounded with increasing rhythm. And before he knew it, one of the long spears was sailing towards the middle of his chest. He ducked quickly to the right, but it was too late. The weapon hit his left side, and he cried out in deep pain as he folded forward. His brother laughed again.

As twilight now quickly surrounded everything on this starless night, the tall grass blades in front of him suddenly shook to the left and right. Slight shadows moved between the thin poles. Then he saw the first pair of glassy, round eyes off to the right. They gazed steadily at his silhouette and quickly blinked. He could hear nostrils moving fiercely to catch another sniff of his blood. Then a second pair of glassy, round eyes appeared directly in front of him; and yet a third pair arrived slightly to the left. Tough, hardened breathing came through the tall grass and multiplied quickly.

He felt himself inhaling more deeply and slowly as if to try and hide himself against the night. His back grew straighter up the tree as he dug deeper for more strength. Their grisly feet made no noise, no effort, as they silently drew closer to his scent. Then one started yipping and howling, which began a chorus of similar sounds as ten pairs of glassy, round eyes came forth from the bushes. They all ran around him, joyful predators circling their nightly kill, stopping to smell him from the back and all sides. He kicked a few of the mangy creatures away to at least put up a temporary fight.

In these final moments, he recalled his stupidity for attempting to trust his brother at all. He had always been willing to see the best in people, especially when dire circumstances had the potential to unite family. But even his father had told him he was too trusting and too generous in judging another's character at times. A silent shame crept up into his mind. He had let down his whole village. He had been too kind at the wrong time, and now they all would pay for his mistake. He could never forgive himself for this horrible error.

The wild pack was now circling closer and faster, and he kept kicking them away to demonstrate he had some fight in him. The bleeding in his side had stopped for a while, having dried up in the sun, but now his leg motions had jolted the wound awake. Fresh blood was in the air again, exciting his killers and creating more mayhem.

Then unexpectedly, suddenly, the circular laughing went silent. All ten bodies stopped moving. In the solid dark air, he couldn't see their stiff ears, or raised fur, or erect tails. He jerked his head to the right; listening and sensing for clues. Another infusion of silence surrounded him as the predators quickly disappeared into the night. He felt a moment of relief, even disbelief, at this sudden turnaround. Maybe his men had returned early from the hunt and saw the footprints in the dirt. Maybe his villagers had sent out a signal for help to their closest allies. Maybe he would make it until dawn and was being given another chance to escape his fated outcome.

But then the hairs on his neck stood straight up as a cold wind blew over his skin.

Right in front of him, slowly emerging from the endless void, a pair of dark orange eyes came into view. A strong, steady gaze locked with his. A slow blink followed as the beast took another step forward on silent padded paws. All air escaped his lungs as a deep fear rose up in his body. He had never been this close to the thick bronze mane of hair, or the giant meaty muscles of the front legs. The animal smelled of dirt and urine and dung and dried blood. Its nostrils flared openly with each step closer to his carcass; his blood a decadent scent and enticing treat. The lion walked towards him with a slow, intentional hunter's focus.

He felt a tear slide down his cheek. He hated himself for being in this situation, for failing as a leader, failing as a man. He looked up to the sky for any final prayers. Then with the first sensation of the beast's hot breath and sharp, crushing teeth on his leg, he yelled fiercely up to the Gods and demanded the night to take him away. Tears cascaded down his body; the pain unbearable and nauseating. A second gnawing bite removed his full consciousness from his body.

Everything went black.

Then in a mere pulse of time, as if he was now the rising sun, his awareness brought him to a point of light above the acacia tree.

He could look down and see the lion tilting his head into that body, chewing on that skin.

He could see above the night sky to where the dawn was breaking off in a distant land.

He could see above the earth's atmosphere as if he was no longer a part of that place at all.

Then he felt himself being lifted up into other realms

where everything was only white light and an indescribable essence of energy filled every direction. He was surrounded by everything and nothing, and he was that essence too. He was light and joy and peace and happiness. He was pure with himself and in love with everything. The feeling of contentment was so familiar and loving as if it was the only thing he had ever known. He was that same pure love; he was in his natural state as everything.

In that void of everything and nothing, he heard his inner voice say, "I want to go back and do this again. I want to make a new decision this time. I am ready for another opportunity to grow. I choose this lesson again."

Everything went white.

Then in another pulse of time, his awareness brought him to a completely different experience.

The tall silver pillars of the New York skyline filled every window. The dark-paneled room was decorated with dark suits, grey hair, stern looks, and an upbeat jazz music dancing above their heads. White jacket waiters stood on the sidelines until summoned for service, as the regulars didn't want to be bothered until they decided when they needed attention. At a few tables, discreet numbers were scrawled across pieces of paper and passed between hushed voices.

"We know he is family, Fred, and that that means something to you. But we're talking about millions of dollars at stake here, as well as the impact this choice will make on millions of people. We can help them. We can do good in this scenario, Fred." Jim swirled his Manhattan with his right hand while gazing intently at Fred with his piercing blue eyes.

A second man spoke. "Your brother made some shitty decisions before and screwed you over; no one is disagreeing with you about that, Fred. But ultimately this isn't about revenge or betraying him. This is about what is best for everyone. We just need you to vote yes with us, and then let the pieces fall as they will." JP's hands folded together on the pristine white table cloth, demonstrating that he was content with his position.

"I need at least 24 hours to think about it, gentlemen." Fred slowly took a sip of ice water. They had been trying to intimidate him for over half an hour now; circling him with smooth words and convincing viewpoints.

"We don't have that kind of time. The board meets at 9 a.m. tomorrow." Jim took another sip of his now-empty Manhattan. The remaining ice cubes tinkled loudly between the four sets of shoulders.

"Then it sounds like you have two choices: either reschedule the meeting for later in the day, or take your chances on not having my vote." Fred took a moment to glance directly at each man before turning his attention to his watch.

"I need to get to my next meeting now, gentlemen. Thank you for lunch." He stood up and walked away with three sets of fierce eyeballs on his back.

Fred stared at the cold elevator doors while waiting for them to open. His older brother had always been a ruthless bastard. Hard, mean, bullying, selfish. He knew the choice here could be incredibly easy and straightforward: vote yes and his brother loses everything - his power, authority, reputation, contacts - and yet he would still keep his inheritance so he could spend his remaining days on Montauk and St. Maarten. But so what? He would be gone from the family business once and for all. Here was Fred's ultimate opportunity to demolish his brother; an opportunity he had dreamed about for nearly his whole life as his older brother beat him at everything, took nearly everything he had cherished, including his high school sweetheart, and had always landed on top no matter what he did or who he screwed over to get there. Fred wanted this potential outcome more than anything. It was as if justice was finally opening her doors to him and he would be the one on top who had the final say. It was finally his time to give his brother exactly what he deserved.

Yet at the same time, Fred kept feeling an inner hesitation to vote no. He couldn't explain it. It wasn't due to his own selfish needs, or family dynamics, or long-term planning, or anything noble at all. It was simply this silent pause that kept him in a place of reconsideration, but also created an inner battle. He really, truly wanted to screw over that asshole. Not to be the righteous good guy, or the better example, or even to get on his high horse, although that may feel satisfying for a while. He sensed, on some level, that he also knew what would unfold if he stayed in this place of tension and power games with that jackass. He didn't want to always be watching his back or stressing over his brother's next strategic, destructive antic. So why was the answer still not completely clear?

Fred considered a quiet truth. Maybe it wasn't so much about his older brother or wanting revenge; maybe he was afraid of only being this version of himself in the world as a result of this relationship. He found himself pondering a terrible possibility: *Was he just a giant asshole, too?*

As the leader of the last merger, Fred had to make the tough decisions and hard calls no one envied. He had to fire thousands and cut budgets and tell pregnant women their insurance was over at the end of the month. He had to change retirement plans for thousands of employees who lost thousands in their savings. He had to close factories and rearrange personnel. Fred had always considered himself a warrior for the company, no matter what it required him to do. Even though his brother had always held more power, he knew how to move the company forward, hold his own, and not be taken over by another's will. He was strong and determined.

Yet somewhere in his heart, he knew this company had only made him a clone of the very man he despised.

Now, he finally had every opportunity and desire to royally screw over his brother, and to emerge the new hero. To steer the family company in a whole new direction and demonstrate his leadership abilities. This was his chance; the opportunity he had dreamed about for nearly eight years as he watched that jerk throw around his power and selfishly act with no regard for anyone else's needs, much less the future of the company. But would he also turn into that type of monster just to prove he was a better man? Or was he that person already and his ego was preventing him from seeing his own participation in this family war?

The elevator finally dinged open as he stepped inside its empty tomb.

And although it went against everything his ego was wanting him to do, Fred felt the greatest peace when he considered just walking away from all of this. Yes, he would be misunderstood for that choice and be viewed as weak, but those perspectives and opinions no longer got to him like they did when he was a younger man. Those people didn't know about the health issues this stress had caused him. They didn't know how much sleep he had lost, or how he had endured periods of counseling to work through the anger. They didn't know even half the story, so he wouldn't give their opinions even half a thought. He had to follow what was best for his sanity, his health, his psyche, and his conscience. The elevator ascended to the top floor as he tossed all of his options around in his head again.

The best choice wasn't the right choice. And the right choice wasn't his first choice. But why did he feel such a hesitation to make a choice?

The following afternoon, his assistant Gina connected him with the video conference service. His crisp navy blue suit looked sharp on the screen; the bright orange tie drew every eye to his straight posture and firm jawline. Ten pairs of glassy eager eyes stared back at him, blinking quickly. Dollar signs hung over all of their heads, as if they were circling around him like monetary predators.

"Good afternoon, gentlemen, and thank you for your cooperation in rescheduling this meeting. I know you are each very busy, so I will cut right to the chase, unless there are any further questions or discussion points."

The board members each looked around the table, a medley of brown, grey, and pinstripes. No hands were raised.

No voices rose.

Jim responded. "Fred, I think we're ready to hear your vote. As you know, we are at a standstill unless this decision is decided on by two-thirds of the board. As of right now, you determine what happens next to this corporation and we trust you have arrived at a responsible decision." Jim's piercing blue eyes stared at the screen as his right hand fiddled with a ballpoint pen.

Fred stared straight into the camera. "Thank you, Jim. I have arrived at a responsible decision. My official decision is that I am abstaining from this vote."

A rush of sharp inhales made their way around the table. Ten pairs of eyes blinked in shock and confusion.

"But Fred, you cannot abstain when you are the deciding vote. The governing principles of this board clearly state that in these situations when an integral corporate decision is on the line, every voting member must -"

"Jim, let me be perfectly clear with all of you about what the governing principles state. After reviewing my rights and potential positions with the lawyers, I have the right to remove myself from any voting decision that puts me in a position of potential harm, consequence, or conflicting family dynamics that will affect the long-term integrity and growth of the corporation. There is a loophole in the rules that allows an individual to vote in the best interest of the corporation by abstaining in circumstances that could result in further legal action against them personally, or the corporation in general, and would ultimately prevent the advancement of the company's interests. With my abstention, and now official resignation from this company, the board can now move ahead with appointing a new board member and securing a new final vote. I absolutely have the right to a non-vote for the good of the corporation."

"You selfish bastard! You know what is at stake here and that you have much to gain with a yes vote!"

"Not my problem, Jim. And that is absolutely not true."

A ballpoint pen flew across the room and hit the wall.

"You are putting everyone in this company at risk!"

Fred maintained a strong, even tone of voice. "I am not putting anyone at risk with this decision. If you'll recall, it was eight years ago that I warned this very board not to put my brother in this position, so perhaps you should have listened to me then, but that didn't happen. Then three years ago, you once again followed your greed to his front door and allowed him to destroy a viable part of this company. And just last year, you all approved his desire to take over our rival, and out of fear of being sued, you swept the truth and numbers under the rug so you could profit from the latest IPO. So you have put yourselves in this position and I will not be your scapegoat, nor the one to blame, nor the person responsible for what occurs next."

All ten pairs of eyes stared at the screen in silence, disbelieving in this turn of events. Calls had already been made to secure new homes, and lease new Lear jets, and make additional investments in top Asian markets.

Fred leaned forward into the camera, and without blinking, said in a slow voice, "I think this is the first time in your life, Jim, when you have ever looked integrity in the face."

Then he turned his head to the right and nodded at Gina. The video conference screen went blank just as Jim leaped forward to yell across the conference table.

Fred leaned back and loosened his tie. His back sank into the cushioned chair and he tilted his head to look up at the trompe l'oeil painted ceiling: clouds, blue skies, and birds danced over his head every day as if he worked under a peaceful open sky. Then he stood up from his custom acacia tree desk and let out a slow exhale. The silence in his mind felt like the best victory.

"Do you think that went well, sir?" Gina leaned against the doorframe of his office.

"It went very well for me. And terrible for them. But I leave here with a strong sense of justice and peace, so I cannot complain, Gina."

She nodded. "I doubt they will let me stay here now, considering what has transpired. Will you give me a recommendation for a new job, sir? My husband is out of work, and I hope to have a position secured by the end of the month." Her eyes shifted nervously from his shoes to his eyes.

Fred then reached into his top desk drawer and grabbed a white envelope.

"You've put up with more than you needed to, or should have, in this role, Gina. There aren't a lot of good guys here, and I know I wasn't always a shining star, but you were. You were excellent for all eight years. Let me know of anything you need. And I hope this helps you with the next eight years of your life."

He walked over to hand her the envelope with a reserved smile. She received it with a look of quiet shock and maintained grace. Then he grabbed his already-packed box of frames, Mont Blanc pens, and travel souvenirs, and headed to the elevators. Three minutes later, he emerged out into the late afternoon heat. His driver was already waiting curbside on Lexington Avenue for this last ride home from his family prison.

Fred called his wife from the backseat and told her she should go ahead with her business idea. He would be happy to stay at home with the kids for a while.

Over the following years, Fred still dreamed about revenge. He wanted to take down those bastards and he knew he could; he had the connections, resources, and ability to expose all of them. He could easily do it any day of the week. But that road was only momentarily satisfying and left him starving again for another possibility; another option that did not fire up the parts of himself that he didn't like anymore. In truth, and in the quiet of his own heart, he didn't want to be that same asshole anymore. Because if he did those things - all of the sabotaging acts he dreamed about at times - he was just being them, but with a different haircut. He was just reflecting their own nastiness back to them, circling around on the same merry-go-round, and that was exactly what he had wanted to step away from by leaving the family corporation. He didn't want to be that version of himself anymore. He was ready for the next higher version of himself to emerge, the new man he was ready to become.

Deep in his heart, he believed the betrayal and manipulation could only get his brother so far. Surely the lies had to be revealed at some point. *There must come a day when justice would prevail*, he told himself multiple times.

Every time he went down these mental paths, he kept arriving at new perspectives: What if this wasn't my battle to fight? What if deciding to follow my gut and step away from that asshole was my true power in the situation? What if simply trusting what I knew was best for me was the only decision I needed to make - and ultimately saved me from years of ongoing struggle? It was hard to continually believe in these perspectives when there seemed to be very little confirmation of them in the real world.

Six years later, after he had settled into his favorite family role ever, Fred received the fateful news while he was touring the zoo with his youngest daughter, Brittany. It was a crisp fall day and the sun was falling on the horizon. The top of an acacia tree could be seen on the other side of a low building. Children ran everywhere, squealing with delight at the latest animal fart, or seeing the baby hippo curled up next to its mother.

"Daddy, look!" Brittany ran up to the glass of the next exhibit as his phone beeped in his pocket.

"They're so beauuuuu-tiful!" Her small hands expanded on the glass as she tried to touch one of them.

He toddled behind her, his eyes on the mobile device. "I'll be there in just a minute, sweetheart." An email from Gina buzzed onto his screen.

After parting ways, Gina had used the money to take a year off to travel with her husband, then found another executive assistant role at a new firm. She was still his silent connection to the family corporation's inner workings, but only for big decisions and always in a discreet manner. He preferred to pretend like he knew nothing, anyways.

Hey Fred,

Biggest deal to date was a set-up. Four of them arrested today – Jim, JP, Dan, and your brother. SEC and FBI confiscating everything. Current board members from all companies being indicted. Twenty years minimum in an orange suit. You're the only one from that company who came out a winner. Guess I'm looking for another job again, but definitely in a different industry this time. :)

Gina

Fred gave a silent smirk at his phone and shook his head. It had been so hard to keep believing in justice in this world, but he had kept re-committing to his values of integrity and truth, even to the point of feeling like a naive, idealistic fool at times. "They say" the light reveals the dark, but what if some corners of darkness are regularly overlooked? What if that sweet saying didn't apply to every act of darkness or what happened in private shadows? These were the thoughts that had passed through his mind from time to time, and especially at night when his anger would occasionally swell up unexpectedly. Periods of doubting in justice, and doubting his choice, and doubting himself, had clouded his heart and weighed on his soul, yet he just kept letting it all go. His wife had told him to hand those feelings and thoughts over to whomever might be listening in to his small inner world. He didn't believe in God - he considered that part of his world still "under construction" - but he believed that something greater was out there.

And in this moment, Fred felt he finally received confirmation of that supposed "light" in the Universe and that something bigger *was* out there.

He re-read the email two more times to let the news sink in. Strangely, he only felt an ounce of righteousness and much less satisfaction than he had anticipated. Over the years, his lingering feelings had slowly evolved from being ego-based to becoming peace-based. He was proud that he had listened to the silent pause within himself more than the loud voices of the board room; that was how he had found his peace. He had transitioned to giving himself justice and strength without needing it to be external. He gave himself validation about his choice, knowing it was best for his own growth. He was no longer wound up in the tangled energies that his brother so easily spun. He had freed himself by trusting his gut and following his integrity.

The battle between them was now truly complete, once and for all, but only because he had finished it within himself first.

A sudden flurry of motion caught his eye. Fred briskly looked up from his phone to see a gorgeous, full mane of thick bronze hair standing right in front of him. With only a glass window separating their contact, the deep orange eyes stared at him hard, then slowly blinked in the afternoon sun. Fred gazed back, mesmerized and overcome with emotion. Their eyes were locked together in a sudden stand-off.

"Daddy, the lion likes you! He likes you the beeest!" Brittany giggled loudly and grabbed his free hand. "Isn't he beauuuu-tiful?" She, too, was mesmerized by how close the beast was to them.

With steady eyes, the giant cat held Fred's face; its wide nostrils flared wildly as if to inhale his scent. All of Fred's senses were on high-alert; his heart was beating throughout his whole body as he tried to breathe deeper. His phone beeped again but he didn't hear it this time, although it seemed to create a sudden pain that shot down his leg. He stood paralyzed in wonder.

Then the lion slowly bowed his giant head, as if acknowledging that something between them was now complete, and on his silent padded paws, he turned to walk back into his cool, hidden cave.

Soul Imprint Healing

Separation Consciousness

Separation Consciousness often includes the experience of external forces working "against" you to limit your power or choices. It creates enemies, war, power struggles, and ongoing dynamics of fighting someone, or something. Our Ego-Minds can even enjoy these exchanges because "winning" feels satisfying; there is a sense of proving you are right, better, in charge, and more powerful than another.

Safe to say, many of us have participated in, or witnessed, these situations personally because numerous environments thrive in Separation Consciousness. Anywhere that competition is valued will allowing the flourishing of these energies, including politics, government, sports, corporations, professional environments, and capitalism. All are structured to support a few in powerful, influential roles, and they perpetuate the belief that others do not have any, or as much, power. Power, control, and being regarded as significant become rare commodities only available to those who are the best, brightest, and at the top.

Now look at how this sets up unsatisfactory dynamics as you become more conscious of energies and of yourself. You will arrive at the conclusion that you can only go so far in these environments because they do not embrace other higher energies. You can only do so much within these structures, and to go further, you must remove yourself. This is often why you have to leave a job or situation to fully grow and heal, which is what Fred ultimately realized. He felt a strong instinctual desire to make another choice that took him away from the karmic battle with his brother, but he also felt a powerful inner struggle that challenged him to stay based on the Ego-Mind's desire for revenge, control, and power. This desire to "win", especially in regards to another who has betrayed you and has always triggered your feelings of being a victim, is incredibly seductive. It is enticing to get the last word in and to take yet one more action that will demonstrate your external power.

Yet Fred ultimately made the wise choice to trust another way to leave the dynamic that didn't pull him further into Separation Consciousness energies. As he listened to his inner wisdom, he heard that his brother would continually perpetuate this energy exchange because it is how his brother thrived, and in fact, it was the only form of power he knew. But as he listened and gained further insights, Fred realized that he was only becoming the very person he despised. So he chose to heal Separation Consciousness within himself as a demonstration of his true power. He embraced the opportunity to close out the previous energy experience instead of circling in the same cause and effect dynamic with his brother.

But this is often not an easy decision or action to take at first because Shadow Masculine energies can be brutal.

Shadow Masculine Energies

Bullying, violence, control, domination, personal power agendas, war, and greed. We know and witness these behaviors, intentions, and actions through many areas of life. Shadow Masculine energies are the lowest expressions of male power that have been animated and unconsciously perpetuated for centuries. They initially began as a form of survival as we expanded from insular tribal communities and started to explore the bigger world, thereby interacting with different cultures, ideologies, philosophies, languages, and values. In its simplest terms, life became more threatening when you had to defend your tribe from invaders, and the ability to trust others quickly evaporated. It was safer and essential to protect, defend, and fight at all costs for what was yours in order to survive.

Through the centuries, very little has challenged this mode of male existence because human consciousness was not high enough to see other options and possibilities. Men in many cultures have been trained, programmed, and shown that this was how one must be in order to be powerful in their lives. Yet the truth is that Shadow Masculine energy does not serve the vastness of true male expression and potential. Men are much more than they have been programmed to understand about themselves in these limiting roles. They have the capacity to live with open hearts, feel their emotions, understand their inner world, create from an authentic place, and express their truth with integrity, honesty, and dignity. We are living in a time when many men are awakening to this part of themselves, which can also bring up feelings of vulnerability, overprotection, and uncertainty as these softer areas come to light. It is a beautiful time of blossoming from the male heart. Yet if it is not safe for a man to know himself in this way, for whatever reasons, he will often unconsciously continue to remain in the lower expressions of himself and perhaps even hide behind a false mask that perpetuates the Shadow Masculine version of power.

In public arenas, Shadow Masculine energies thrive in closed systems that are not open to change, evolution, or innovation. Specifically, politics, government, big business, sports, and competitive environments are key areas for these behaviors and actions to continually dominate. Fred came to identify himself as a powerful leader who had to make tough decisions that supported the company's objectives and needs. He was locked into the behaviors and actions that secured his role and domination. This is in stark contrast to his soul's experience of life on the savannah where he trusted others, perhaps too much so. He withdrew into the Shadow Masculine energies and stayed in an environment that accepted and promoted this part of his energy. On some level, he enjoyed fighting with his brother and having a combative person to work against because it gave him permission to be the same way. This is one of the main reasons why another's Shadow Self will trigger our own Shadow Self.

Shadow Self Connections

Welcome to a merry-go-round of unconscious energies! An eye for an eye and a desire to fight fire with fire. Shadow Self connections are an amplification of ego, power, manipulation, blame, and control when both people are operating from, and re-triggering the lowest expressions in each other. They are often highly karmic relationships that have been ongoing for lifetimes, and consequently, it has become normal to interact with this other person in only this way. You can rarely see them in any other capacity or role.

With Shadow Self connections, there is a perspective that there must be a winner and a loser in every situation. It can also appear that there are no other options except to continually engage in this dynamic so you are not the loser, whatever that may mean. Your perspective is so limited that you have no idea that you can make a choice to end the dynamic because there is a part of you that wants to participate and win. You want to have the last word.

Shadow Self connections operate on the Elevator. The Ego-Mind drives the Elevator. Imagine a well-dressed concierge operating an immaculate elevator, and observe how he can only direct the car to go up and down. It's simplistic, safe, and easy to understand; plus, a form of control is maintained. The Elevator provides security because it can only go north and south, and therefore, it is easy to interpret events in a straight-forward manner that supports the Ego-Mind's prime functions. Life is good when things go up; life is bad when things go down. It is also simpler to live life at the same speed as others, and easy to compare where you are at in relation to others. The Elevator supports staying with a peer group, following the pack, blending in with the crowd, and evaluating life based on hierarchy, accumulation, and status.

The Elevator thrives in Separation Consciousness and Earth Consciousness because it is looking for safety; evaluating what can be gained and lost; and determining how to get ahead for survival. Because the Ego-Mind is primarily concerned with its needs being met, it will create expectations and attachments and goals and resentments. The Ego-Mind is always so, so busy.

For example, the Elevator is not motivated to travel off the known path or push beyond the boundaries. Safety is preferred. Don't rock the boat. Stay in control. Why step outside the comfort zone and explore something foreign or odd or weird? In terms of spiritual growth, the Elevator wants to stay with the masses and be connected to what everyone else is doing. The Ego-Mind thrives within a pack and looks for competitive opportunities to stand out within the group, but it won't go off the Elevator's route. This can also lead to denying authenticity out of fear of the unknown and a perceived loss of control or power.

Just as the Elevator can only go to the top floor of a building, the Ego can only go to the highest expression of itself within a limited dynamic. It thrives in Shadow Self dynamics.

The first thing you can change when you observe a Shadow Self connection within yourself is to ask: *How can I act more consciously going forward?*

Interacting Consciously with Another's Shadow

Let's just cut to the chase: interacting consciously with another's Shadow is not easy. This is not the feel-good, light, and pretty stuff that we seek to work on as we journey along a spiritual path. This is the tough inner core work that takes you to your own dark corners and asks you to shine your own light on yourself and another. It can be a point of ongoing struggle as you do battle with your Ego-Mind, wanting to still win and experience a certain level of ego satisfaction. We have multiple layers within ourselves looking for validation, justice, and significance.

Yet changing the dynamics with Shadow energies is also where our greatest soul growth lies. In order to do this, you have to go up higher on the spiral of energies and possibilities.

You have to get off the Elevator and open up to a new perspective where you are a detached observer seeing all parties involved and what they are learning. What are you understanding and seeing in yourself? What behaviors are you enacting that do not truly serve you in the long-term? What choices are you unconsciously making that you may be willing to change now?

Higher answers reside on the Spiral. Soul energy guides the Spiral approach to moving through consciousness. The Spiral is a continual movement of energies: fluid and flowing, graceful and continual. The Spiral *is* connected to all types of consciousness, but the energy must be invited into the space. You must initiate the request. For example, when you experience a fear around money and temporarily move into Separation Consciousness, you have the option of inviting in a higher perspective around the gifts of these feelings. *What am I learning about how I use money? Where am I perceiving myself as powerless with finances?* These questions open you up to your internal power, and then the Spiral can spin you up to a higher energy source of Love, Peace, Gratitude, Joy, and Abundance. This is where you connect with the wisdom of an experience.

Regardless of anything that has happened, your power is in your energy and choices now. As you leave the Elevator and evolve up the Spiral to higher ways of looking at these Shadow Self connections, you will begin to see new choices you can make that are more powerful and in alignment with your true Self.

When we interact and engage with another, we are energetically co-creating with them. Think about that for a moment. Think about all of the people you co-create with on a daily basis when you interact with them. The two of you together form a third energy that is a combination of your individual intentions. Look at how this understanding can change what you respond to and direct energy towards, especially in regards to Shadow Self connections. One of the most powerful questions you can ask yourself is: *Do I want to keep co-creating with their Shadow energy?*

It is wise to not expect the other person to understand, appreciate, nor connect with the conscious perspective that you are focused on. Chances are, they will not be able to "hear" you, either energetically or literally, and a direct conversation with them may not change anything. Fred had to make an independent choice and leave the merry-go-round.

One exercise you can do is to imagine speaking to their Higher Self. What do you hear? What do you understand in a new way? And what does your Higher Self tell you about this situation, too?

Most importantly, remember that we all have Shadow Self energies within us as part of this human journey. Yet we are not truly our Shadow Selves. We are all beings of light in physical bodies who are learning, growing, and experiencing a variety of energies. With this understanding you are more able to see that they are not their shadow; they are just having an experiencing of hiding from their own light.

This understanding will assist with calling in higher energies to work through karmic relationships.

Initiating Integrity into Karmic Relationships

Initiating integrity into karmic situations is often a lonely road. It is a stepping away from unconscious, often revolving choices, and instead following what you know is best for yourself and/or for the best of everyone involved. It is the higher evolved soul who can see this possibility and feels the responsibility to make this choice. But that does not mean it is an easy or even satisfactory choice at first.

Integrity calls you forward into a new energy domain that is free and clear of previous lower entanglements. It is a bit like re-booting a computer so a new program can fully load. You have to turn off the current system, wait 3 seconds, then start it up again so the new download takes effect and the new version can begin. Integrity is those 3 seconds of waiting as you switch between systems.

Even when integrity is initiated into a karmic relationship, you may still feel the pulls of revenge, sabotage, or a desire to harm. You may still feel deep emotions and triggers around a situation. (Put down the kitchen knives...) You may spin in the "what ifs" and feel that perhaps another choice would have been better or more fulfilling.

Yet you, as the leader of consciousness in the karmic relationship, have made a choice that is actually beneficial for everyone involved. By withdrawing your energy from the ongoing dynamic, you have also freed up everyone else from interacting with you at that level of consciousness. Since you have shut down the old computer programming, so to speak, there is no way for them to connect with you through that old system. You upgraded to a new version and the previous version is now incompatible; there is no connection. This also offers the other people involved an opportunity to upgrade, too, because you have initiated a new possibility into the karmic merry-go-round. This is a huge leap forward for karmic relationships that have circled for lifetimes.

As you initiate integrity and trust what is true for you, you may feel waves of doubt, loneliness, and confusion at times around your choice. The loneliness aspect is working with you on a bigger scale to untangle you from what you have experienced across all lifetimes, and to reconnect you with a higher truth that you are ready to embrace now. These are the times when you do more of your inner work to strengthen your belief in yourself. This is an opportunity to affirm that you've acted in a manner that can benefit everyone, regardless of what they choose or do next. Give these messages to yourself. Be your own source of knowingness. Integrity speaks for itself; listen to what you are hearing about this empowering decision.

Another important quality to recognize in yourself is that the more advanced soul in the dynamic feels the stronger pull of responsibility to grow. He senses there is an opportunity to make a new choice; to move away from what he has done before and venture into what is right at this time. He feels a sense of moving a situation forward because he is connecting with a higher aspect of himself. He reaches up to those higher ideals and senses that he can make a new type of powerful choice to walk away and step out of the dynamic, no matter what another is choosing. He feels stronger in following what is true and best for him because that choice alone is connecting him with his true power.

A Gateway to Higher Consciousness

An inner pause is a gateway to higher consciousness. How many intentional pauses do you take in a day? They may be fleeting and very hard to recognize at first, especially because we can override them and ignore the inner messages. We are so good at that as we move through our modern lives, filled with screens and sounds and unlimited distractions. Yet this beat of stillness is also where you connect with more messages around a situation and your potential choices in it.

The soul whispers softly, yet it is also direct. It is that flash of something in your gut, or the moment when you want to hesitate and consider something. The pause is an entrance to your higher consciousness when you can sit and be in that space with your full presence. It takes practice, and it won't always be your first inclination to listen to it. But the more you do, the clearer, louder, and stronger it becomes.

The gateway also occurs when you are saying "no" to a current version of yourself so you can step into another choice and expression of yourself. Saying "no" to your Shadow Self energies may be hard at first because they can be unconscious, reactive choices. But the more you practice staying in that space of pause, the more you will intentionally slow down and hear the other possibilities that lead you to a gateway of higher consciousness.

Reincarnation Retracking

Many people are choosing to clear energies and imprints through multiple lifetimes in this one lifetime. To do this, we elected to take the biggest serving, so to speak, of imprints and do a lot of conscious healing work at once. Instead of only committing to, say, healing one lifetime of forgiveness, we find ourselves having to forgive 23 different times and/or we experience an intense emotional situation that pushes us to forgive on the deepest levels of our beings. (Clearly, we are very optimistic souls when we agree to do this work.)

This is also why the hardest situations in one's life requires a lot of ongoing inner work and multiple layers of understanding. We are moving through that "biggest serving" in order to completely learn, heal, and complete it across multiple lifetimes, once and for all. That means you don't have to come back and do the work again (yay!), but it also means you don't want to leave anything unfinished or with loose strings hanging out. You have an inner conviction to really, truly be complete with a relationship or former aspect of yourself. You feel guided by an intense need to "clean it up" once and for all. It will be most evident to you because you will feel compelled to make a certain choice or that you must intuitively do something that might not make sense to your rational Self.

As we do this deep work, we set ourselves free from reincarnation retracking. Reincarnation retracking is when we have to go back and clear something, or complete a soul contract with someone, or do something we committed to doing in a previous incarnation. At a soul level, we can choose to come back and make another choice in a similar situation, just like Fred did after his experiences on the African savannah. You want to "clean up" what you previously forgot to complete due to your free will choices. Reincarnation retracking is how you make something right for you and it does not necessarily involve someone else. It is similar to karma, except instead of balancing energies, you are remembering something you forgot or failed to do in another lifetime.

Once you step off the karmic merry-go-round, consciously choose to not engage with another's Shadow Self, and make new choices that support your energy now, you won't have to retrack through the same imprints again and again. You will feel that certain relationships and themes are really done (*done, baby, done*) for you as a soul across all incarnations. Then you'll find the next area of energy to master.

JAPAN
{Solitude}

Swirls of inky black encompassed every direction. Shades of darkness expanded and contracted in front of him and up beyond his head. A tight cramp slowly formed in his left leg from the paralyzing confinement. His spine, a brittle chicken bone attempting strength, pushed back against the walls that were trying to close in on him. Across from him, somewhere, there was the locked steel door, cold and creaky and heavy with rust.

Drip.

Drip.

Drip.

When the rhythm of the dripping picked up, he learned it meant that the rainy season was here again, howling through the country and bringing welcomed water to the rice fields. This visual alone brought him back to the bright green sprouts protruding through the wet fields and soggy soil.

He had grown up working in his family's endless rice fields, and in an instant, he could feel his feet in the sinking soil again, hours spent pulling, pushing, prodding the seedlings. A whiff of fresh morning air invaded his nose with the remembrance of his youth; a mirage of sensations overwhelmed him. He would envision the endless freedom of each row of seedlings growing higher and higher in preparation for harvest.

And just as quickly, it was gone; the smell of mold and dank water returned to his lips. A humid stupor sat on his nimble shoulders and invaded his coarse beard.

He opened his eyes; two almond shapes of stark white and warm brown glistening with the only life in this living tomb. The perpetual darkness had required him to rely on his other senses for survival and mental stimulation. He could feel the mud with his tongue; a hardened cold texture he knew just as well as his own weakened taste buds.

As he did multiple times every day, he silently quivered up to a standing position, one hand on the brick wall for balance, and gingerly stretched both softly wrinkled arms up into the abyss, allowing them to reach without restriction, each finger pulling away from his toes. A slow steady breath guided the movement. A pull moved up both arms until he felt a tensing in his shoulders. His head fell back with abandon, as if the view was spectacular and enchanting and an amazing spectacle to behold. Then he closed his eyes again in   the   moonless   room.

Drip.

Drip.

Drip.

After three counts, his small frame began to bend forward and the stiffness in his back created a tight grimace on his face. He returned to his breath, allowing the murky air to fill his lungs. A paralyzing sensation set in often since he had very little space to walk or move around, so these soft movements helped keep his body in motion. The rats would return soon, and he would need to dig more holes for their burial. Some days, he realized this was all he had become in life: a collection of weak muscles; bumpy, itchy skin; lungs of musty dark air; and a rat killer.

But when that cloud of despair began to move in, he returned to his inner harbor of hope. A world where he was still the brave, valiant leader of his people. A time when he roamed freely and bravely anywhere he pleased. He had travelled great distances and saw foreign sites others could never even fathom in their small village existence. He knew what it meant to live fully and to be one with the earth, the people, the country.

Until he had made one fateful choice and it was all gone.

Drip.

Drip.

Drip.

He never knew when, or if, she would arrive. Occasionally he would hear a voice in the distance, but it was only a passing buzz, a hive of temporary whispers that disappeared before he could pick up any information. His heartbeat made waves in the blackness when he felt the possible presence of another person. The solitude was beyond loneliness at times, but he always had the power of his mind and his carefully constructed thoughts. He would never allow himself to go into some of his darkest private caves as he knew they would be difficult to exit. Instead, he would sit absolutely still in this eternal moonless night and visit every place he had loved until —

Bang! Bang! Bang!

Craaaaank.

Claaank.

He knew he was expected to stand when a guard was opening the door, but this time he did not move. His hands remained in their prayer position against his chest.

A slice of light cut into the solitary confinement cell; the black closet suddenly exposed with a flood of yellow strokes. His eyes blinked wildly with retraction, confusion, relief as his back remained steady against the dirty walls.

Then her hard eyes darted aggressively into his space, moving from the dirt mounds on the floor, to the red marks on his toothpick legs, to the tightness of his fingers interwoven above his knees, pressed to his chest as if to cover his heart from her evil gaze. His long, tangled, tough beard rested against his hollow chest, slightly rising with each intentional inhale.

Bang! Bang! Bang!

Her clenched angry fist pounded again on the steel door, demanding attention and respect and servitude. His eyes evaded her capture.

"You will never have more than this! Never!"

Her fury pounded through the jail and hit the bricks yet again, just as they did last week.

"This is all you are! You are nothing!"

Again her tiny fist slammed on the nearest surface. Just looking at him instantly brought out her rage, even after all these years.

He slowly unclasped all nine-and-a-half fingers. The other half-finger was safely buried in the far right corner with rat bones. He again found a steady place on the wall to balance against as he rose up to his feet. He allowed himself three deep breaths into the light. She watched, glaring through the crack, entranced by his weak movements, as her nostrils rose and fell. She crumbled the ball of rice in her silk pocket, smashing it to nothingness as he continued to disrespect her.

"No one in the country cares about their forgotten hero anymore. They all say you are *dead*." Her hiss whispered at him with steady vengeance.

He slowly limped forward, intentionally taking his time to allow more fresh air through the cracked door. His eyes took in the accumulating mud pit in the corner where the water leaked in; the old rat piles; the shapes of the bricks; the height of the walls. It was both familiar and new, just like the hardened eyes staring in at him, waiting for his weakness to be revealed. She was a few inches shorter than him, but her tight black bun and supremely decorated headpiece made her appear taller, like a rising black moon. Her favorite deep red silk kimono reflected the light beaming into the cell and turned it warm; a vertical dance of regal waves he silently enjoyed.

He hobbled forward until he could hear her breathe into

his own lungs. Slowly, his eyes rose to the dark beads glaring through the yellow streams. Her sharp eyes smelled of floral incense and expired mud and cowardice, and he knew them well.

His captor. His master. His wife.

With a steady gaze, he whispered, "I have more now than I have ever had before."

Then he pivoted right, his shoulder passing through the shrinking ray of light, his foot stepping on a high mound of dirt as brittle rat bones protruded into the arch of his frozen foot.

She hurled the crumbled pieces of rice into the room, a shower of tiny snowflakes in a blackout, and slammed the door shut with surprising strength. Her headpiece continued to dangle for moments after the physical exertion. Anger festered through her fists.

No matter what she took away, she could never remove his inner peace. Ever. She had continually downgraded his life from slave, to prisoner, to solitary confinement, and not once did the light in his eyes dim. Never.

A fury roared in her, and blazed up higher and stronger each time she visited his pathetic self. After all *he* took from her. After all *he* did to her life dreams. After all the ways she suffered, he still had peace, and she only vibrated with vengeance. She stomped her tiny wooden *geta* into the ground and marched back to the staircase. Tonight they were entertaining important guests from a nearby clan, so she must now focus on the evening's needs. She would not give him another thought. Her headpiece and tiny wooden shoes created a symphony of sounds as she stomped up the hollow stairs and returned to a world where her husband did not exist.

Drip.

Drip.

Drip.

He stood in the corner, toes sinking deeper into the softening mud, and captured drips of rain water into his open mouth. The wetness hit his throat, nose, arms, as he turned in every direction to receive the blessings of this shower. Years on the battlefield had taught him to never waste an opportunity to touch water, no matter how it arrived or how long it lasted. It would always give you more than it took; it would cleanse you, renew you, sustain you, support you.

In these instances when he was blessed by an abundance of water, he felt like he could actually identify with the rice seedlings he grew up cultivating. This is what it felt like to be receiving heavenly drops that brought you to life.

Then he flashed to another moment in his life when he exuded *bushido*. Samurai training had prepared him for all types of battles, especially in the ways of self-sacrifice and moral principles. He had learned to lead his men during the toughest encounters because he knew they were each prepared to die for their purpose. As he witnessed a man surrender his life one time, and he had to carefully close both of his eyelids as the blood rushed out of his stomach, he gave the man one last sip of water on his drying lips as a form of respect and gratitude for his warrior work. The last drops ran into the dying man's mouth just as he took his last breath and then his chest stopped. Water had been his last living blessing. It was the very least he deserved for a courageous life of honor.

Drip.

Drip.

Drip.

His eyes eventually adjusted back to the darkness of his current existence, and he now realized that every visit from his wife brought greater light into his cell. He never took the light for granted; he never turned away from it; and he never gave in to the blinding foreign rays. Every yellow beam infused his life with new hope and possibilities and faith; all of the qualities she could never take away from him no matter where she sent him or how long she kept him locked away.

After each unexpected visit from her, he made a vow to continually forgive himself because he had not always been good to her. He had not always been the husband he could have been. He was not always the best man in life. She had every right to be furious with him, and he accepted her anger. He forgave her for keeping him in this solitary cell. He spent many hours reminding himself of this thought.

As a young man, all of his conquests had been physical and imperial. The focus on power, acquisition, and achievement had brought him many rewards. He was a hero to the country and had enjoyed all of the pleasures of a regal life due to his fighting talents. But he had learned through the years that his work now was not on the outer battlefields; it was on the inner ones.

He had known his life would significantly change at some point because of what the medicine woman had told him when he was five. She sold herbs to his mother in a backroom of a hotel. Visitors and warriors wandered in from distant lands to find magical concoctions, and she always had the right medicine for their ailments. Her dry, crusty hands would reach for a small container on the high shelves. She would move briskly to mix a recipe, muttering out loud to herself the whole time, repeating each ingredient three times, and jolting her head wildly as if in a trance. Then after stirring and mixing, she would bark loudly at the patron to consume her creation now, right here, in front of her. She never trusted them to walk away with her signature remedies; they must be taken on the spot or the person was a liar. She always squinted her eyes with skepticism until the vial was completely empty and back in her hands.

His mother would visit the old woman a few times a year, holding a small jar of their family's savings in one of her hands and his small fist in the other. He stared up innocently at the grouchy lady who only glared back down at him in return; her left eye bigger than her right one. His mother would turn away to drink the special prescription, coughing afterwards, and he never knew why she drank that slushy brown liquid. The medicine woman's big eye always twitched as she leaned in to make sure his mother drank it all; he hid behind his mother's scratchy dress, yet was still close enough to smell the earthy herbs, plant roots, and animal hides in the vial.

Then one time, the old woman stared down at him with fierce intensity. A bony finger appeared in front of her big eye. "You will be a great samurai someday, son, but lack inner peace. A woman will change all of that so you can come into balance. A lotus flower must bloom from the inside out, not the outside in!" She snorted wildly and threw back her stringy black hair. "You will lose everything, but find even more. What a life you will have, young boy."

Then she placed the palm of her hand on his head and his mother yanked him out the door, his eyes terrified by both the crazy medicine woman's touch and her prediction.

Many years later, when he was stronger than the winds, taller than the trees, and more determined than the ocean, he had made his way up the clan's ranks to become a noble samurai leader. His greatest victories were found fighting the invading Mongols, but it was through training his mind that he experienced the greatest advancements in his career. He required his men to understand the principles of Zen Buddhism, and observed that only those who practiced regularly held up the highest possible morals and mental strength. The rest were victims of mental fragility. He would occasionally remember the old medicine woman's words, but remained confused about how he "would lose everything, and then find something even better."

The raindrops had stopped falling on his skin. A small puddle had formed below his ankles, so he cautiously squatted down to scoop the ground water into his mouth, both hands cupped together, savoring the wetness as it moved from palm to mouth. After each scoop, his cupped hands formed into prayer hands; an intentional blessing for this gift.

He hadn't always been this thankful. He hadn't always been connected to his blessings in the moment. He had previously been ambitious, and eager, and disciplined without perspective. He had fought on the battlefields and knew the extremes of human emotions. He knew the complexities of one's inner world and how the fear could rise up. When he saw her eyes, he understood her anger. He understood why she spit and cursed and hated him.

He had killed their only son, after all. He bowed his head again in forgiveness.

Upstairs, she stabbed a comb into her tight black hair, securing yet another layer of locks up into its normal pristine position that would sustain hours of entertainment in her popular teahouse. Her nightly preparations always began with her dress, then hairstyle, and finally densely-packed makeup applied to her face, neck, and upper back. For years she had followed the same routine, yet harbored a deep dislike for the whole process because it always reminded her of her wedding celebration. Of the young woman she used to be who had love in her heart and hope in her eyes about the new life she was blessed to be beginning with her warrior groom. She could still effortlessly recall the week-long celebration to commemorate their union and the ongoing evening events that required her to meticulously prepare herself for a proper presentation every time. Her mother had whispered relentlessly in her ears how to behave, what to do, whom to thank, how to be proper in this new family, and had tinkered with her hair piece and final adornments until she was nearly late to the next event. She was the bride every woman in the country wished they could be.

And when she looked at herself now, years later, she was still reminded of that former status and the promises that were not kept. The duties that were not honored. The blessings that were brutally taken away from her. But she would never cry nor show weakness about those losses. Instead, she smashed tea cups and broke combs and hissed at her servants and kicked floor cushions. She kept it all inside for decades, never once allowing herself to feel anything.

She reached up to secure her selected obi for the night, and felt the familiar tumor on her right side, two inches below where she comfortably secured her kimono. It had been four inches below her obi last year. Soon she would need to have every gown custom altered so the obi could be secured without pain or discomfort. The doctor spoke nonsense when he said she may not be around the following year for her tea house's twentieth year celebration. She just threw money at him for the visit, and turned abruptly to leave his pristine office. No man would tell her how to run her business or what she would be able to do in her life.

Three *maiko* and four *geisha* were currently on her payroll, but only one was the true star of her house. Visiting men requested her star performer regularly, and she made that geisha work almost nightly to meet the demands. There were only so many years a *geisha* would be popular and it was not an option to waste an opportunity to receive money for her talents. The star performer was lucky to have her as a mentor, after all; she was the reason the woman rose to such notoriety in the first place, and therefore would always be in her debt. This was simply how she ran her business.

She finished applying the deep red lip stain, and performed one final brush of her dark eyebrows. Her night servant brought in a tray of nigiri, rice, and tea, then silently scuffled back into the hidden rooms of the house.

Of all the people who came and went in this house, only two people knew about her captor in the basement: the house's bodyguard and her highly observant cook, who became curious why extra servings of rice often disappeared.

One rare evening when she had consumed a little more *saki* to cope with the pain in her right side, she mentioned how expensive her captive would be over the course of the next few years as the price of rice kept climbing at the market. The cook stared at her in confusion and fear, bewildered by the omission, but she never elaborated or mentioned it again.

After she had retired that night, the cook had looked for a doorway to the basement; tiptoed down the hollow stairs with a glowing lantern; and saw a heavy steel door deep in the shadows of the dark passageway. He stood frozen with fear. At the sight of a giant rat scurrying across the dirt floor, he turned to go back up the stairs before he could possibly feel responsible for what he knew. He decided he didn't know anything.

Once fully prepared for the evening, she began her nightly rounds of checking in with her entertainers and surveying the performance room with scrutinizing eyes. She would have to raise rates next month to cover the need for new silk cushions and polished tables. And new instruments would be required by the end of the year.

Out of nowhere, a jolting pain moved up her side. She breathed deeply and counted to five, then proceeded on with her required duties. The guest list was then presented to her on a wooden tray with a deep bow, and she noticed they had three new visitors attending this evening. Her eyes scanned the names and then -

The wooden tray crashed to the floor. It was not possible to see those names in front of her eyes, in her very own home. The shock sunk her body to the ground.

The drips had completely stopped for hours now. He knew they would return soon enough, so he made a conscious decision to enjoy the silence. The peace of the space. His Zen teachings had greatly assisted his mental acuity beyond what he thought was possible. But it was in this extreme silence that he must also face his own inner battles that wanted to rage on if he fed them.

A rat scratched by his left side, digging or climbing or burying something. He knew the sound just as he knew his own breathing. Soon, the animal would make its way to his own flesh and scratch again at his legs, but he had a perfectly timed routine for ending the pain on his skin and reducing the ever-increasing rat population. He had even developed a gratitude practice for these nightly killings.

The significance of a burial ritual had never been important to him until his confinement. When his father died, he had attended the ceremony and fulfilled his role, but his mind had still been out on the battlefield. When his soldiers died, he had honored them briefly and respectfully, but typically had to tend to the next battle, the next territory. He was always thinking of the next obligations and duties of his life.

Now, he was present. Now, he was connected to the experience. Now, he was fully aware of what it meant to bury another former living thing in the ground and respect the completion of its life. And so with each rat he killed, he intentionally focused his energy on a proper burial ceremony as a way to also continually honor his young buried son.

As the rat's scratching came closer to his skin, he reached down to sense its movements and warmth. They were fast little beasts, but his hands had grown just as fast. He grabbed the round chunk, broke it in the appropriate places, and felt its squishy innards spill over his hands and onto the ground. He worked quickly to dig a shallow hole amongst all of the other mounds; firmly pressed the matted hair creature into the earth; then filled in the remaining parts of the hole with dirt. With both of his shriveled hands on top of the warm earth, he would close his eyes and began his official ritual.

In his inner vision, a vast field of green grass and pockets of red amaryllis extended as far as the eye could see. He was walking with his ten-year-old son on a winding, weaving path that dipped lazily above and below the horizon. The air was as blue as his favorite *kompeito* sugar candies; sweet, indulgent, decadent. They walked along together as the wind moved the grass and flowers in dancing motions; his son pulled him forward to their favorite destination under the gigantic cherry tree.

By the time they reached the familiar spot, his son was always confident and fearless and strong. His precious boy laid down on the hard dirt, his angelic face looking up at the candy blue sky, and he brought his soft arms over his chest. With a final smile, he stared up at his father's face and said, "I am ready to be brave now, Father." Just like every time before, this was where he had to say goodbye.

On bended knee next to his beloved boy, he placed his own hands on top of his son's delicate chest and simply felt the warmth of his little body until it eventually melted away under the rising dirt. Until he could no longer feel the life beneath him or the frame of his child. Until the only connection he had to his child was the earth. Every burial ritual ended with silent tears blessing the ground. Then he leaned back against the hard wall of his reality, and dreamed of meeting his son again.

He realized the only way to find peace with his life was to accept his choices and actions, no matter how difficult or shaming or terrible they were. So to cope with this objective, he had created new versions of his life in order to be at peace with himself and to find the love in everything. This was why he did not kill himself. This was why he did not give up, or give in, or lose hope. This commitment to peace was his ultimate reason for living in this horrid situation.

The truth around his son's actual death was much different. The young boy had drowned in the ocean while fishing on a secret day trip. A gust of wind rocked the small boat violently as they were returning to shore, and without his father's knowledge, the child had fallen into the giant blue abyss like a feather coasting down from heaven. The choppy white waves swallowed him up before his father even knew he was gone.

The news swept the country in days. The loss brought shame and great public disdain to the family, as the boy was the heir to his father's role. His wife's grief was violent and abrupt; his whole family scorned him publicly and privately. Fearing for his life, he planned an escape one night to discreetly travel to the countryside and disappear into another world. But his wife's guards surrounded him after dinner on the night of his departure, and he was locked up and moved to another property far away from the family. They would control his destiny now, they all told him. He must pay for his carelessness, his mistake, their unbearable loss.

Within months, rumors spread that the great warrior was sick and dying after the loss of his son. Not a single soul in the country suspected that he was being held captive by his own family. Years of slavery and solitude followed, and the ongoing loneliness taught him a great deal about his inner world. He learned where his samurai training had taken him away from his heart. He came to understand that he had the power to balance his warrior energy with peace. He had since learned, after years of battle, that his ego was a false soldier.

The old medicine woman's prediction not only stunned him, but also gave him hope. If he chose to embrace this fate and experience, she said he would be given even more than he had lost. How could that possibly happen? Perhaps the curiosity alone was what kept him going forward into the black void of his existence.

Now, this disgusting confinement space had become sacred ground to him. Every hump and bump and mound was a place of silent honor for his only child who he was gifted at burying almost every day. He had decided what his private world would mean to him, and regardless of what was really under those dirt mounds, he would choose to see each element as a blessing of some kind. Otherwise, he would surely turn on himself and never survive the torture.

Suddenly, a shuffle and clang were heard outside the door. The removal of silence stirred his being. The lock on the door was being tampered with by clumsy hands until a stream of light poured inside the dungeon.

"Hello?" A man's voice entered the dark chamber. A small head peered into the space, searching for anything to focus on.

He started to stand up, yet felt uncertain about this stranger. Was this someone to trust or to resist? His samurai instincts guided him forward slowly.

"Yes?" He whispered back.

The small head jolted in surprise. "You are here?"

"Yeesss…" He whispered slowly. "And who are you?"

"Sir, I am the cook. I - I - I can get you out of here now. Follow me quickly, please!"

The old prisoner moved towards the light as fast as he could, but his legs were not able to carry his weight well. His muscles had evaporated and his malnutritioned frame was frail. But he strengthened himself with his mind and charged ahead with all of the force he could muster.

"I am coming, cook. But please be kind. I have not moved fast in years."

The cook could not hide his stunned reaction when he saw the meatless man in front of him. His coarse beard looked like charred broccoli and his weakened frame resembled the evenings thrown out fish bones. Yet his eyes glowed with a resilient light of peace and promise.

The two shadows made their way up the hollow stairs in silence, one hobbling, one guiding.

"Wait." The old man stopped on the third stair, out of breath. "Please close the door and lock it."

The cook nodded rapidly in agreement. He turned to go back and make sure nothing looked suspicious from this side of the steel door.

They continued the slow dark climb up to the kitchen. The cook opened the cellar door slowly, listening for any movements, and as he did so, the old man was overcome with the aromas of fish, rice, and jasmine tea. The warmth of the kitchen seeped through the door opening and he felt his skin want to eagerly move into the air's inviting embrace. Such warmth had become a foreign commodity. He reached to steady himself on the top stair, then followed the cook into the dimly lit room. The kitchen was spotless and barren, and quite possibly the most beautiful thing he had seen in years.

Without saying a word, the cook motioned for him to go to a side pantry which was hidden behind a bamboo screen. He slowly shuffled towards the closet, hunched over with a curved spine, but his physical self was not in his awareness. He was overcome with the sensations of a cozy room and a clean floor and smells from the evening's last meal and the soft light of a corner lantern.

Inside the pantry, a low table sat on the ground offering him a bowl of rice, hot tea, and a warm cup of fish broth. A worn cushion was nestled up to the table. He looked at the cook with emerging tears in his eyes, and all he could do was nod his head in extreme gratitude.

The cook nodded in silent response, amazed at both the frailty and strength of this man who had somehow survived beneath his feet for years. He wished he could have freed him sooner, but Madame was present in his kitchen on a daily basis. Now that she was permanently bedridden, he had the freedom to prepare for the man's escape, just in case he actually was in the cellar. Just in case a prisoner did exist in the basement of the city's most popular and expensive tea house.

The old man sat down slowly on the cushion with great care, his body weak and thinner than a noodle, but his spirits higher than the moon. He slurped the warm fish broth first, closing his eyes at the flavors and sensations of nutrients running down his throat.

"It is best if you stay here for a few days to regain your strength a little. I live in the room right there." The cook pointed across the hall. "No one will come into the kitchen because the girls have left to visit their families and Madame is bedridden. I will check on you in the morning." He gently shut the bamboo screen as the rice bowl was nearly emptied.

The next morning, the cook rose early to go to market and select the day's ingredients. He returned home to find the man still sleeping, almost fully curled up on the soft cushion. He placed fresh rice and tea on his table just as the cook's mother used to do when he was a sick little boy. He had learned that the body can only handle simple foods when it is recovering and weak, so he intentionally rationed food that would not harm the old man's body. Hopefully the warmth and comfort of his little pantry would fortify him back to strength soon. He did not have a plan for him after this.

By mid-day, the prisoner had awoken, and again ate all of the food placed in front of him. Then with a slow, diligent effort, he carefully stood up in the pantry and opened the bamboo screen. The cook was chopping green vegetables and smiled at his new occupant. He brought him more rice and tea, as well as a small piece of fresh pink salmon.

After consuming it all in mere moments, the man began to carefully shuffle his feet around the kitchen. He walked five feet to the other side of the room and leaned on the counter, completely exhausted from the effort. He rested for minutes, then turned around to walk back to the pantry, gently sliding each foot forward while focusing on his balance. He finally leaned up against the other wall for support. He looked up at the cook, smiled and nodded, then proceeded to walk back to the opposite side of the room. He could regain his strength in this small room by walking more than he had walked in years.

They co-existed in the kitchen for three days as both men performed their work and focused on their priorities. No words were shared as they were not needed yet. The cook brought trays of food up to Madame five times a day, and only witnessed her sleeping head and stagnant body in the giant bed. She was never awake when he visited, but the trays were always empty when he returned.

Muscle was slowly returning to the old man's body. He slept throughout the day, then ate, then walked around the kitchen for nearly two hours, and then took another nap. He awoke at the darkest hours to watch the rain drip from the cherry blossom trees and to witness the clouds cover the night sky. Sunshine flooded the clean floors nearly every morning, so he stood in the window to drown in their rays.

On the fifth night in the kitchen, he sat on his cherished cushion and finished all eight pieces of fish, two bowls of broth, and two bowls of rice. The cook had literally saved his life, yet had asked nothing of him nor any questions about his captivity. He finally inquired about Madame's health while the cook put away the last clean rice bowl.

"She is very ill and the doctor does not expect her to live through the week, Sir. She has a tumor that is now taking over her ability to breathe. And last week she had to close the house because of two guests that she would not permit into the nightly ceremony. She has never closed the house before." He straightened his knives, then wiped down the counters.

"Why would she close the house because of incoming guests?"

The cook stopped moving and whispered, "Because the

two men who were coming that night had the names of her former husband and dead son. She knew it was a bad omen. She fainted and hit her head."

The old man held the cook's gaze evenly for a long pause while hearing this news. "I must visit her."

"Then it must be tonight, sir. She may not make it through many more days." The cook began sweeping his pristine floor, his brow furrowed in concentration. "But may I ask, sir, why was she keeping you as a prisoner?"

The old man waited two beats before responding. "Because I am her husband."

The cook's brown eyes expanded to the ceiling. His hands fumbled with the broom.

"But-but-but, Madame was married to a royal family and her husband was the amazing samurai warrior -" His hand covered his mouth in shock as he stared into the old man's soft eyes, and began to recognize the hero's forgotten face.

"But you-you-you are dead. You died years ago of a sickness, the whole country knew this to be true..." His voice trailed off.

"I am here and I am alive, kind sir. And I must visit her tonight." He bowed with respect. The cook bowed in return. Then the prisoner motioned to exit the kitchen, and the cook led the way to Madame's room.

Her private quarters were hot and stuffy; a heavy jasmine incense sat in the air, covering her tiny shape like a sixth blanket. The old man shuffled in slowly, his posture slightly more upright and his legs feeling stronger than ever before. He stood at the foot of her opulent wide bed. Her small head rested against a buffet of silk pillows like a doll propped up to be played with. Her whole body was hidden underneath layers of comfort. A side table held a pitcher of water, the last delivered food tray looking completely untouched, and a red lamp cast a hot glow across her pale face. He stared at her with rising compassion.

Bang! Bang! Bang!

His fist pounded on the end of the bed.

Her head jolted left.

Bang! Bang! Bang!

She opened her eyes with a glare, trying to determine what was disturbing her. Her blurry vision finally saw a shape at the end of her bed but she could not make out the person. Her doctor was taller; the cook was wider; the guard was heavier.

"Finally, we are now both free." His voice glided above the incense and landed on her ears in confusion. She squinted forward. He started to slowly move to her side of the bed. As he turned in profile, she began to recognize the shuffling and curved back. Her mouth dropped open but no words came out. The medication had taken away her external fire and venom, but she still felt it rising within.

He stopped three feet from her. "Now we are both free, but our prisons were very different, my wife."

A shape that could possibly resemble her right arm moved under the blankets.

He whispered on. "My prison was external and dark; years of hell spent in the worst possible of conditions for a horrible accident that I took all of the blame for. Your prison was internal and dark; also years of hell but the experience was created by your own anger as you lived tormented by your rage and your body morphed into self-destruction."

Her right arm slid again under the blankets.

"Yet both of these prisons had something in common, my wife. Both were of your making." Her eyes squinted in response. "The only difference is that while you blamed me, I did not blame you."

He took a step forward.

"I have come to believe that our beloved son was our greatest teacher for he revealed who we really are. He exposed what was in our hearts and what lived in our cores. Our dear son brought us to our deepest lessons."

Her tiny white arm moved outside of the silk blankets and up by her shoulder.

He took another gentle step towards her, holding her

glaring gaze.

"I have become a new man after losing everything, but I have never lost my warrior spirit. I fought every day for my survival, and as I did so, I came to believe the only way to fight was through surrender. I surrendered daily to the darkness and turned inward to the light of my being. I surrendered to the present moment and allowed it to carry me forward each day. And I surrendered the death of our son to peace and compassion. I chose to believe that he would not want either of us to be suffering while we still had the promise of a next breath."

Her little doll hand glided up under the biggest purple pillow and stopped moving. Her neck stiffened, her nostrils flared. He was now only inches from her bed and could hear her deeper inhales.

"I do not hold any anger towards you, my wife, for I promised myself I would not burden my life with that inner pain. Daily, I forgave you, and daily, I forgave myself. Because while I had no control over my living conditions, I vowed to myself I would remain in full control of my inner conditions."

Then with a sudden, wild jerk of her arm, a searing long silver blade appeared from under the pillow. For a split second, the shiny surface reflected the glowing light from the red table lamp and blocked the gaze of her venomous eyes.

He reached out to grab her arm, but in an instant, it was too late. The sharp blade slid across her white, exposed neck as she coughed and let out a silent last scream. Her little body sank even deeper into the pillows. Then her loose arm fell to the side of the bed and the dripping knife dropped to the floor, sliding under the table.

He stared down at her as her final breath escaped through her mouth. She had been trained by his family to commit suicide if taken as a hostage or if danger attempted to get her. Knowing this, he had been prepared to take the knife away so she wouldn't allow anger to end her life, too. But perhaps this was exactly what needed to happen. He would honor her choice to live and die with anger, blame, and pain pulsing through her body. He could not save her from herself. He bowed to her in gratitude for the lessons she had taught him.

He turned around to see the cook standing in the doorway in shock, a witness to everything. The old man silently shuffled to the door, his head down, and made his way back to the kitchen.

Two days later, the news of the warrior's return shocked the country. The story of his captivity escalated in tales and extremes. The suicide of his wife was deemed perfect justice. He was offered riches, accolades, rewards, parades, honors, and royal privileges. The recognition, appreciation, and loving return surely lifted his tired energy, but he declined everything. None of it interested him. That was no longer who he was. He had a new mission in his life now.

The old warrior purchased an abandoned rice field in a remote village. The field stretched as far as his old eyes could see, which made it the most beautiful sight in the world to him. On the left side of the property, he planted his favorite red amaryllis flowers and tall grass, intently ensuring each bulb and seed would grow eagerly in the soil. On the right side of the property, he tended to the rice, just as he did when he was younger. The land bloomed in only a few short years to become one of the most impressive fields in the province.

As the sun sank low one spring day, the cook stopped his evening kitchen chores to gaze at the horizon.

"Sir, by now I must ask. Why did you change half of the field to grass and flowers? We would have made more money if all of the land was still rice fields, so I am curious what you were thinking." He stared out at the fields, one arm resting on a kitchen broom.

The old man paused with intention. "It is simple. The land holds everything. It captures everything from every day - the sun, the winds, the rain, the seeds - and it turns every day into something more beautiful than the day before. The land tells many stories, and I decided that I wanted to create a story about balance within ourselves."

A puzzled look moved across the cook's face. "Please tell

me more, sir."

"I want to show the importance of balance visually. Look at the contrast between each side of the field. Each section of land holds a different side of the same story. The right side of the field is about what lies beneath. What we cannot see, yet what we absorb like the water on top of the soil. What we cultivate and grow under the surface is what leads to a new bounty. The rice is essential to our daily lives, but it must do its own work. In this way, I see the rice as warriors. They are little bits of food that do much to be cultivated and grown, yet their efforts are not seen until the harvest. They are fighting to develop every day, but they are also supported by the land and rain.

"The left side is what blooms. It reminds me that life offers us beauty in many forms, right in front of our eyes, and that we must be open to seeing it as it arrives, no matter how it appears. When we take the time to notice how effortless life can be, we incorporate surrender and trust into ourselves. Just as there are warriors in nature, there are also peacemakers in nature. And where there is peace, we bloom.

"When I look at these fields I see how being both a warrior and a peacemaker contribute to our lives. Sometimes we must fight and continue on with a battle, while other times we must surrender and forgive everyone in order to be at peace with ourselves. We cannot fight all of the time, nor can we only exist in a state of passiveness. We must be both. We must be everything. We must be the land."

The cook stared ahead into the distance, silently marveling at the wisdom of his master's vision. He had no idea a simple plot of property could mean so much to one person. "That is quite lovely, sir."

The old man smiled at the land.

"Through the years I've experienced life in multiple colors, and so I have come to see the soil as my being, and the choices I can make demonstrate how I am cultivating it. No matter what the external conditions are in my world, I choose to understand that everything has the potential to nourish my growth. Just as the soil receives blessings in all forms, from rain, to heat, to death, I, too, receive all of the conditions of life as opportunities to cultivate what lies beneath. From these choices, my soul truly blossoms in all ways because I am able to work with the conditions of life. I am able to experience the full bounty of being present in all of life. And I never knew this was possible until I had the gift of solitude."

He stopped talking long enough to witness the cook nod in agreement, and to watch a bird dip low in the sky, as if its wings were grazing the tops of every soft petal.

"These are my Warrior of Peace Fields, cook. And to me, they are the most beautiful sight in the whole world because they remind me of all the blessings I have experienced in my life."

Then he shuffled back into his small home and began his evening preparations for sleep.

Soul Imprint Healing

Divine Masculine Energy

He is clear and solid in his sense of Self. He holds a firm connection to his own inner leadership, his own guidance system. His true strength comes from integrity and he isn't afraid to fight for justice, be it grand or small, personal or collective. He is a regal King who connects his loving heart with his seeker's mind. He holds an inclusive vision for his family, tribe, company, community, and is determined to safeguard them when necessary. He works for the best interest of many, knowing that real power comes from inclusive intentions and focused actions that support the betterment of All. Divine Masculine energy is a warrior who fights for higher principles and right causes. At his core, he knows he is here to serve and lead; to feel and act from a place of purpose.

Divine Masculine energy reveals a man who is connected to something bigger than his human self, and he integrates this connection into his daily life. He is part of a larger whole and requires himself to be an active contributor to the collective. He works with a sense of self-value and self-confidence that supports others. There is an ownership over all of his actions, behaviors, energies, and choices. He knows he is responsible for all parts of his being and all aspects of his life.

Ultimately, Divine Masculine energy is the man who knows he is an important physical embodiment of God energy. This is not about, nor connected to, religion or dogma; this is a spiritual perspective that reminds him that he is not alone in his purpose or on his journey. Even when he is confused, lost or afraid, he believes in his ability to figure it out; that he will know his answers and next steps in due time. He knows challenges, setbacks, and detours are all part of the winding path, yet none of these temporary experiences define the heart of who he is at his core. He is here in human form to make necessary and useful contributions to humanity, in whichever ways that inspire and motivate him. Although he will have to voyage on alone at times, it only makes him stronger and more connected to his own God energy.

As much as we may recognize Shadow Masculine energy, there are many examples of Divine Masculine energy in the world, too. Mythical and fictional examples are commonly found in "the hero's journey" stories, while Real Word examples can be found throughout business, community, social, civic duties, and family endeavors. Divine Masculine energy can be found in numerous industries and areas of life. They are men who are trustworthy, honest, perceptive, caring, and open to their own personal growth.

Just as the old man consciously chose forgiveness and peace during his years in solitude, Divine Masculine energy looks for ways to rise above troubling situations as a demonstrations of his own internal power and strength. He will still feel anger, pain, hurt, betrayal, and fear, yet he pushes himself to be stronger than these fleeting aspects of Self. He recognizes the truth of his feelings with responsibility. He intentionally focuses on how to care for his inner world so he can then move forward triumphantly in his outer world.

Divine Masculine energy does not deny any part of himself. He values his emotional needs and listens to his heart. He is in touch with the fullness of who he is, and even if those areas are kept private and protected, he honors them all as valuable parts of himself. He is open to knowing himself better and to evolving into a stronger sense of Self as his personal identity grows and matures throughout life. And despite anything that comes his way, he remembers that he is alive to experience all parts of himself as God energy.

Shadow Feminine Energy

She attacks. She actively uses her tools of emotional abuse, taunting, criticism, and judgmental tendencies against others. She is the mean girl who participates in or initiates bullying; sabotage; salacious gossip; or enjoys manipulating others to get what she wants. She feels jealousy, often unconsciously, and will act from a competitive place to dominate and win. Her behavior is rooted in control over others and she does not work in the best interest of all. She has a powerful Inner Bitch who does not believe she is loved, valued, or seen.

Shadow Feminine energy is similar to Shadow Masculine energy, but tends to be more subversive and hidden. There can be a greater focus on relationship dynamics and working behind the scenes to gain more power or control. Shadow Masculine energies are often more external and obvious because there is a central focus on winning, conquering, and overpowering in a manner that asserts obvious domination. Shadow Feminine energies, on the other hand, are more covert. They focus on discreet techniques that are often not visible to others; an emotional or manipulative tactic is skillfully employed.

Shadow Feminine energies are Master Manipulators who prey on the unsuspecting innocence, naiveté, or purity of others. These undercover dynamics are also why many men cannot see what women do to each other; there is no obvious proof. If a female were called forward to explain these energies, she may sound ridiculous because it can quickly turn into a game of "she said, she said." How can one prove what was said behind closed doors or demonstrate intention when these behaviors can be defended with lies and denial?

Shadow Feminine energy is a by-product of patriarchy where survival needs were altered away from community connections and mutual support, and transferred to power within a few and success of the individual. The focus shifted to competition instead of collaboration. Openness and vulnerability became weaknesses; expressing emotions made you prey. Other women became threats. Within this system, Shadow Feminine believes she has to compete for a husband and fight to keep him; she has to fight for her job, or title, or position, or clients. She believes that she cannot truly trust anyone and she must do anything and everything to get what she wants. And all of this feels powerful to her.

It is also realistic to assert that most, if not all, women have learned this behavior as a form of survival in their lives. Whether it was on the playground, in the classroom, or in a meeting, most women have had to employ Shadow Feminine survival tactics to assert themselves in patriarchal structures that support competition, winning, control, and being the best. Sometimes this is necessary and important; it is not to say that being successful in these areas is always "bad" or out of place.

But the difference is found in her intentions: *Am I leading and contributing for the sake of everyone involved, or only for my own egoic gain? Am I listening and respecting all involved, or do I only care about my own needs? Am I a strong, confident participant who is making decisions based on integrity, or am I trying to "game the system" and manipulate others to get what I want?*

It can be difficult to change one's behavior within systems and structures that thrive on these energies. Oftentimes, she is required to leave them altogether when she has reached a higher state of consciousness about her own participation in them. She must leave the job, the friendships, the family, or the life that thrived on these behaviors and find a new way to exist in the world that is actually more powerful than the false ego energies she has known up to this point. And that is a huge risk.

So why do Shadow Feminine energies thrive and continue on for some women?

Ultimately, she feels extremely disconnected from God, Source, the Universe, and the All That Is. She believes she has to fight for her own survival because nothing else has her back. She does not trust anyone. She is not connected to her own light. She does not see nor value the power of her heart or true feelings because a part of her authentic self-love is dormant or dead. She cannot - and will not - receive from others. She must always be in control. She does not trust anyone because she does not trust anything outside herself, nor does she trust within herself. She does not know who she is on the deepest, purest levels.

So she continues to fight for her own survival. And as she

denies her feelings, her truth, her light, and her connection to the Universe, she develops energies within herself that slowly kill the beauty of who she really is.

Inner Merging of Masculine and Feminine Energies

Humanity is moving forward into new, higher expressions of gender roles that embrace the inner merging of Masculine and Feminine energies within oneself. The warrior of action and external achievement meets the inner well of receiving, trust, and safety. The ability to self-lead mingles with trusting higher connections to God energy. Creativity meets action. Initiation works with receiving. Talking couples up with listening. External goals are supported from a pure, loving internal knowingness. The outer world and inner world are both honored and respected as necessary parts of a full life. One knows when it is time to make something happen (Masculine), and when it is time to allow something to happen (Feminine).

No one here is a half human. You are a full human with connections to all of the energies on the planet. You have access to the fullness of yourself as an individual light and as a being who is connected to All That Is. When you open up to more of yourself, you activate more of your pure Self. You discover that there is no polarity within yourself when you accept all that you are naturally. Instead of seeing yourself as one side of the coin or the other, you view yourself as the whole coin. And both sides have value.

The merging of Masculine and Feminine energies is an advancement in consciousness. You see that it is within yourself that all things must be in balance and in place as this is the source of your true energy. You mine from within and believe in your own supply.

Men and women are doing this inner merging in opposite ways in order to connect with these energies. Women are being encouraged to emerge out into the world with stronger voices, bolder actions, higher goals, and stronger demonstrations of renewed confidence. Women are ready to take their wisdom out to a bigger audience and share authentically from their heart space. *What does it mean to stand up and declare your needs? How does it look to require equality, respect, and recognition for solid contributions and leadership? What does it mean to offer your authentic self to the world?*

Women are birthing their full I AM presence.

Men are supported with turning inwards to connect with the truth of themselves and to know their inner world on a deeper level. They are being pushed to feel into themselves; to hear their hearts, their emotional voices, and to understand how valuable these parts are in their self-identity. *When the masks are stripped away, what lies beneath? What has been covered up as weakness or denied as too painful to examine? What has been sacrificed as part of patriarchal systems that reject the fullness of who you are?*

Men are gestating their full I AM presence.

Men and women are beautiful teachers for one another in this way as we each focus on developing the strengths of the other. We can demonstrate and support these merging areas for each other with love and respect. As we each do this, we evolve humanity into a fuller, more accurate representation of our individual and collective powers. We expand our I AM presence to be more truthful, honest and love-based because it encapsulates all of who we are in our fullness. It honors all of who we are in our Godness.

The Power of Daily Forgiveness for Shadow Energies

It is not our first instinct to practice forgiveness of another's Shadow. When vile, mean words are being hurled at us, or cruel actions are being done to us, we have other reactions that will impulsively come forward, perhaps involving a four-letter word or physical response. When we are experiencing another person's Shadow expression it will trigger our own Shadow side, too. But with higher consciousness, we can make other choices that support Love.

We always have power over ourselves, our actions, our words, and our responses, yet Shadow energies will create a temporary separation from this power. You may instead feel that the other person has more control or power in a situation, and that may be temporarily true. But it is not eternally true. It is not an ultimate truth. You are experiencing their ego, or false self, and this is a gift for you to see the experience from a higher perspective.

What you are experiencing is someone who is not connected to their light. You can close your eyes and visualize them as a being of light that is not seeing their light; they are turned away from it. They are not able to see more of who they are, nor can they see other choices that are available to them.

Forgive them for this. Forgive them for being turned away from their light. Forgive them for being in this other space that is not the truth of who they are, even though their free will is perceiving that this Shadow energy is their power.

Forgive them daily as a way of loving yourself and accepting them. As you do so, visualize them turning towards their own light. Visualize yourself opening up that connection for them as you forgive them. See them embracing more of their light in a beautiful, open manner.

And then release your expectations and attachments to a particular outcome. This can be the hardest part! You may certainly want proof of what is changing or evolving. Yet simply know that you are being of service in the highest possible way through the use of energy, and you are not ultimately responsible for anything else. You do not have control over their choices or next steps, so free yourself from those expectations or attachments. One of the most powerful things you can do is choose to control the energies within yourself by not absorbing their Shadow energies, and instead respond with higher light and love. You are sending their Shadow energy away with forgiveness and consciousness.

This is a spiritual perspective, but we must be responsible about our human needs, too. If there is abuse involved, please know that other practical steps are required for you to take care of yourself. Please take those actions, whatever they may be, that support your self-care, power, and safety in an abusive situation. Talk with someone; ask for help; file a report; get yourself away from there. It is incredibly important to take care of your practical needs in these situations and not only rely on the spiritual understandings.

As you work through daily forgiveness, you will feel a lightening of your inner world. Greater peace will emerge and you will more easily connect with what you are learning spiritually. Forgiveness is one of the toughest lessons we learn because it typically works against our ego's perspective.

And let's be real. Forgiveness is also an ongoing practice, so do not have expectations of yourself to be "over it" quickly or to never go into your ego energies again. That is not realistic. Instead, see yourself moving through the energy of forgiveness as if you are sailing on a river. There are twists and turns; rough rapids and slow sections; and yet you stay the course knowing that it is leading to a more peaceful place within yourself. You continue to sail forth with forgiveness as your guidance system because it is truly best for your soul, and for theirs.

The Gifts of Solitude: Separation Consciousness or Awakening Consciousness

Being completely alone on a planet filled with billions of people can create many different reactions within oneself. It may feel inspiring and needed; a relaxing respite from the world; a time of reflection and contemplation. Or solitude can feel completely lonely and difficult; a boundless emptiness or torturing separation from life; a painful phase of solitary confinement and deep fears. Perhaps it is accurate to say solitude is all of these experiences, as well as a balance of them.

From a spiritual perspective, solitude is a gift of being in your own full presence. You can hear yourself, listen to yourself, speak to yourself, and tune in to the energies that are alive within you. It is also a time to receive messages from Spirit and connect with your own guidance. When you are alone in your own energy, you can tune in to what is animated within you.

However, solitude can also trigger a deeper truth about being human: Do you feel separate or connected to the Universe when you are by yourself?

Solitude offers a check-in point for what you truly believe, trust, and feel in regards to your connection to God energy. It is in this space that you consciously, or unconsciously, choose Separation Consciousness or Awakening Consciousness. Separation Consciousness is when you feel your power is outside of yourself and that you are not connected to the Universal whole. Awakening Consciousness is when you see yourself as a powerful soul who is in charge of your energy at all times because you are always connected to the Universe. When you are alone with yourself, you reinforce either of these perspectives.

Until we understand what lies within our psyche around these deeper feelings, they are animated unconsciously within us. We are afraid to be by ourselves for a weekend. Or avoid going to a movie alone. Or cannot imagine taking a trip by oneself, much less moving somewhere new and starting over. On a bigger scale, your feelings around solitude set the foundation for your life. You are the single steady companion for your life's journey, and that will involve phases of being alone at times. Do you go into a downward spiral, or an upward spiral, about this?

Solitude also offers the opportunity to claim full responsibility for your power, just as the old man used his time in solitude to develop a stronger mind and to consciously choose the feelings in his inner world. He intentionally focused on forgiveness, honoring his son, and choosing to find peace within himself when he could so easily resort to anger, fear, and intense reactions. Instead, he developed daily rituals and visualizations, and connected with the simple elements in his very small world, such as water and dirt. He used solitude as a time to fortify his inner well of strength, control, and self-respect.

Solitude offers a contradiction. Although you are alone, you may also feel more connected to the Universe than ever before. You can tap into the understanding that no matter where you go, or where you roam, or what may be happening in your life, you are always innately connected to the All That Is. You are never lost, forgotten, or invisible to the Universal whole because you are just too darn important for that to occur. The Universe will never lose its connection to you, but are you choosing to lose your connection to it?

Global Energy Healing

When a soul chooses to heal a soul imprint, they are also choosing to clear it for humanity. We transmute an energy within ourselves so we no longer carry it as an active contributor in our life. This work is based on intention, of course, but it is one of the powerful ways we each contribute to Oneness on our individual journeys.

The earth has been living longer than any other species here. As the host of all microorganisms and life forms, the planet has the innate wisdom to work in energetic cycles to continually evolve and develop itself as needed. This evolution happens across all energy forms, with physicality being the most visibly obvious, but it also occurs through dominant human energies and behavior cycles.

The world has known destruction and creation; renewal and death; cleansing and growth; and all variations in between. We have polarities in everything from actions such as war and peace, to the physical locations of the North Pole and the South Pole. Our planet is continually working with energies in all forms, and then working with other planets and luminaries to incorporate their energies too, such as the solar flares from the sun.

In terms of gender roles, the earth has also hosted the rise of patriarchy in modern Western times while also nurturing matriarchy in other tribal or remote cultures. Countries and cultures move through different global energy balancing cycles at various speeds. Some countries are more progressive and active in social areas, for example, and integrate gender needs into their political, governmental, and societal systems.

Collectively, we all co-create Oneness and global energy. We see it most evidently through mass consciousness and popular culture topics, although that is only one way the energies manifest around us. There are multiple layers of Oneness, like a multi-layered cake with some layers being thick and dense, and others being light and soft. Together, all of these energies create the current Universal whole. As we each make conscious choices around healing ourselves, we contribute greater healed energy back to the dynamic, evolving energy of Oneness.

How do you know an energy is healed for you? You feel a neutrality around it with no intense emotional responses. You are detached and observing of something that no longer activates a deep response in you. The old man was no longer triggered by his wife because he had accepted who she was, focused on forgiveness, and consciously choose to keep his mind in a higher place. He did not perpetuate anger, hate, or any intense reactions to her because he knew his power was in himself and how he used his energy; not in staying entangled with her. It would have been a very different story if he had responded to her with the need for revenge and hateful behavior. His conscious choice to move forward in his energy ultimately contributed to global healing because there was one less angry, vengeful person contributing that energy to the multi-layered Oneness cake.

HAWAII
{Heart}

ANOTHER SOFT OCEAN WAVE rolled in, hitting the strong calves of every member of the large *ohana* (family) as they stood in a semicircle, brown feet sinking into the shallow sand. Ipo held the tiny baby firmly with his loving hands, extending the newborn over the water. The little naked soul closed her eyes, the rhythm of the tides rocking her back to sleep. He felt her soft spine relax even more in his massive palms. Nearly thirty people from the tribe were gathered for the ceremony as dawn emerged on the horizon; every male wore a ti leaf garland; all women adorned themselves with a single white hibiscus flower behind their right ear.

Ipo's eldest son, Kale, the future leader of the tribe, waited patiently for the next wave to arrive, and then carried the powerful healing conch shell over to the little one's body. He held the coral, pink and white swirl steadily above her body to cleanse her spirit and bring her full consciousness into the *Pa'a* (the Now) as her new life began. This sacred blessing welcomed the new soul to the earth and called all of her energies into her physical body, ensuring she began her journey with love, abundance, and family. After the third wave ebbed back, Kale nodded his head in respect to the newborn and retreated to stand with the *ohana*.

"We gather to welcome the arrival of a new blessed child," Ipo's voice boomed across the water and echoed deep into the valley.

"The gods have granted us this life after our recent shared losses because we know the *akua* (gods) are always guiding us in a Divine manner. This precious one will be called Alana, and we recognize her as a gift from our great ancestors."

The newborn rested peacefully in Ipo's wide hands as he spoke. Every person began quietly chanting in unison a soft song they had carried to this new island from their Polynesian homeland. *Pohaku* (stones) had been arranged on the shore in the traditional manner for sacred *keiki* blessings. Kale raised the same conch shell to capture the singing alongside the energy of her soul. The singing voices continued to rise and sail above the waves, out into the sunlight, beyond the mountain top's foliage.

The child was born two nights ago just as the sun began to sink into the ocean. The midwife, Meli, guided Kaimi through labor just as she had done eight times before; six of those children had been successfully delivered in ten years, and the other two had been returned to the gods within hours of their arrival. Kaimi had experienced every possible emotion during her years of delivering precious new souls to the island, from extreme joy and calm for the first baby, to intense heartache and loss for those she only held for mere minutes.

But she knew this child's birth would be different. This baby she had been growing was to be a gift to her older sister, Maka. Kaimi knew it was the best choice, even as she gently rubbed her belly each morning and felt the pounding kicks each night. As she walked through the quiet tropical forest, her other children trailing behind, she held her womb and told this little one that she was blessed to be her birthing mother in this life, but that she felt a different path ahead. This baby was a sacred gift of love, hope, and renewal for Maka, and the whole tribe.

Maka had been named *favorite one* because she was their

mother's first live child after three babies left her body during labor. And then the same fate struck Maka after three of her own died in her arms, the most recent death being only one month ago. Maka was tending to her daily duties carefully during the whole pregnancy, making sure her body was always protected and safe, until one afternoon a gripping pain moved through her womb. Hours later, after rushing to the birthing hut as deep pain overwhelmed her small frame, Meli guided her through the premature birth and Maka watched her stillborn baby return to the *akua* (gods) as an eternal blessing.

Following the birth, Maka's grief had rolled in and out with the ocean tides, and she continued to pray to the gods to be worthy of blessing her with a little one someday. She was failing her husband's legacy; failing her duties as a wife; failing as a woman. It was excruciating to watch her sister's belly grow riper with each passing day while she was punished by the gods.

After Maka lost her tiny daughter on that devastating day, Kaimi awoke suddenly in the middle of that same night. Ipo's hand was sleeping on her hip and she felt a new sensation in her womb. The baby was moving in a different way; she could feel it roll and turn inside her with greater strength. She practiced the deep breathing Meli had taught her years ago, and as she closed her eyes, she felt a strong message come into her *mana* (spiritual energy). Kaimi listened quietly, and then slowly turned her head towards Ipo, shaking his hand to wake him.

"*Ke aloha* (beloved)," she whispered. Ipo moved slightly. She repeated the words again and pulled on his arms. His deep brown eyes opened slowly to look at her. "Yes, my queen."

"I have received a message from spirit, *ke aloha*. About the baby." Her hand continued to rub her belly.

"Tell me."

"The soul of Maka's daughter just entered my womb tonight. The baby's energy changed greatly and I believe this is her child I am now carrying."

She slowly propped herself up and stared at his face, searching for a response. Then he sat up and placed his hands on her belly and felt the warmth, the softness, the life within. He closed his eyes and waited. Then suddenly two kicks landed where his palms sat.

Ipo laughed softly, his eyes squinting, and he began to massage her hips just as he had done during every pregnancy.

"I feel a different power in my hands, too, it is not the same as last week," he said, staring at her intently through the gray darkness. "It appears the gods have possibly blessed Maka in an unexpected way."

Kaimi nodded in agreement. She knew in her soul this child was for her sister; a quiet message she intuitively felt, but could not completely explain.

Ipo laid back down. "But we must wait to see how this child arrives before we know for sure, my queen."

She completely trusted her husband's guidance. He had always protected her, their family, and every member of the tribe with great love and wisdom. "Yes, you are right. I will keep this knowledge to myself, and we will know when the new one arrives if this baby must go to Maka."

Her heart thumped with a quick pang about handing over the newborn.

"And if so, we will do what is right for everyone, my beloved, but I will need your strength and guidance." She grasped Ipo's hand. Within a few moments, this upcoming birth had become foreign territory.

It reminded her of the sensations she felt when they had arrived on this foreign island years ago as children. Their native ship had sailed from their home island to explore the great seas, a voyage so big and new and life-changing that she had no way to prepare for it. Ipo's father was a distinguished navigator who yearned ceaselessly for new adventures. He studied the stars in the sky, and watched bird's migratory patterns, and after numerous long voyages where the tribe had doubted his return, he decided to move his young family and village to new territory in the hopes of discovering prosperous lands. Five families had gathered together on the beach in the early morning hours and filled the expertly crafted double-hulled canoe with supplies, food, livestock, and themselves. Kaimi sat two people behind Ipo during the endless voyage and watched his muscles glide the oars forward for hours at a time, looking for any distractions to ease her seasickness and fears. Even as a boy he knew how to provide safe passage for her.

She turned to look at those same muscular shoulders now. "This will be hard, my beloved. But if it is what *akua* is requesting, I will trust our guidance." Her voice trailed off in the dark hut.

A sliver of stars could be seen through a familiar crack in the hut's entryway; her private portal to the heavens. As chief, Ipo had made separate huts for his children, storage, tribe meetings, and their private quarters. Each one was constructed with wood and sweet-smelling grass, and protected them from the intense heat and unexpected storms. Tropical breezes blew in regularly to clear out most of the stagnant air that lingered in the late afternoons.

She laid back down gingerly, allowing Ipo to curl up behind her. "If your sister is blessed with the soul of this child, then the gods are watching over all of us." Ipo whispered, then leaned over to kiss the nook of her neck. "We will fulfill our duty together." He inhaled her skin, moving her carefully to her side as his desire for her grew in the darkness. His chest muscles pressed into her back as his lips glided across her shoulders; his hands pulled her hips to meet his. "We are blessed with many gifts, my queen, including a great love." Then passion overtook them as a heavy rain started to pound down on the A-frame's thick leaves.

Kaimi's labor pains began late one afternoon, nearly a month later, and she was guided to the same sacred place in the forest she had visited eight times before. She arrived with the assistance of other women in the tribe, each one accustomed to playing a role during childbirth and learning how to properly participate for the benefit of the tribe's legacy. With each birth, new skills were taught to the women who were selected to assist Meli. Her midwife knowledge was being passed down to as many women as possible to keep the traditions and wisdom alive for generations to come.

As Kaimi breathed deeply and slowly, her dark eyes stared intently ahead as the tree leaves moved in the wind. A spicy aroma floated in the air as Meli massaged a medicinal oil into her skin. The deep contractions picked up just as she expected, and she alternated her focus from the tree leaves, to closing her eyes as if to escape from the pain, and then back to the rooted strength of the trees. A collection of hands supported her legs, massaged her hips, and rubbed her neck through the contractions. She allowed her body to roll with the movements, knowing she was strong, and blessed, and loved, and alive. Tears started to roll down her cheeks as she surrendered to this mighty physical force that was bigger than herself.

Meli moved into her authoritative position, and with the assistance of gravity, Kaimi was propped up onto birthing stools so the baby moved through her with greater ease. Fingers gently stroked Kaimi's scalp and hair; her nostrils flared with intense breathing. As Meli chanted louder, the other women followed her lead and a chorus of Feminine voices filled the forest and the valley and spiraled up to the young moon hanging on the horizon.

The tribe's men and children could hear the singing down on the waterfront, and continued to prepare a feast for when the women returned from their birthing duties. Tables of fish, corn, bananas, taro, and taro bread would be ready for them all. Extra torches were being set up and would be lit as signs of blessings and gratitude to the gods if the new child survived.

The intoxicating chanting from all of the women around her encouraged Kaimi to push harder, and stronger, down into the earth with as much force as her tired body could summon. Her eyes remained tightly shut; her breathing enveloped her full body; she felt deeply connected to nothing and to everything at the same time. She felt the movements happening inside of her, felt the child sliding down to exit her inner world and meet the outer world. Her head reeled back with loud screams and the women chanted louder in sisterhood support. Their singing voices continued to soar up the mountain side.

Then a fresh, sweet sound was heard in the world for the first time. A tiny, high pitched squeal screeched into the tropical foliage.

Kaimi yelled in pain, in relief, in exhaustion, and fell backwards as four arms caught her worn out body. Meli swiftly moved through her process of cutting, cleaning, and checking the newborn for any signs of danger. Then with wrinkled fingertips and strong arms, Meli handed the baby to Kaimi.

"A blessed girl, momma." Both of Meli's ears rose as she smiled widely, her kind eyes conveying the good news. "Healthy, strong, small." The newborn sat on Kaimi's chest, screaming wildly, her tiny fists flailing about.

Exhausted, Kaimi turned to the youngest girl next to her who had been stroking her hair. "Please... get Maka..." She could not summon any more words. The girl nodded in eagerness, then ran back to the village. Maka had asked for forgiveness for not being able to be present for this birth. Kaimi held the little warm body as tears streamed down her face.

"Momma, the child needs your breast. That will calm her down." Meli looked at her quizzically, knowing that Kaimi fully understood what to do at this point after delivering many children.

"Wise Meli, would Maka's breasts still have milk even after losing her baby a month ago?"

Meli furrowed her brow. "Yes, they would. Why?"

Kaimi looked down at her perfect daughter with a patch of black hair, tight puckered lips, and dark glowing skin. "This little girl will be her child, Meli. It is a blessing from the gods and it is the right thing to do. I will explain later." Her face was covered in sweat and tears as she stared back up at the leaves in the trees while the infant's warm body snuggled up to hers. Meli held her hand in support.

"What is it? Are you okay, sister?" Maka stood breathless after rushing from the village. "Is the baby okay?"

"Sit down, sister. Here." Kaimi pointed to the ground on her right. Maka looked at Meli for approval, who pointed to the same place, and then Meli lifted the newborn from Kaimi's chest and placed her gently on Maka, who was completely confused and silent.

"The child needs your milk, Maka." Meli quickly removed the top of Maka's dress. She felt her breasts change as the infant squirmed and squealed in her arms. Maka looked to her left. "What is happening, sister? Why are you not feeding your daughter? Are you okay?"

"This is the soul of your unborn daughter, dear sister. I will explain more later. Right now, I must rest..."

Kaimi turned her head away from her sister, away from her little girl. The tribe of women continued to clean up the space. A young girl massaged more oil into Kaimi's hot skin as she fell asleep from deep exhaustion.

Maka felt a warm suction on her left breast as this precious little being eagerly looked for food. Her head was spinning as shock, confusion, and the reality of feeding a baby sank in. A deep warmth moved through her whole body as she stared down at the newborn girl her sister had gifted her with. *The gods do love me.*

Now, two days later, as the group stood in the water to welcome the cherished infant into the world, they opened their arms to receive blessings from all elements of the earth. The water healed the child's spirit, washing away all negative energies, and the child's energy healed the water with fresh air. The flames from the tiki torches burned away any lingering fears and instilled courage into the newborn's spirit. The lemon sun bestowed a gentle warmth across the tops of the palm trees, and together, the sun and the earth would provide roots and grounding for the little one's lifelong growth.

Then Ipo handed the infant over to Maka's husband, Pono, who was seeing the young babe for the first time. When Maka was summoned by Kaimi after the birth, Ipo visited Pono with the news of the newborn. Pono kneeled down in speechless gratitude to the tribe leader, two tears streaming down his hard cheeks. *The gods do love us.*

With the infant now in Pono's grasp, Ipo addressed them all again. "We are a strong community, beloved by our ancestors and *akua* for our ability to care for one another in times of need. The child Alana is a reminder that we are small compared to *mana*, and we must continue to pay our respects."

Pono held the infant against his chest awkwardly but firmly, the ocean tides moving around his knees. She was the smallest living thing he had ever held. His heartbeat sped up as she nestled toward his bare nipple.

"We care for each other and raise each other together as one family. Alana is ours and yours because this is how we experience more abundance together."

Ipo then signaled for Maka to approach. Pono handed Alana to her gingerly, and the baby intuitively opened her mouth to feed. Then Kaimi slowly moved forward in the water, a well of emotions in her spirit, and she stood facing her sister, her eyes wet and strong. Ipo moved behind her and placed both of his hands on her shoulders as she began to speak.

"My dear *ohana*, it is with great blessings that you receive this precious daughter. I believe she is the soul of your unborn child because on the night that you lost her physical body, I felt a new spirit arrive within me. I knew in my being the two events were connected and I have faith that it is truth because you are loved by the gods just as we all are." She paused to turn and face the whole group.

"We are all *ohana*, and we are all responsible for our lives together. This child is one of us, a symbol of our shared home. Please, let's all care for her as we care for each other. May we continue to be blessed and loved."

As the sun blazed higher in the sky, a celebration of life was held on the beach. Singing, dancing, and a special feast overfilled with bananas, coconuts, fish, and taro was shared for hours. Alana was personally welcomed to the tribe by each member, and the children took turns counting her toes and moving her little arms. Kaimi watched in wonder and emotional gratitude as her new daughter brought much-needed joy to her tribe. Yet she held back from getting too close and allowed Maka the intimate joy of this time.

The evening celebration finally grew silent as the full moon rose and the wild tides came in. The children returned to their bamboo mats, the older ones taking care of the younger ones, and the men sat pensively around the fire pit. Women returned to their huts after a long period of birthing support and celebration.

In the silence of their hut, Kaimi turned to Ipo. "But how do we know we are doing the right thing, my beloved? Children are not possessions we can trade and share, and yet this decisions feels right and I know it is the best thing to do. Yet it brings up confusion and many emotions in me..."

"Understood, my queen. Children are not commodities in any way, but that is not our intention. We are connected to the gods and we are trusting this message from them. And by doing so, look at all of the joy and love we have created for Maka and Pono and our tribe."

Kaimi nodded as her long hair fell forward over her shoulders. "I understand this with my head, but it is my heart I must also listen to."

"Absolutely, my queen."

They sat in shared silence. The valley was finally silent after hosting the sounds of the birth. The inky sky was exceptionally wide and blank and hollow with potential. Waves continued to crash and pound off in the distance as they did under every full moon. Kaimi and Ipo moved to their sleeping mat and curled up together like two giant ti leaves.

Kaimi's voice, even and strong, finally broke through the warm dark air.

"I must leave in the morning, my beloved."

With these words, Ipo knew what she must do. His arms tightened around her waist. "Yes, my queen. You must."

She intertwined her slender fingers between his firm ones, and allowed sleep to lift her away from the inner heaviness.

Kaimi awoke before dawn with her hand resting instinctively on her belly. Their hut was shrouded in early morning darkness, but the birds outside were singing and chirping erratically as the sun began to rise and the ocean brought in new bounty. Ipo was softly snoring, his long black hair lying on the ground like a sleeping snake. She gently rose and grabbed her bamboo sack, the one she used every day to scavenge for fresh bananas and fire sticks, and filled it with the same essentials she took each time: an empty coconut shell, a knife, pieces of taro, and two beloved conch shells. Ipo sensed her movements, and instinctively sat up, his hair slithering from the ground to meet his back. He reached over to a dark corner.

"Please take this with you, my queen." He placed a small packet in her hand, wrapped tightly with a bright green ti leaf. "I have been saving these herbs for you. Maka said that they greatly assisted her last time, and I believe they will also nurture you." He leaned in to kiss her forehead, her nose, her lips.

"Thank you, my king." She placed the packet inside her bamboo sling. "I will return when the Heart Flower's leaves begin to curl."

"*Me Ke Aloha Pumehana* (With the warmth of my love)," Ipo whispered, and pulled open the stiff hanging curtain to their sleeping hut.

Kaimi walked quietly to the sandy edges of the village, the ocean at her back, and looked up at the majestic *mauna* (mountain) covered with green foliage and high water falling in the distance. She closed her eyes and inhaled the *mana* (spiritual power) of her surroundings. Then she proceeded to the far edge of the forest where a collection of bright red Heart Flowers (anthuriums) sat at the opening to the sacred path.

Their bold, shiny leaves form an open heart shape and a long spike protrudes from the center; the deep red hue making a striking contrast to the dark green leaves. Since arriving on the island many years ago, the tribe has watched as nature sends signals and messages. Flocks of seabirds fly together when a storm is approaching. Fish swim into shallower waters twice a day to signal tidal changes. And this flower has come to symbolize abundance, luck, and blessings. It is highly revered as being connected to messages of *mana* from the gods, for when the waxy leaves of the Heart Flower begin to curl, it means rain is approaching soon and a cleansing energy will be arriving.

Kaimi followed the winding path as she ascended higher up the mountain, walking across boulders and rocks, crossing over two shallow flowing streams, and passing through countless bushes and flowers. Heart Flowers paved the way up to the sacred *heiau* (temple) where she would speak to her ancestors and the gods. Taller trees appeared as she traveled further into the island's womb. Occasionally, she saw a small female footprint hardened in the mud, a reminder of her sisterhood with other women. *We must each be alone during this cleansing, but we are still deeply connected to one another as sisters.*

She stopped and picked a young orange hibiscus bud to place behind her right ear. As the sun rose to the still point in the sky, she paused in the shade of a plumeria tree to rest. She grabbed as many plumeria branches as she could carry and continued on her way to the private temple.

By mid-afternoon, after climbing and dipping to the mountain's dance, Kaimi arrived at the end of the dirt trail. A sturdy, wide wood platform sat above the ground, looking out to the sea, and behind it was a tiny A-frame hut covered in long leaves weaved together to keep out the rain. A small fire pit was off to the far side, and on the edge of the cliff, eleven *pohaku* (stones) were cradled gently in the earth to show eternal respect for every *kaleiokalani,* child of heaven. Kaimi had arrived at their sacred grieving space.

Just as nature showed them the cycles of the earth and the

wisdom of change, the tribe's elders have taught every clan member that the same cycles of change exist within themselves. They were one with nature, always in alignment with the earth, the animals, the plants and trees and flowers. They all shared the same precious island, and were constantly learning and teaching each other in the ways of natural existence. The tribe ate twice a day in accordance with the ocean's tides, and slept with the rhythms of the sky. They watched for input from the gods about how to organize and run their daily lives, including the honoring of intelligence, skills, and leadership gifts. Women were taught to trust the right men and honor their instincts, protective nature, and strength. Men were taught how to care for their mothers, sisters, wives, and daughters with an open heart; to allow her to feel her emotions and flow with the tides.

As a result of this wisdom, a sacred *heiau* (temple) was built to allow anyone private space to be with their ancestors, the gods, and the earth when they felt a calling to do so. The necessity of this grieving space had become even clearer after one woman refused to participate in a clearing ceremony.

Kamila, Kaimi's aunt, had lost her infant son one week after he was born. She had cradled his little cold body for hours, and for days afterwards, refused to grieve for his return to the gods. She stated it was not necessary to grieve as she would rather not think about it, not focus on the transition, not dwell on the past. She pretended she felt strong and fine, and as a result, Kamila took on more duties around the village to demonstrate her strength. Her husband, Lopaka, insisted she must go to the sacred temple in order to care for her spirit, but she refused, day after day, night after night. She told him, and everyone, that she was fine and strong and did not need to connect with sadness.

Kamila's grief and emotions slowly turned inwards as she rejected the natural mourning process. She chopped down excessive amounts of trees as her inner aggression grew, and soon, other tribe members had to prevent her from destroying their abundant resources. She became known as The Angry

One by the children, and was avoided by other women as she lashed out aggressively at them. Kamila's rage began to destroy their connection to nature and divided the tribe. Loud arguing, blasts of words, and her daughter's crying echoed over the tides nearly every night from her family's hut. The elders noticed there was no cleansing rain for their crops and daily needs for weeks. Kamila's inner grief was harming them all.

Finally, after Kamila's emotional turbulence had swept through the village yet another day, her husband Lopaka knew he must follow the elders' guidance. He must force her to do what she needed to do, or watch her destroy everything they needed and cherished. He had no choice. It was for the good of All.

Lopaka led Kamila into the forest canopy after the evening meal, holding a single torch to guide the way into the approaching darkness. He held her arm tight as he pulled her forward; she tried to backtrack to the village, resisting and struggling with him the whole way. She shouted loudly up the mountain. Lopaka marched on; a fire torch in one hand, a fiery wife in the other.

One hour later, they arrived at a small clearing miles from the beach. Kamila collapsed on the ground in protest for being taken to this place, although she had no idea what was happening. Rage sat on her face and her eyes steamed with anger and fear and contempt. It had now been exactly 19 days since she had lost her newborn. She still thought about him every minute of every day.

Lopaka sat on the earth facing Kamila, their knees touching, her head turned away from him. The final rays of the setting sun gleamed through the thick green brush creating strips of light on the ground.

He reached for her hands and unraveled them open slowly from their tight fists, one finger releasing at a time. He softly caressed her palms and inner forearms, and watched her breathe deeply as her body slowly relaxed, unfurled, released its clenched turmoil.

Lopaka pushed strands of hair from her stiff shoulders. "Please, beautiful one, may I have the gift of your eyes."

She slowly turned away from the forest to face him, her long black hair hanging limply, exhausted, against both cheekbones. Her eyes trembled with fear. She had no idea what was happening here or what her husband intended to do.

Lopaka held both of her hands loosely, staring deep into her black eyes, and began to slowly say the words as the elders had instructed:

"I love you. I am sorry. Please forgive me. Thank you."

Her eyes squinted shut. He grasped her hands tighter.

"I love you. I am sorry. Please forgive me. Thank you."

Her head fell forward. Her hair touched their knees.

"I love you. I am sorry. Please forgive me. Thank you."

Her shoulders started moving up and down as her body shook with a quiet force. Tears grew in his eyes as he witnessed her release. His voice remained strong and steady.

"I love you. I am sorry. Please forgive me. Thank you."

Then she fell forward into his strong embrace, sobbing and heaving with the grief she had been carrying for 19 days. Lopaka continued to repeat the sacred blessing five more times as his wife finally gave herself permission to feel what was in her heart.

Then Kamila also summoned the strength to repeat the phrase aloud with him over and over again. She said the words to her lost son, to all of her children, to her husband, to her whole tribe, to her ancestors, to the gods. They sat there for hours as the stars emerged in the dark ocean above them. She allowed the feelings to be felt and her true emotions to be released. They remained in the cleansing space until the next morning, crying, sleeping, and sharing.

Upon the rise of a new sun, they felt their spirits had been brought back into oneness with nature and truth. Kamila had finally acknowledged what her heart needed to say.

As they walked back to the beach, Lopaka stopped and pointed at a cluster of Heart Flowers. Each one's waxy red leaves were now curling. The rains finally came and the whole village was blessed with much-needed fresh water. Kamila's emotional cleansing had moved the *mana* through her and re-connected her to a new place of healing. Lopaka was praised for leading his wife forward, and Kamila was praised for her brave authenticity. The whole tribe celebrated their healing process. One year later, Lopaka and Kamila were blessed with a healthy baby boy named Pono.

This story was regularly shared in the tribe for young ears and old hearts to remember how they were always connected to everything. The importance of honoring their natural cycles of celebration, grieving, releasing, and beginnings was to be cherished regularly.

Kaimi arrived in this space with a willingness to be, and stay, open.

Even though Maka had been in the grieving space only a month ago, it still required fresh clearing and cleaning for Kaimi's personal ceremony. She cleared fallen leaves from inside of the hut, and wiped off the debris on the platform. She arranged the plumeria branches along all four edges to claim her protected sacred space. She settled into the land and felt it settle into her. Then she began her opening ritual by taking the two shells from her bamboo pack and placing each one in front of a *pohaku* (stone) to signal to each child's spirit that she was here. She lit a fire in the fire pit, and watched the top of the trees dance in the ocean breeze. She believed that was a signal from the gods, waving hello to her through the tree branches.

Aloud, she asked, "Dear Spirit, dear Ancestors, dear Gods, please guide me during my sacred clearing time. Please provide the answers I seek around giving this precious daughter to Maka. Why am I being guided to do this? What is the bigger purpose of this child? Please show me peace around my decision, which I know and feel is the right thing to do. Thank you for your blessings and Love."

With her hands resting calmly on her knees, Kaimi sat in silence for an hour as a demonstration of supreme trust. Then she retired to sleep.

Kaimi emerged from the hut at sunrise, and after eating a small serving of taro, she sat on the platform surrounded by the plumeria branches as the sun's warmth hit her feet. She began her ceremony the same way she did the previous two visits when she had been here to say goodbye to her babies, but she knew this time was different. She had been guided to gift the child to her sister, so this birth was a blessing in many ways. But as her mother had taught her, she must always honor the truth of her feelings as messages from her *mana* (spiritual energy) and not *mana'o* (think) too much about them or she will go *pupule* (crazy). *Allow yourself to flow with the streams, the tides, and the winds.* It had been her wise grandmother who had brought this grieving ritual to the new island from their homeland. *Our traditions and wisdom were the lightest things we carried on the boat,* she would say with a soft laugh.

The deep emerald valley and wide sapphire ocean stretched out in front of her as a new day was birthed. She closed her eyes to feel her physical self. With every inhale, she summoned the wisdom she was now meant to receive, and with every exhale, she released the thoughts and emotions which no longer served her. She asked for the highest possible *mana* to flood her soul now. And as she opened her eyes, she began to speak the meditative cleansing mantra aloud to the world:

"I love you. I am sorry. Please forgive me. Thank you."

The words stirred a dormant volcano of energy within her.

"I love you. I am sorry. Please forgive me. Thank you."

A soft breeze moved across her face.

"I love you. I am sorry. Please forgive me. Thank you."

Her eyes began to feel the energy of handing over her precious daughter. Even though it was the right thing to do, she was opening to the loss. Opening to the pain, opening to the hollowness it left in her, opening to the change.

"I love you. I am sorry. Please forgive me. Thank you."

She kept repeating the words to her new daughter, her

children, her sister, her husband, her tribe, her ancestors, the gods. She was clearing all emotional energies from all connections each time she said the phrases.

And then she said the mantra nine times to herself:

"I love you. I am sorry. Please forgive me. Thank you."

With tears streaming down her face and dripping onto her knees, she allowed everything to open and flow through her. She did not fight it, nor deny it, nor try to control what was coming through her. She simply allowed it all to drain through her as she trusted the clearing experience. Then exhausted from the hours of chanting, Kaimi returned to the hut for an afternoon nap and hours later, woke up to darkness. She ate another serving of taro and drank water from a nearby stream. She watched the stars dance and twinkle as they quietly rotated in the heavens. Hints of plumeria lingered in the warm air. A shooting star jetted by, waving vibrantly at her. She imagined Ipo's warmth engulfing her as she fell asleep feeling emptied and open.

Kaimi began the second day with the same ritual. She sat and repeated aloud the meditative cleansing mantra to everyone, including to herself. She opened the herb packet from Ipo and rubbed the blend on the soles of her feet. Rich and musky, grounding and strong, her connection to the earth embedded her skin. She placed a dab on the very top of her head and ran it down her long strands of strong black hair, rubbing the healing herbs further into her energy.

She listened for answers to her questions, but did not hear any yet. Her grandmother always told her the true answers would only come when she returned to a place of real peace, forgiveness, and healing. Her work was in getting to that place no matter how long it took. *We always have time for all of our healing, Kaimi.* So again she chanted the phrases that cleansed her:

"I love you. I am sorry. Please forgive me. Thank you."

"I love you" is the opening statement of *aloha* and Supreme love; a unifying connection of energy between her and all elements of the earth.

"I am sorry" clears away any and all lingering grievances, anger, hurt, pain, or blame. Stating "I am sorry" expresses all hidden shame or regrets, sincerely and simply.

"Please forgive me" is the request for atonement for any and all actions, known and unknown, seen and unseen. An acknowledgment of all conscious and unconscious choices to be forgiven and released, healed and completed.

"Thank you" is the recognition of gratitude, peace, and forgiveness. A completion of a cycle that began with love and returns to love. A sacred blessing to the gods, to nature, to All That Is for the abundance of everything in the world, including eternal connections.

Kaimi continued on by honoring each of the souls of her unborn children, and focused on many blessings for Alana. Then she fell into another deep sleep, with her final thoughts still wondering what the bigger purpose of this situation may be for her growth.

On the third day in the grieving space, Kaimi again moved through the same rituals and applied more sacred herbs to her body. After chanting, and listening, and blessing everyone, she sat on the platform and inhaled nature's *mana* deeply. She began to feel a deeper peace and emerging lightness inside her heart.

When the sun was at the highest point overhead, and there were no shadows on the earth, she walked down the path to look at the Heart Flower for guidance, but it was not curling yet. Feeling a pang for completion of this cycle, yet a deeper trust that all was happening in perfect timing, Kaimi returned to her sleeping hut for a late afternoon nap. And as she drifted effortlessly off to asleep, the answers she wanted arrived through her dream state.

Kaimi saw herself as a being of light surrounded by many beings of light all around her. They were all connected as a soul family that intended to allow every member to feel deep Love while in physical form, yet each would do so in a unique way. From her awareness, she noticed two beings from the circle who had volunteered to work with her through the next cycle of life together: one being was Maka, the other was Alana. All three held the intention to give and receive selfless Love in order to connect their tribe and advance their own capacities to Love.

The being of Alana stepped forward. She held a higher energy frequency that spun a little faster than others in the group. She volunteered to be the catalyst that could heal hearts, strengthen relationships, and build bridges between souls in their tribe.

Then Kaimi saw her own energy become clearer. She would play a role of generosity and learn how to give love in a whole new way in order to experience how love only multiplies when it is shared. Within the dynamic, she may feel that she is losing something at first, but ultimately she will connect with the Eternal Truth that lack of Love is never a reality. She was, in fact, creating more Love with her heart-based generosity and healing the tribe's grief.

Maka had volunteered to learn how to receive Love without guilt or shame, and she would truly tap into the power of being supported by her community. Maka's soul was used to working hard and struggling for what she wanted in life, so she was ready to balance that energy by easily receiving what she wanted more than anything in the world. Her soul's growth would come through the process of loving this child as a true blessing, without feeling that she must do something to be worthy of it.

Alana's mission was to push them all to open up their hearts more and form a stronger bond of connection with her arrival. Even though it would not be easy at first, it would be worthwhile and bring about even more happiness and abundance as each soul would see and feel even more love in her life.

In her dream, Kaimi saw that precious newborn Alana was actually their tribe's wisest teacher. Alana was here to assist every person to grow, heal, forgive, and find peace within themselves because the tribe was ready for communal advancement. The wise elders of the tribe would even have an opportunity to learn more as this situation had not occurred in their community before. Many gifts would come to everyone with Alana's birth.

Then Kaimi heard her soul asking questions. "But what if I cannot let my newborn go? Or what if I regret doing so? What if I grow to resent my sister, or the baby? How will I return to this higher understanding once we are living it?"

Alana replied, "When these raw emotions come up for you, honor them. Allow them to be heard and acknowledged as beautiful messengers from your heart. We agree to these areas of growth as souls, but we forget them in our human skin, so it is normal to question all of this. Your heart will be full and even heavy at times as we all adjust to this new development, especially as you, more than anyone, will feel like you have lost something that you once held. The only way to move through those real and true emotions is to feel them and allow time for grieving. Your tribe knows this, and it is why a sacred space has been honored for healing purposes."

The soul of Maka then said, "And what if I do not feel worthy of receiving such a blessing? Or if the guilt overcomes me, especially as my sister grieves? How will I arrive at my own inner peace around becoming a mother without giving birth to the child?"

Again Alana spoke. "By also honoring your feelings, too, but allowing them to be a starting point for your heart. If you feel guilt or doubt, allow yourself to go into those emotions and see where they stem from. You are worthy of being a mother in this lifetime even if it does not happen through your own body. Remember that I, Alana, wish to help you heal this part of your heart by showing you that you are ready and able to be a wonderful mother, and it is only your job to stay open to the experience and to receive this gift of life. Your soul has experienced much loss, and now it is time to re-connect to a deeper heart healing. It is the generosity of Kaimi that allows this soul growth to benefit all of us."

Kaimi's soul then asked a final question of Alana. "And what if I do not choose to let the baby go? Or if something changes while I am pregnant?"

"At higher levels of consciousness, there is no wrong choice. There are only different paths of healing, love, and joy to experience. Any choice you make will be perfect for all involved because we know that your intention is ultimately loving and heart-based. This is also how you will know that it is wise to give your sister the newborn. You will feel it in your being as the highest and best for all involved, and this strength will carry you through the adjustment phase."

"How will I really, truly know this is the right choice? Will there be something that brings me inner comfort during this difficult period?"

"Yes, you will know it is the right choice because you will intuitively know to name me Alana, which means *awakening*. You are awakening all of us to even more love."

Suddenly Kaimi sat up in the hut feeling dizzy and confused. The warm sun was moving across her feet, but she was disoriented and light-headed from the deep sleep; unaware of where she was or what her dream messages meant. She emerged outside and stood up, stretching lightly, and then walked to the nearby stream to wash her face with cool water. The fresh liquid trickled down her skin and cleared away the cobwebs of sleep.

Kaimi returned to the platform with a handful of bright flowers. She began creating a lei as the afternoon hours stretched into early twilight. She sat on the platform's edge overlooking the valley and allowed her fingers to work hypnotically while she gently started to recall the messages from her dream with greater clarity. With each twist and push of petals onto the lengthening necklace, Kaimi slowly remembered everything about her soul's agreements with Maka and Alana, and how she has been guided by her soul to make this choice. She saw the three of them as beings of light and remembered how Alana was their tribe's teacher. She could hear their questions being answered about this experience, and connected to a deep peace that arose from her Soul's energy. She felt in her being that all was unfolding perfectly.

As she weaved together this new necklace, she also weaved together the fuller insights about her soul's story and the purpose of this decision to give Alana to Maka. Even when her human Self went into all of those various deep emotional spaces, she calmly re-directed her knowingness back to her soul decision, choosing to believe that all was right and perfect in this scenario even when it tugged at her heart strings. She allowed herself the space to be honest about the emotional complexities of this choice while also choosing to trust that she was following her soul's guidance. Kaimi then started to chant aloud the *ho'oponopono* blessing with new strength in her voice and fresh clarity in her heart as a beautiful display of blooming beauty continued to come alive in her own hands. She began to feel different and cleansed; whole and serene.

The night eventually settled in around her like a clean navy blanket. She retreated back into the comfort of the hut, exhausted from a day of deep and meaningful change.

Crisp rays of sunlight woke her in the morning. Kaimi ate more taro for breakfast, drank from the fresh water stream, and then held her fragrant lei, blossoming with fuchsia, orange, and yellow petals, up to examine in its completed state. She walked over to a giant blossoming tree perched on the edge of the cliff, and added her lei to the growing collection of necklaces left by other visitors. Every lei was a traditional blessing given to this sacred space as a demonstration of gratitude, respect, and love for all it provided each temporary resident.

Kaimi then walked down the path to look at the Heart Flower's familiar red waxy leaves. And with joy, she noticed the plant had started to curl along the edges. The giant petal was turning in on itself, revealing a rough under skin, and forming a tight fist. Kaimi looked up at the sky to see a gathering of dark clouds off in the distance. *She did it!* She had made the gods happy by cleansing herself and allowing her grief to be transformed into healing for the tribe.

A wide, beaming smile overtook her whole body as she

ran back up to the site to gather her belongings before the rains arrived. She collected her cherished shells in front of the *pohaku* (stones) and filled her bamboo bag with everything she had carried here. She offered one final blessing to the gods, to nature, and to the space before turning to head down the mountain. With every step, she felt lighter, clearer, and cleaner, as if a new layer of her soul was weaved into her being. A peace had settled into her heart and a surge of hope lifted her up into the light.

As she approached the village, she saw Maka and Pono bathing Alana in the ocean's soft blue waves. She intentionally walked a little further to avoid intruding on their family time, and to honor the freshness of her experience. She was not yet ready to interact with them, but she trusted she would be able to when the timing was right. No need to rush or force anything right now.

Kaimi saw Ipo preparing the fire for the evening's meal, and ran to him with open arms.

"My queen! I am so happy to see you!" He lifted her up in his strong embrace, smelling her hair, and holding her heart to his. Then he gazed into her happy, teary eyes, and said, "You feel different, my love. You feel lighter and more peaceful."

She held both of his worn hands. "I am. I am all of that and more. We are going to be an even stronger tribe now."

He kissed her warmly on both cheeks, then her children ran up to hug her legs.

Ipo turned back to the emerging fire as something off in the distance caught his eyes. He squinted, trying to decipher the shape. He walked to the water's edge as the object bobbed out in the ocean. The dark clouds were now closer, approaching with rapid speed, yet providing enough time for the tribe to prepare for the evening's downpour. After another moment of watching the horizon, Ipo exhaled slowly.

"My queen, there are ships approaching in the distance. I have never seen sails this big."

Kaimi stood next to her husband on the shore. A second ship had now appeared, and both were headed in their direction, possibly to outrun the approaching storm.

"Please tell the elders and other families about these visitors, now! We must not assume anything." Then he urgently put out the fire he had just created and ran to do the same at each torch, hoping the weather would make it difficult for the ships to see the shore and their flames.

Kaimi ran to the tribe's main lodge as huge pellets of cleansing rain fell on her shoulders, legs, and feet. No matter what these unwelcomed guests may bring with them, or what their intentions were, Kaimi knew the forces of nature and the gods would guide and protect them.

The village men sharpened their spears fiercely as the women collected food and supplies in their bamboo packs. The children were ordered to tie blankets around their bodies. All valuable possessions were taken to the forest's edge for hiding. The tribe knew where to go if the visitors were threatening.

As the ship's wide white sails grew bigger in shape, Kaimi looked up at the mountain and quietly asked for its protection as her tribe was about to meet the next chapter in their evolution.

Soul Imprint Healing

Love and Abundance Imprint

You have had happy, joyful lifetimes. You know what it means to feel peace and love and safety. You have experiences of being loved and cherished by partners, family, and a community. Love and abundance are imprinted within you deeply.

So you may wonder why you do not feel those energies at times, or why they have been so hard to connect with, especially in recent years. Why have you experienced struggle, loss, hardship, loneliness, or depression when you also carry these higher energies, too?

The truth is more likely that you have forgotten your power and connection to these energies because you have set the intention to do deep healing work in this lifetime. Lifetimes of joy, abundance and peace may have felt 'lost' or overlooked because there has been an intentional focus on healing karmic energies and lower vibrational unconsciousness within yourself first. Your soul stories include both sides of the coin, so to speak, so you could work with all possible energies to support your soul growth. Many are present on the planet to activate greater consciousness within themselves and complete these other soul energies across all lifetimes. You wanted to clean and clear first, then move back to these energies that you know so well. You wanted to do your chores first, then go outside and play.

Please bear in mind, you are not a victim in anyway if you have not experienced love, abundance, or happiness in your current life. You are always powerful, and the Universe sees you this way eternally. In fact, you are loved and valued even more for choosing to do your hardest, most intense work now. And remember, you are only experiencing these energies as temporary sources. You are none of them; you are only the one choosing to move through them for greater soul wisdom.

Bigger cycles are also at play here. Humanity's collective

growth has involved many periods of intense learning and evolution that were designed to support everyone's free will and highest good. Most notably, we have been given opportunities to see how powerful we are within all energy spectrums, including the denser, harder energies that can feel like a never-ending cycle. As you continue to grow and evolve based on your personal timeline and needs, you will have more opportunities to rise up and live from your higher consciousness. You will activate more love, abundance, success and joy in natural, organic ways, and you will be able to live from these places more effortlessly. There are many rewards for doing your chores first!

No matter what is happening in your life now, remember to focus on your joyful incarnations and to call in those experiences. Ask to be guided to know those parts of your soul story, too. Ask to be shown locations on the map, or cultures, or people whom trigger these incredible feelings of happiness in your soul. These parts of ourselves are here and alive right now, too! Everything is connected with our intentions. After periods of deep work we can forget to call in joy and happiness because we have felt disconnected from these parts of ourselves, yet it is also our responsibility to do so. It is in your power to claim the very best times, places, and experiences that your soul has ever known. They are waiting for you to remember them and to embrace them open-heartedly.

Divine Feminine Energy

She allows and attracts. She opens and receives. She trusts and accepts. Divine Feminine energy is in the flow of life and connected with God and her unique essence. She is magnetic and alive with her own intuition. She loves herself as a creative being and accepts the truth of who she is in all ways.

Divine Feminine energy is connected with the flows and cycles of life, knowing she is an integral part of the All That Is.

She expresses from her heart, uses her mind, acts with confidence, and trusts in Spirit to guide her in the best possible ways. She feels and honors her emotions. She is not afraid of crying. She is not afraid of grief. She is not afraid of anger. She knows these are each cherished parts of a bigger mosaic. She knows these are messengers of her current truth, and yet they are only passing through. They are only temporary visitors on this endless journey, so she can see them, experience them, and embrace them as aspects of Divine wisdom, knowing they are not to be feared or denied. Each expression of a feeling only makes her fuller in her Self.

The biggest difference between Divine Feminine and Shadow Feminine energies revolves around intentional actions. Shadow Feminine attacks; Divine Feminine intentionally expresses. Shadow Feminine controls and deceives; manipulates and plots. Divine Feminine trusts; she acts in integrity with an understanding of how energy works and that everything she initiates always comes back to her. Shadow Feminine unconsciously feels jealousy, revenge, anger, or pain; Divine Feminine consciously feels these same emotions and allows them to be without taking the energy outside of herself. She doesn't act on them.

In our modern times, most women have been in contact with their Shadow Feminine energies. These are the aspects that have had to compete, fight, and emotionally manipulate to get what she wants or needs. Many women have been conditioned to act this way as a consequence of patriarchy and Western cultural ideals. The energy shows up as bitchy comments, malicious gossip, excessive criticism, mean girl antics, jealously, and verbal, emotional, psychological, or energetic attacks. And to be realistic, it is a part of Self that may continually be activated and triggered throughout life. Shadow Feminine energies do not simply disappear forever when they are deeply conditioned and/or believed to be essential for survival. A woman can exert mostly Divine Feminine traits and yet still have an active Shadow Feminine side.

However, the central differentiator comes down to her intentions and if she chooses to act on any of those unconscious impulses. Even if she feels jealous, she contains it. If she doesn't like someone, she doesn't spread terrible gossip around the playground. If she feels threatened or competitive, she comes back to the bigger picture that there is room for everyone and she is lovable as she is. Even if she is feeling mad, or pissed off, or hurt, she doesn't throw the energy around outside of herself unconsciously.

A fully conscious Divine Feminine energy asks herself: *How can I change this energy within myself? How can I evolve and elevate this reaction I am feeling? How can I take responsibility for this part of myself and learn from it?*

Divine Feminine knows she is seen and loved. She feels safe in herself, safe with God, and safe in her soul. The world may be hard, difficult, trying, and challenging at times, so she knows she can turn to her Spirit as a blessed sanctuary. When she feels fear, she returns to Love. When she is afraid, she comes back to trusting God and the Universe. When she feels lost, she finds herself again internally.

Divine Feminine energy is a master creator, open-hearted lover, and beautiful embodiment of God energy in female form. And through her presence and conscious expression, Divine Partnership can be shared, cherished, and experienced.

Divine Partnership

Divine Partnership is when Masculine and Feminine energies are equally open, symbiotic, supportive and loving with each other. Divine Partnership is an intermingling and interaction between Masculine and Feminine energies that allows for the authentic expression of both. Each brings something to the table that the other needs and values. You can't carry everything on your shoulders, so why not allow another to provide what they can uniquely offer? When you are able to receive another as an equal component of God energy, you are opening to the beauty of Divine Partnership.

Feminine expressions in Divine Partnership include feeling open and trusting of yourself, your partner, the Universe, and life. You feel expressive in your creativity, intuition, and ability to feel your emotions authentically. You also have the power to share these parts of yourself with confidence and strength. The Feminine receives and surrenders; she trusts she is taken care of and valued. She knows she is connected to the Universe. She feels safe in being vulnerable and expressing from her heart because she loves herself enough to be open and strong.

Masculine expressions in Divine Partnership consistent of strength, protection, stability, and providing for loved ones. He is focused on his purpose of safety and security, and believes in his ability to take care of what the family, tribe, or group needs. Masculine energy is loving, respectful, and supportive of Feminine energies. He guides and supports because he believes in his ability to solve and provide as necessary.

Regardless of gender, the basis of this Divine Partnership dynamic begins with your relationship to God, Spirit, the Universe, or the All That Is. Do you believe that you are loved and seen by the Universe? Do you believe you are always cherished by God? Do you believe you are valued by Spirit? And do you see yourself as an unlimited vessel of Love? The way you view your partnership with the All That Is ultimately determines how you experience and create relationships in your life.

As you love, value, and respect yourself more, you call in a partner who offers and reflects those same energies back to you. Yet in order to call in this type of partner, you must also see the same qualities in them that you experience through your connection to God energy. For example, if you want an open, trusting, loving, and respectful partner, do you also have that same relationship with God energy? You must already know what that dynamic is and how it feels in your life to trust Masculine energy in order to recognize it when it shows up in your life.

Ipo and Kaimi are depictions of Divine Partnership because they support each other as individuals, as parents, and as contributors to the tribe. Ipo could hear Kaimi's pain around giving up her child, and knew it was important for her to honor her emotional needs and grieving process. He supported her in all ways and was the strength she needed to take care of herself during a very hard time. Kaimi trusted Ipo with the complexity of her feelings and felt safe opening up to him about her truth; she did not put on a mask or try to carry the burden on her own. She was strong enough to be vulnerable, and this dynamic created more love between them. The experience of Divine Partnership allows each person to be their whole, full Self with love and acceptance.

Another key aspect of Divine Partnership is that because this person is an energetic equal, they will challenge you to grow. They will see all faucets of you, and push you to be more conscious in your life. A relationship among equals opens doors and removes barriers that you may have been unconsciously using to protect yourself from being hurt, or seen, or truly loved. You will be encouraged to grow in this partnership like no other connection you've had before because your partner is intentionally supporting your soul growth with their own soul energy.

Divine Partnership is not gender-specific. In every lifetime, you have to choose a gender role to be here; that is just part of the game of being human. But when you choose a gender, you still have access to both energies of each gender, even though you are more likely to embody one more than the other. At this time, we are moving through a grand cycle of uniting energies within ourselves that are both Masculine and Feminine. As we do this, we attract and bring in partners who are equally whole and balanced. Divine Partnership is when these energies work together to support, love, and provide you with a greater connection to God energy and to Heart Consciousness.

Heart Consciousness

Heart Consciousness is an energy connected to universal Love-based feelings: Compassion, Forgiveness, Joy, Gratitude, Abundance, and Success.

Heart Consciousness is a voice that talks above the noise of the Ego-Mind and guides you to do something that is best for everyone. A feel-good component is active, from donating monthly to the Humane Society, to volunteering two years in the Peace Corps, to choosing to see the best in people even when you're having a rough day.

Heart Consciousness is energized by inclusion, similarities, and connection. We see this energy come alive every time there is a natural disaster of some sort: earthquakes, tsunamis, flooding, and hurricanes offer humanity the opportunity to support each other in times of need. From a spiritual perspective, the higher purpose of these events is to unite people and remind us that we all occupy this blue-and-green marble together. International and domestic travel may open up Heart Consciousness energy as connections with other individuals around the world may remove preconceived notions and stereotypes.

Heart Consciousness removes boundaries and labels, and identifies us as brothers and sisters with similar needs of Love, Joy, Forgiveness, and Success.

Communal Wisdom

We all come from a lineage of ancient wisdom and teachings. Throughout your incarnations, you have been a key contributor to global wisdom, and you have received insights from others' wisdom. We have had lifetimes filled with community support, ongoing caring, exchange of resources, and tribal connections. Soul groups incarnate together to take care of one another and to provide a remembrance of connection to Oneness. We support one another by sharing our stories, truth, and wisdom, as well as honoring our individual viewpoints and value systems.

Communal wisdom includes ancient traditions, group teachings, tribal knowledge, and collective understandings. Ipo and Kaimi's tribe had communal wisdom from their native land, and made sure it was passed down to other tribal members and kin. They viewed nature as a wise teacher and ally; a source to respect and honor. They also shared tribal knowledge about childbirth practices to ensure information was being passed down to more women. Many cultures around the world have these verbal traditions of sharing collective wisdom with younger generations, yet in modern times it seems we have less connection to our ancient roots and practices.

Depending on what we are here to learn and heal in this lifetime, we may forget our communal connections. We may forget that we belong to a bigger tribe and are always connected to others because we may first have to heal abandonment, persecution, alienation, loneliness, or separation of any form. The journey may take you far away from the experience of being connected to others, but the truth is found in re-connecting to your eternalness as a soul. You are an integral part of the whole and no other soul can fill the unique space that you occupy.

Another aspect of communal wisdom is being open to the offerings that others bring to the table. Even if you do not immediately agree or understand, you may find that their message is the beginning of something new for you, or that you will connect with it in a deeper way at another time. Or it could be that it never fits for you and that it is just about being in acceptance of another. There is no single way to quantify it, of course, other than to respect them as a fellow traveler on this crazy-train human journey who also comes from a rich history of ancient knowledge.

You will have hints about your communal wisdom and tribal knowledge based on the cultures, practices, and philosophies that you are drawn to throughout your life. Trust what piques your curiosity and where you feel a desire to investigate further, whether it is a book, class, or area of study. Follow the cultures and traditions you are drawn to exploring. You may be opening up to an area of your soul's experience that is extremely timely for you.

Honoring of Emotional Cycles

Focusing only on happiness is a modern day perspective that does not serve us in the long term. Do flowers only bloom? Do the tides only rise? Does the sky only have room for the sun to shine? Of course not. There are cycles and phases in all natural areas of life, and each one provides a necessary component to the fullness of life. Only wanting to experience happiness or positivity is a disconnection from the fullness of who you are as a human being.

In Western culture, we have turned our attention to creating, doing, making, and accomplishing. The Industrial Age brought in a new focus on productivity that revolutionized how we spent a typical day and what it meant to be successful in life. As our collective values and daily needs evolved, we turned away from the natural cycles of life and started imposing requirements on life that supported achievement, professional success, power, and daily conveniences. All of this took us further away from our hearts, emotional wisdom, and acceptance of the complexities of being human. We pushed away what was inconvenient or distracting so we could get back to work and be productive, successful citizens.

Now we are in a cycle of returning to the wisdom of our emotions. Being vulnerable is a sign of strength and confidence. Feeling anger is a sign of authenticity. Owning your creative expression brings more joy. Sharing your true Self with the world is a sign of empowerment. Allowing yourself to be sad or to process grief is normal and to be expected at times.

As we evolve to higher states of consciousness, we understand how every part of ourselves is a beautiful messenger from the soul that is always supporting and loving us deeply. There is no need to impose forced happiness or feigned positivity because we are open and accepting to every color of our emotional Selves. We become more in tune with natural cycles and phases, and how these cycles are an integral aspect of Oneness. Honoring our emotional cycles ultimately unites us and is a significant connector of our similarities. We are made of all colors of the rainbow; why deny some and only highlight a few?

Following your bliss and being happy are important parts of the human journey. But from an energetic viewpoint, they are no more valuable than allowing yourself to experience other emotions authentically, too. You will know yourself better and feel more powerful the more you are open to the various emotional cycles of life. You will tap into the wisdom of your soul and begin to love yourself even more for practicing this wisdom.

For those periods of time when you are stuck in the lower expressions of anger, blame, pain, resentment, or any fear, one ancient tool that will support your healing is the *ho'oponopono* prayer.

Ho'oponopono

The ancient practice of *ho'oponopono* has been linked to numerous South Pacific Island cultures, including Tahiti, Fiji, and Hawaii. It is a simple prayer of four phrases that are intended to clear blame, anger, pain, and hurt between individuals. When spoke aloud to another, especially in person, it energetically gets to the heart of a lesson or learning opportunity by moving away from the unconscious energies that are often passed back and forth between people.

In this story, the four phrases were used in this order:

"I love you. I am sorry. Please forgive me. Thank you."

However, these four phrases are documented as being said in other variations, too, such as beginning with "I am sorry" and ending with "I love you."

Ho'oponopono is intended to promote forgiveness, reconciliation, healing, and completion of unhealthy interactions. When spoken multiple times, such as 10 times a day for a week, it has been known to shift energies and release one from the root cause of an issue. Many use this prayer for karmic healing, ongoing family battles, and even for illnesses. It brings release and peace as the energy within you shifts and you re-program your feelings and perspectives. Just as Kaimi used the prayer to process and release her grief, you can actively move through any darker feelings with intention when you make this a daily healing practice.

This is also a prayer you can say to God and the Universe when you are feeling fear on your path, heaviness in your being, or any type of disconnection from yourself. *Ho'oponopono* allows you to move from Separation Consciousness to Heart Consciousness with grace, authenticity, and power.

EGYPT
{Strength}

Hookah smoke slowly coasted up above his hard nose, smoldering eyes, bushy eyebrows, bald head, and disappeared into the backdrop of his dark olive skin. The afternoon heat was deathly intense this time of year, so he retreated to his office for a mid-day smoke and to bully his political assistant into getting more done for his upcoming campaign. The Old Kingdom fell years ago as the beloved Pepi II had left his earthly body and ascended to his Ka, leaving power to ruling monarchs such as Naeem. His self-appointed duty was to control the whole valley and all of its resources while also establishing a new legacy of power in the country. With his wealth and access to anything he wanted, there was no way he could lose control over the region. He would bring greatness back to the land and begin a long legacy of dominance. Perhaps one day his son Issa would be blessed with influence and power, but that possibility only made Naeem smirk. He would live to be a very old age and his son would be lucky to gain a quarter of the power he possessed.

"Do you want to make changes to the incoming shipments now, sir?" Omari sat across from Naeem, making marks on papyrus paper. A slight sweat bead collected at his left temple.

"No, we will wait until after the water level sinks lower, and then impose a higher tax on the imports. Ship captains will have to pay then because they will be desperate to unload goods when the river is difficult to navigate and their boats are heavy."

Naeem smiled at his own genius. He had been in politics long enough to know that his reputation traveled up and down the Nile. As the biggest landowner in the region, he felt great pleasure in making others poorer while he accumulated more taxes. His acres of flax plants were used to create linen for the whole region, and over the years, he had hired teams to travel far and wide to kill the flax plants of competitors. He took a slow inhale on his beloved hookah pipe. Everyone was viewed as a competitor, but not really as competition. Another puff of smoke weaved up above his ears.

"Father, may I have a moment of your time?" Issa stood in the doorway, his brown shoulders wide and strong. On the day of his birth, Naeem declared his son a gift from God, and so the child was bestowed with the name Issa, meaning *God saves*. But as he grew up, it became clear that Naeem was not interested in having a strong son at all; he preferred having an accommodating servant instead.

"No, you may not, Issa. I am in an important meeting." Naeem inhaled again and looked at Omari as if he was nothing more than yet another business liability. Omari kept his head down, reviewing his marks and wishing to disappear into the vapors. When Naeem was agitated, he hurled hurtful remarks at everyone. Omari learned to avoid eye contact as much as possible. *Ruthless men are never pleasant company.*

Issa turned and walked away, but did not allow his father's rejection to sink into his skin. In fact, it only confirmed that he was doing the right thing. *The plan would unfold perfectly regardless of what his father said.* Issa returned to his bedroom and grabbed his favorite knife as one of the house cats sashayed into his room, ready to curl into the coolness under his bed.

"Omari, we have reviewed enough for today. At the

upcoming meeting, I will announce the changes that are to be carried out by everyone in the town. There will be no negotiating anything."

"Yes, sir. I understand." Omari stood to leave the room, his wide sandals accidentally kicking the desk.

Naeem glared at him. "Do not touch anything in my house. You are still only a servant."

"Yes, sir." Omari nodded with respect and made his way to the door.

A timid house servant silently appeared to escort Omari through the compound's labyrinth. Naeem's compound was so big that Omari always had to carefully consider which direction led to the exit, afraid to make a wrong turn and suffer the consequences. Omari wiped away the sweat on his brow that had accumulated from surviving another meeting with his employer. He had only worked for Naeem for a few months, all due to a debt his father had to pay off. Since Omari was more intelligent than most people in town, he was a top resource to offer; otherwise, the family would have lost their remaining sections of land. His unpaid term expired in less than two months, which was also the time when the Great River would be safest for passage out of town.

As he wound through the home, Omari passed Pakhet sitting in the shade in one of the courtyards. Pakhet was Naeem's only daughter, and Omari stopped in the doorway to acknowledge her. She looked up, and their warm brown eyes connected briefly; he nodded to her as a gesture of a blessing. He had no idea how any female survived in this household.

Pakhet quietly smiled at her father's assistant standing in the doorway, his hands together in a prayer pose in front of his chest. She returned the gesture, and when their eyes met again, she silently showed him two fingers; their code for meeting again in two nights at their special gathering place. He nodded again, and was gone.

Pakhet returned to her quiet meditation, pushing her long black hair off her shoulders and returning to peace. From this corner of the courtyard, she could see an expanding moon hanging low in the sky. Pakhet always had a special connection with Ra, the Sun God, and she felt his presence through the moon, too. Her studies with Omari had opened her up to even more mystical understandings and she was excited for their next meeting during the full moon. It was the one time every month that she felt closest to her mother. Pakhet completed her afternoon prayers, and after taking the long way around the compound to avoid her father, she returned to the kitchen to help the other servants prepare the evening meal.

Every night after dinner, when the house was cooling off, Pakhet left the family compound to secretly descend to the Great River. Since she was a young girl, she had created different pathways down to the water, some winding along a steep hill through high grass and rattlesnakes; other paths smoother and intuitively easier to find because they flowed with the natural growth of the reed planets. Pakhet loved exploring the water's edge whenever possible and often ventured much further down the river than she ever revealed to her family. When the water was high, it roared with authority and she dreamed of floating away on its steady waves. When the water's movements were a bare trickle, she scoured the mud and sediments for new discoveries like shells, fish, and anything thrown over the edge from a passing ship. She sat next to the Great River, stealthily watching the grand ships sail on to an exciting place, a new land, a foreign destination. After watching hundreds of them pass by, she had finally decided it was time for her new life to begin, too. One day, she would set sail on the Nile and discover even more than she could see from this place on the shore.

For months Pakhet had been collecting necessary supplies from the house, and anything she found in the streets, to prepare for her grand adventure. Her brother was often careless with his possessions and always wanted something new, so Pakhet was able to occasionally snatch a few pieces of twine and tools when he was too busy with his latest weapons. She discreetly hauled every found item down to the water's edge. After pulling back the blades of reed that covered her secret, she would work on her small boat. It was crafted with wood planks and woven straps to secure the multiple layers together; grass and weeds were stuffed into all gaps and cracks. Looking more like a raft than a boat, Pakhet built it wide enough so her five-foot-frame could lay down in the back, but it had a pointed front end like the grand ships that sailed by. She didn't know why the boats were designed this way, but she decided it was best to emulate them. Her boat had two-foot-high raised edges to protect her from high waves, and to hopefully keep water from flooding inside. She crafted two oars out of long sticks and found a way to tie them each to the boat for extra security.

Pakhet tested the boat as she built it, ensuring it could float and even hold twice her weight, if needed. She would tie the helm to a boulder on the shore, then push the boat out into the water's flow, getting used to the movements under her feet, allowing herself to trust the river like never before. In her seventeen years, she had seen many sides of the Nile, but she had never been on top of it like this. A growing thrill moved up her body as she stood atop the river's waves, her huge smile beaming back up to the sky. The boat was ready, but it was not time to leave yet. As her mother had always said, she must have the blessings of Ra before embarking on anything.

Ra the Sun God was the entity who would grant her safe passage, especially on water, as he was known for possessing two boats himself: *Mandjet*, the morning boat, and *Mesektet*, the evening boat. The morning boat carried Ra through his day travels, and the night boat brought him down into the underworld. Then the sun would rise again and Ra would reappear as a rebirth of the new day beginning. She could feel her rebirth approaching, and was simply waiting for Ra's blessings.

As Pakhet returned to the shore after testing her boat once again, she asked Ra for his guidance and perfect timing. She wished to set sail up to Memphis and she knew it was important to honor the cycles of the stars. Omari would assist with this blessing tomorrow night.

Pakhet covered up her boat again, tucking it into the shoreline just as another ship appeared from around the river's corner. She stood in the shadows as the light from the almost-full moon revealed a sole captain silently steering his possessions and staying far away from the upcoming port. He had no intention of stopping anywhere that Naeem ruled.

The following night, after Pakhet cleaned up the dinner and was dismissed with a grunt by her father, she gathered together her most prized artifacts. They were each kept in separate hidden compartments in her floor so that if someone found one, they did not find all of them. She dug up a gold charm from her mother, a rolled sheet of papyrus paper, a small vial of mead, and a delicate box with a shoulder strap that held everything for easy transport. Once her father retired to sleep, she silently crept out to the courtyard closest to her bedroom, and just as she did nearly every night, scaled the wall in the corner. An old palm tree hung low in defeat in that spot, and Pakhet knew exactly where to place her small feet so she could scurry over the top of the high structure. Then she carefully slid her body down the other side of the wall, her arms now strong after doing this maneuver for years, and landed with a quiet thud on the desert floor. She always paused to listen for movements. The air was heavy with stillness.

Issa silently watched as his sister expertly abandoned the house yet again one more night. He waited a few moments, then walked to his father's bedroom and banged on the door.

"Tonight is the night, father! The men are waiting for you." Issa's eyes glowed with vengeful power as he spoke. Naeem swung open the door, and pushed past Issa, knocking him over with a cold shoulder. Issa maintained his posture at the disrespect and resolved to stay focused on his next tasks. *Everything will change soon.*

Pakhet's mother loved sharing with her that her name meant *Night Huntress*, so it was no surprise that Pakhet preferred the company of the stars nearly every evening. Her intuition guided her effortlessly through the desert as she made her way to a little known sun temple. She and Omari had been meeting under this pyramid for many cycles now, and she was grateful for his spiritual guidance. He came from a long line of mystical teachings, yet he had to keep it private in this town or risk a terrible fate under Naeem's rule.

Pakhet approached the temple's secret entrance covered with worn stones, loose branches, and heavy sand, and peeled through the layers before descending down into the Wisdom Chamber, being extra careful about where she stepped in the darkness. Rattlesnakes loved the stones and the vicious rats grew big quickly, especially with fewer predators down here. She knew this walkway intimately; its silent curves and rising mounds etched into her mind's eye as she traveled into the earth's depths. She kept her right hand on the rough dirt wall, her fingertips scraping the surface, and her left hand grasped the leather shoulder strap of her box.

After precisely three minutes of following the dark passage, a soft glow started to gradually appear. As she turned a corner, a full light emerged ahead of her. Omari was standing in the Wisdom Chamber, both hands out to his sides, palms up, his head tilted back. She knew this stance; he was invoking greater power by opening up to the earth, the light, the energy of the space. Four candles burned in the chamber to recognize the four directions on a map, as well as the four elements of the natural world: earth, air, fire, and water.

Pakhet removed her box of artifacts from her shoulder, and began to lay each item out on the circular table in the middle of the room. Omari unrolled the astrology maps onto the table.

"Welcome, sister. It is a magical night, isn't it." His wide smile instantly softened his hard features and brought a caring hue to his dark eyes. Omari was a rare force of male energy in these warrior times. He kept his caring, generous spirit tightly guarded around fierce, power-hungry men who wished to dominate and conquer any hint of softness. Instead of following those pursuits, Omari devoted his mental genius to self-knowledge, spiritual wisdom, and harnessing his inner power to guide others. He was greatly respected by each person who met him here in the Wisdom Chamber.

"Yes, it is a lovely evening. The full moon is quite powerful tonight and I am wondering if leaving for my adventure will happen soon?"

Omari consulted his astrology charts and closed his eyes to breathe deeply.

"Dear sister, Ra is protecting you in all ways, but you must know that there are great forces who do not want you to leave."

Pakhet stared at him in disbelief. "But what do you mean? Who?"

Omari looked at her with a steady gaze. "Your greatest power is found within your instincts. You are entering a new era where you must trust yourself more than ever before. This will be a lonely period, but you will also reap great rewards from it."

Pakhet felt her heartbeat picking up speed. In all of their meetings together, she had never before sensed danger like this.

"Is this a message from Ra, soul brother?" She stared at him, looking for any signs he would give her.

"Pakhet, your life is blessed by Ra and he will always appear when you need a sign from him. This is part of your ability to trust yourself." He reached for the papyrus scroll.

"Tonight, on the Pisces Full Moon, we will do something different. We will leave your precious artifacts here in the chamber as offerings to all of the gods who will bless your travels and guide you to a rebirth."

"So I am to leave tonight?"

"Yes, it is imperative that you leave tonight. You must leave directly from here. Are you ready?"

Pakhet nodded in response, excited about her new beginning but unable to understand the danger she was feeling. Omari reached for the vial of mead.

"Let's drink to your rebirth, Pakhet, which is divinely

guided by Ra. But first, a blessing to your mother for her guidance and all she has allowed us to experience together." They were each introduced to this Wisdom Chamber because of their mothers.

But before they could begin the blessing ceremony, the south candle suddenly blew out. Fear ran through Pakhet as she instantly locked eyes with Omari. He scanned the room, then instinctively reached for all of the artifacts.

"Quick, sister! Put this in your pocket!" He handed her the gold charm, and grabbed the papyrus scroll.

Suddenly the west candle went out. Pakhet's eyes grew bigger as she understood what was happening: Ra was giving them a signal to leave the chamber now.

Omari drank half of the mead in the vial, then pushed it into Pakhet's hand. "Now!"

She downed the medicine in one gulp as Omari took the papyrus paper to the north candle and completely burned it. As she was trained to do, Pakhet threw the empty vial fiercely at a hard wall to break it, then she picked up the biggest pieces and quickly dug a hole in the wall to bury each segment.

The east candle blew out just as she finished.

"Sister, we must go! Now!" He grabbed the astrology maps and rolled them up, stuffing them in his belt.

"What do I do with the box? We weren't trained to destroy this artifact!"

The box was hanging from her hand, her eyes wide with fear as the Wisdom Chamber descended into more darkness. Only one lit candle remained.

"I will take it, but you must leave, and do not look back. Do you understand?" His eyes were fierce and strong.

Pakhet nodded obediently, then he grabbed her arm and they ran up the pathway just as the north candle blew out behind them. They followed the passageway only on instinct, their heavy breathing filling up the pathway as they quickly reached the secret doorway. Omari halted, his heartbeat racing, as he listened for voices, footsteps, anything outside. Nothing could be heard. He turned to Pakhet, both hands holding onto her small forearms.

"Sister," he whispered slowly, looking deeply into her eager eyes. "Tonight is your night and Ra is here blessing you with these signals to leave now. You and I will meet on the other side of this rebirth. Remember everything you have learned and allow nature to guide you."

He stopped to listen again. Nothing.

"But what do I do now?" Pakhet's hushed voice was filled with panic, terror surging in her eyes. Maybe she was not as ready as she believed.

"Breathe deeply and go to the river." She again nodded, knowing it was simple, but feeling a heavy dread forming inside her stomach.

They pushed open the secret entrance quietly, and allowed the full moon's rays to reveal any shadow movements before exiting the space. Nothing moved. Pakhet stepped forward, then ran to duck behind a low bush. Omari made brief eye contact with her, just as he did only days ago when she was sitting in the shade. Then Omari and his ancient wisdom silently ran in the opposite direction of town. Pakhet watched as he laid low in the night, dodging between any shadows he could find in the desert, until she could not see his shape at all. She turned toward the river and listened. Nothing.

Pakhet moved effortlessly in the night shadows she could find, trying to see any other movements or changes across the land. After all of her years of visiting the Wisdom Chamber, she had never experienced a single candle going out during a ceremony, much less all of them extinguishing within minutes. It was a sure sign that change was on the horizon, and happening quickly. She would now leave on her boat tonight; there was no choice but to follow this guidance. A flurry of movements suddenly appeared in her right peripheral vision.

"You are a disgrace!" A loud booming voice commanded from behind.

Pakhet instinctively turned around and was blinded by the unexpected light of roaring hand torches. A strong hand clamped onto her arm, swinging her off her feet with its brutal force, and in an instant she was forced down onto her knees. Her heart was in her stomach and panic overtook her body.

"What sinister acts are you performing in the chamber!" His rage-filled voice echoed across the desert. A small tribe of men stepped in closer, creating a semi-circle of dominance.

She stared at the dirt between his feet. Panic turned to rage at the sound of the familiar voice.

"Father, I have done nothing at all to disgrace you. In fact, it is I who is disgraced by your -"

A tight slap hit her right cheek, knocking her down to the cold desert dirt, covering her linen dress with shades of brown filth. Pakhet's head spun with the unexpected blow. Her cheekbone was flaming from the impact, but she tried to focus on the ground. The medicine from the Wisdom Chamber was greatly assisting her with clarity and inner strength.

"No worthless daughter of mine can speak such words to me. You will now be put to use for a true purpose. Grab her."

A thick-necked man pulled Pakhet up to a standing position while she stumbled over her feet. He shoved her to walk in front of his shadow. Her father led the tribe, the bright torch flames reflecting off his bald head, as three men walked in front of her; the fourth behind her. Each one glanced back to smirk at her and she recognized them all as associates of her brother. They had all attended the same school, played together in family courtyards, and shared their first round of beer in a teenage drinking game. She recalled how the youngest male had been kind to her as she gingerly sipped the strange taste in the glass, coughing on the hops, yet not wanting to appear weak in front of the group. It was during those times that she had spent among groups of men that she felt a deep ache for her mother. How was she to be a woman when all she saw were the fierce acts of men? How was she to be Feminine when they were constantly telling her she needed to compete for survival?

Now, as older teenage men under her father's growing power, these same boys saw her as yet another foreign land to conquer. In the private rooms of the city, where the night seduces young ambitious men with beer, opiates, and dancing women, she had no idea that her brother had regularly offered an award to the first male who could conquer his virgin sister. He laughed loudly while sharing the prize, taking an extra-long pull on his favorite black hookah, and watched as this conquest became the most desired prize amongst his soldiers. If the girl became pregnant, then that soldier became family; a very smart political move for any ambitious colleague. The young men cheered at the idea and took a ceremoniously long inhale together while a woman of the night began her next performance.

As they marched back to the family compound, Naeem considered which secret room to lock his daughter in: the one behind the office bookcase with a high window, or the one below the kitchen with greater privacy. He would keep her in a room until after the upcoming election, after his new power had been granted, and he would use the disappearance of his daughter to evoke sympathy from the city. He smiled smugly at the thought of manipulating the public to simply hand over this position to him as he explained that he must be in power to ensure this type of situation does not happen again to any citizen. Then, after the election, his daughter would be miraculously found and returned as a demonstration of his Divine power, a public blessing from Ra that the Gods supported his rule. *It was almost too easy.* This brilliant plan was yet another reason why Issa was his favorite child. He will make a formidable General one day if he continued to create such devious plans for power.

"Stop! Get her!" A loud booming voice shook the desert floor.

Every member of the tribe halted and tried to look at each other through the darkness, their torches now only specks in the horizon. The thick-necked man was on the ground, trying to stand up and wipe dirt off his legs.

Naeem barked, "What is going on!"

"She ran, sir! My torch light suddenly went out, and she kicked me. Then she disappeared this way!" He pointed towards the river.

As the men started to run toward the river, the remaining lights from their torches were extinguished, and for a moment, the desert fell into complete darkness. Their eyes slowly adjusted to the broad light of the full moon that opened up the horizon. A small shape was running in the distance.

Pakhet charged ahead without stopping to look behind her. She ran fiercely to her forever friend, the Nile. The friend that had been there for her all of the seasons of her life; the friend that she could rely on night and day; the friend that would save her tonight as she escaped the darkness of Masculine brutality. With aching thighs and a burning chest, she pushed forward, trusting the river to guide her survival. She heard a stampede in the distance as the soldiers followed in determined pursuit. Her father was surely trailing behind the pack, his heavy stomach an anchor to the ground.

She reached the shore and paused for a second to catch her breath, trying to discern which part of the river this was. Her eyes squinted as she looked to the other side of the shore for orientation. She had not explored this section fully, but she knew it would lead to her familiar ground. The men's breathing was arriving right behind her.

The river bank was extra thick with bushes, palm trees, and grass, so Pakhet grabbed a long stick, and reached out to her right with the stick to create a potential path in the high grass. She jostled the stick back and forth to give the appearance that her body went through the tall reeds to the right. Then she dodged to the left and ran against the flow of the river, doing her best to move with silent feet. She dashed below the foliage, an advantage of her height, and allowed the moon's light to reveal where to step next. The men must have gone to the right because she didn't hear their voices after a few moments.

She stopped and dropped down into a bush to breathe and listen. The night offered a slow breeze, and as she peered through the reeds, on the other side of the river, she saw a heron sleeping along the bank. *It's a sign*. Ra takes many forms at night, including as a heron, and she knew this was a sign that Ra was supporting her journey. Pakhet scanned the Great River and realized she was not too far from her boat, but she didn't want to lead the group to her secret place.

"Then she went this way! Come on!" The voices sounded like they were only meters away.

Pakhet bolted from her resting place and stayed close to the river's edge, knowing the mud would support her lightweight more than it would support the heavy bastards who were trailing her. She kept her breathing inside her body, steady eyes on the ground, as she came up to the familiar territory near her family compound. To throw the men off a second time, Pakhet grabbed rocks in her hands and threw them further along the river bed as she moved up to higher ground on the steep hill. This was her territory, the land she knew the best, and there was quicksand along the sections where she tossed the rocks. From her high perch on the hill, she watched the shadows move down to the water.

"What kind of girl runs along the river? Maybe Issa lied to us. She must be a hermaphrodite!" Loud hearty laughter rolled over the top of every wave.

Issa. Hearing her brother's name sent a heavy pang into Pakhet's stomach. A shock rolled through her lungs, and tears suddenly emerged from behind her black eyes. Then her father's voice boomed above the trees.

"We are near my home and I know this part of the river very well. Pakhet will definitely be along the edge. She is afraid of the water, so we will find her soon."

With those words, Pakhet dashed forward, moving almost directly above the gang as they scoured the edge. She rapidly dodged between the trees and bushes she had memorized for years, and as the men stepped into the quicksand, she maintained her quick pace past the boat's hiding place, past the oldest palm tree, past the curve where the grand ships make their impressive debuts. The river was moving fast tonight with the pull of the full moon.

"I'm stuck!"

"Me too! I can't move my legs."

"You idiots!" Her father yelled. "Get out of there!"

Pakhet found the familiar brief opening in the bushes and reeds that created a path right down to the river's edge. Her heels sank into the mud, but she knew how to balance her body along the river's incline. She took a deep breath and tilted her head up to the moon. *What would my mother do this in situation?*

Pakhet paused to hear an answer, a whisper, anything from Ra. She stared up through labored breathing to consider her next move. And just then, a muscled arm grabbed her waist as a large hand covered her mouth, muffling her impulsive scream. Pakhet's head turned with wild alarm as the youngest male in the group stared back at her and winked, his cold dark eyes glimmering with desire. Salty sweat from his palms sat on her lips.

"This has been a fun game, Pakhet. You and I always played together well." He whispered roughly in her ear and forcefully pulled her back into his strong chest.

"But I won't tell them where you are yet because I want to collect my prize first." With one hand still covering her mouth, he violently yanked up her dress, and she suddenly realized how truly sinister these young men were, despite knowing them all of her life and playing childhood games with them for years. This was no longer a game.

And in that split second, she also remembered Omari's wisdom from a previous ceremony, words passed down from their mothers: *I am my own heroine.* She would not be anyone's prize. She would not succumb to anyone else's desire, or plans, or power. She would not be paralyzed by fear under his strength or weight. And due to her intense training, she knew how to fight the dark with light. *There will be more light than darkness tonight.*

Out of the corner of her eye, she spied a nest of glistening white eggs.

With stealth quickness, Pakhet used her size, gravity, and the tilt of the river's edge to her advantage. She bit his sweaty hand while simultaneously lifting her small foot high and stomping violently on his toes. Then she dropped to the ground and rolled to the right, up the river bank. The man yelled out loudly and stumbled forward in blinding pain, losing his balance and wading into the river as he carelessly searched for relief.

Without even knowing it, his splashing stirred up the water's sleeping giant.

As she took two large steps back up the river bank, Pakhet heard a devastating scream as the jaws of a female crocodile opened up from under the river's midnight sleepiness. The ferocious mouth clamped onto the man's leg, an agonizing sound emitting from deep within his lungs, and he was pulled underwater as shock and fear overtook his eyes, his face, his body.

Pakhet looked at the water for a brief pause, breathing intensely, then scampered further down the river bank as she heard her father's tribe yell in response. The crocodile's nest was typically further down river, but the high water level must have moved it upstream where more mud collected. Pakhet silently smiled to herself as she realized the momma croc was the affirming sign from her mother that she had been looking for. *Don't mess with my daughter, fool.*

Back at the family compound, Issa marched up and down in front of the rows of soldiers, each one holding a burning torch with flames that waved wildly up, up, up to touch the sky.

"They will return soon, men! Be ready for their approach from any direction."

Issa adjusted his knife holster and scanned the street for activity. Since the family lived away from town and closer to the river, they did not have to worry about villagers watching what was about to happen. Issa stroked his chin at his own genius. One of his greatest blessings was that he was born in a family of fools.

"Issa, what is this!" Naeem appeared from around the corner, sweating and dirty but still not defeated from the night. "We have just lost a man to the Great River. Send these men to the river to find him and your sister now!"

Issa halted in front of his father, his eyes steady, his shoulders solid. In a cold voice, he announced, "That won't be happening, Father. I am officially taking over the rule of this family and this town tonight. These men are here to arrest you. Grab him!"

Eight men circled around Naeem instantly, grabbing both arms, blocking his ability to move. Naeem's eyes turned to fire.

"What is this?" His father's words seethed from his mouth like a rattlesnake's tongue. "You cannot take power from me! No one will believe you can rule this land."

"It is unfortunate that tonight, you left into the desert with a group of men, and you never returned. Ra cursed you with disaster during the full moon, removing all of your power because he no longer deemed you strong enough to lead our people. You were never heard from again, presumed dead because of your corrupt ways."

Issa looked at the three soldiers who had returned with his father and asked, "Where is Pakhet?"

"She ran away, you fool! She escaped to the river!" Naeem's words curled through the air.

Issa looked to his right and nodded; a fabric was violently placed around Naeem's mouth.

"Then my sister is also smarter than you, and for that, I respect her more and will let her run away."

Naeem's eyes burned with rage as he realized how his son had set up this coup.

"Father, you will be placed in a location far from here. You will never receive a tomb in your honor, nor will you be remembered or recognized in any way. You have failed because I am the powerful one in this family. I was born to lead the province to greatness. And as the sun rises tomorrow, I will be rebirthed as the ruler of this land."

The soldiers cheered wildly with this announcement. Issa smiled smugly at his father's wild eyes, and then nodded to his left. Four men then hoisted Naeem up on to their wide shoulders and carried him to a horse. They tossed him over the saddle, securing him with ropes, and Naeem gagged with the brutal discomfort. Issa reviewed with the soldiers their extensive three-week journey to dispose of his father from the territory. The soldiers were ready to embark on the adventure, travelling through the desert and mountains, voyaging on a river barge, and upon returning to the town, they would be hailed with higher rankings and victory for their mission. The torches blazed high, high, high in the night.

From under a low bush, Pakhet heard cheers echoing down the river. Her father and his men had retreated back to the family compound, so she found safety in the shadows. A wild adrenaline still pulsed through her body as she stared at the Nile's simplicity. She aligned her breathing with the pace of the waves to calm down her heart. She couldn't believe how this night had unfolded. It had turned into a nightmare in all ways. A darkening from light. A removal of everything she had known and thought was real.

As her body sank a little more into the earth, she started to cry. First quietly, not wanting to interrupt the night, and then the sobs grew louder, deeper, more intense as anger, pain, and grief rolled through her. She cried for the loss of a loving mother. She cried for being rejected and betrayed by dark men. She cried for the complications of life. She sobbed for the loss of safety and simplicity that she wanted from a family; the feeling of being abandoned by all of her comforts. And then she cried for not being stronger, for being emotional when it made her appear weak. Her cascading tears fell to the ground, creating fresh mud in the old earth.

As the heaving in her chest eventually slowed down, a tall, thin figure appeared through the branches. A heron stood incredibly close to her on the river bank, swiveling its long beak in staggered movements. Pakhet stared at it in wonder; she had never been so intimate with the bird before. Her breathing continued to relax. Her pulse calmed down. She felt her chest move with the river's motion. And then she remembered her last conversation with her mother.

She was only seven years old, but a keen observer to everything her mother did, from the steady way she cut and sliced dried fish, to the purposeful manner of brushing her silky hair in the twilight. When Pakhet's mother made the bed, her long black hair falling to touch the thin mattress, she did so with intense focus and presence as if it was the only act in the world. One afternoon, after pulling the light bed blanket tight, she invited Pakhet to sit up on the bed with her. Her illness seemed to slow her down a little more every day, but she always tried to stand strong in front of her daughter.

"Dear star, I see your curiosity growing every day. Come sit with me." She lightly patted the bed as Pakhet crawled up to join her. Her mother's wide brown eyes always contained a loving smile. Pakhet leaned into her soft arms, inhaling her sweet fragrance, and rested her head on her mother's shoulder. This was her favorite place in the whole province.

"Mamma, why does Issa speak so strongly to everyone? Why is he so mean to me? I hated him today at school."

"Dear child, your brother has a much different path than you. He was troublesome even while in my belly, and I knew that he would create much turmoil in his life because he was born under the Mars moon." She laughed calmly in Pakhet's ears, stroking her daughter's wispy long hair softly. "He is part of the shadow Masculine energy, but perhaps that is too much for your young ears."

Pakhet was listening intently, savoring every word, trying to grasp each sentence and store it in her memory bank. Her mother was so wise because she was trained in the ancient mystical teachings. A lineage of women passing sacred information to each other in secret ceremonies was in her blood, her roots, her dark olive skin. Pakhet yearned for more of it.

"Mother, I feel so different from Issa and Father. I do not like how they want me to compete, how they laugh when I do not want to play their games. They always try to make me look like a fool around them."

A deep exhale came from her mother's chest.

"You must understand how your path in this life will be special, dear star. You are part of the change coming in the Kingdom, and it will not be easy. Men have used power, domination, control, and war for years, and that will continue, but the country will unite itself again. It is part of a bigger cycle the land is moving through."

Pakhet's head felt heavy with the insights, not understanding everything her mother was saying, but wanting to memorize every word.

"Our great ancestors have known about these big cycles. It is one of the ways we are very lucky, dear star. The ancient teachings have been celebrated for thousands of years in our mystery schools, of which I was a revered priestess, and we pass on the wisdom of life's cycles when it is appropriate, and only to our beloved. During the current phase, unbalanced Masculine energy has taken over, pushing Feminine energy away as weak and small, and yet we must stay strong with trust. Ra loves us." Her mother squeezed her tighter.

"Inside our temples, Pakhet, we have sacred sayings that remind us of our lifetime's purpose. One I believe you will need throughout your life is *Always watch and follow nature*. It will guide you reliably. Your Feminine heart will always be your best Neter." She leaned down to kiss Pakhet's hair.

"Sometimes their meanness to me is brutal, Mother. And they encourage it in each other! And with their friends!"

"Men have been trained to believe their power is in their hands, in a sword or weapon, but their real power is truly in their intentions, which is connected to their heart. But men cannot hear this wisdom now; they are caught up in external power pursuits. Issa is not connected to his heart, I'm afraid, and it would be wise of you, as his younger sister, to not expect him to be in his heart space in this lifetime. His environment does not support it, and he is going to be ruthless in his quest for power."

Her mother's eyes stared off through an open window, allowing the guilt of birthing a brutal boy move through her and fly out to the sky. She did not share with Pakhet that her soul had agreed to give life to this child in order to assist in making her daughter stronger. The upcoming cycle needed brave young heroines more than it needed egotistical heroes, and the strongest women were birthed from extreme oppositions. Only those in the inner temples would understand such dynamics.

She gathered her strength back. "But this is how you are special, Pakhet. You must look at me as I say these words to you."

She grabbed Pakhet's shoulders and turned her around on the bed, her young knees pointing out below the rustic dark blue linen dress. The innocent eyes searched her mother's face intently.

"You must stay connected with nature, and you must trust your instincts. You must never, never give up on yourself or your dreams, and you must always love your heart, love your feelings, even if you think they make you weak. Your emotions never make you weak, they make you brave and strong. Do you understand?"

Pakhet nodded obediently.

"The Old Kingdom is ending and Egypt must unite itself in order to prosper. Lower Egypt and Upper Egypt are polarities, but the upcoming great uniting of the polarities is symbolic of the unification of the Divine Female and Divine Male, Pakhet. When it is time, you will understand what this means." Her mother exhaled and looked down at the bed.

"In the meantime, dear star, allow your emotions to flow like the Great River. The Nile is powerful, our ally, and it is powerful because it does not limit itself, nor succumb to its own strength. It flows with grace and a power so deep that no force can stop it. If you hold back your Feminine qualities and resist their natural flow, you will submerge the energy into aggression, which is a shadow Masculine expression. You then become a female version of shadow Masculine energy and this separates you from your heart. You will become more violent internally and externally. Dear star, your greatest power will always be in trusting your feelings and allowing them to flow honestly, even when they are uncomfortable or overwhelming. When you are older -"

Loud feet stomped down the hall.

"Quick, under the bed!" Her mother pushed her away and stood up to adjust the blanket again. Pakhet dropped down to the floor, pressing her body away from every edge of the bed.

"Wife! Pakhet is not in here, is she?" He glared around the room slowly. Women were not allowed to spend time together alone because they were known for speaking untruths to one another. His wife was under constant surveillance to never be alone with the girl in his household.

"She is not here, Husband. I have not seen her." She lifted her head and spoke with assurance.

"Very well. Dinner needs to be early tonight. The meeting starts at sundown." He stomped off back to his office.

Her mother leaned under the bed to see Pakhet's terrified eyes. She whispered, "Dear star, the time has come. I must give you something tonight."

She stopped speaking to listen for any feet approaching. Then she waved at Pakhet to come out from under the bed.

"When dinner is served tonight, you must run down to the Great River, and follow it south past the curve where ships debut."

She stopped again to listen, then continued.

"There is an opening in the tall reeds, and as you go down to the water's edge, you will see a nest. Dig under the nest to find my greatest gift to you and return to the home after sundown."

"Wife!" His voice pounded down the hall again. "Come at once! Now!"

She stood and walked out of the door, her feet elegant and strong despite her weakening frame. Her mother's illness had come on suddenly, and she now needed long naps every day, especially as her appetite decreased and her muscles shrank. Her father never noticed the changes in his wife, or at least never changed his behavior towards her. His demands only became more urgent.

Pakhet did as her mother directed that night as a glowing full moon revealed the path to the river's edge. Only being seven years old, it was the first time she had left the compound on her own, and the only time she had been to the river by herself. She was amazed at how the Nile looked different at night, as if it were more alive and in its natural state. She walked carefully down to the water, uncertain of what to expect below her feet. Discovering the opening in the tall grass seemed to take forever as she tripped on rocks and stepped on sticks. The cold earth was inviting after another smoldering day, and thankfully, she missed stepping on a snake as she tried to find her way in the shadows. After nearly two hours by the river, Pakhet found what was buried under the crocodile's nest, and returned home exhausted and exhilarated from the night time adventure.

The following day, as the sun hit the earth with extreme force, Pakhet searched for her mom throughout the house, glee in her eyes about the nocturnal discovery, but that connection never happened. Her mother was gone forever after taking her last physical breath in her sleep.

It had now been eleven years since her passing. Pakhet blinked back tears at the memory. The heron turned towards her, spying her movement under the bush. The bird extended its wide wings in both directions, and flew low across the water to another point downstream. Then Pakhet emerged from her hiding place, hearing only silence, and decided to venture back upstream to get the box from her mother's secret spot.

She moved slow and low in case the soldiers were still waiting for her, taking a few steps and then listening for any human movements. Nothing. She arrived at the known nest which no longer incubated crocodile eggs, and grabbed a stick to dig into the soft ground. After a few moments of work, scooping the dirt away, the stick eventually hit the wood box with a thud. As she had done every year on her birthday, Pakhet removed the container from its protected earth tomb and lifted the small chest onto her lap, pushing mud and grass off its smooth edges. A symbol was carved into the bottom of the box, and it looked nothing like the hieroglyphics she had seen before in the deep chambers.

Pakhet placed both hands on top of the box in a quiet blessing, and then opened it up. A deep purple coating covered all sides of the box, a representation of Divine protection. A heavy musky aroma filled the container, an invisible vapor from another place and time, and seeped out around her fingers. Inside, a large stack of papyrus papers were rolled together tightly. A dried up scarab, morsels of gold, a crystal quartz, and a quill sat at the bottom.

Pakhet unraveled the papyrus papers as she had done many times before, and because the content was deeply memorized, she flipped past the astrology recordings, animal totems, spiritual laws, and mystical teachings. She sorted through the sheets describing the cycles of nature and spiritual blessings, and finally found the papers detailing ancient goddesses. On one of the sheets, her mother had written at the top in her distinctive lettering: "PAKHET. Your rebirth begins on your eighteenth Full Moon Solstice, dear star."

The scroll read: "And on the dawn of her eighteenth year, Neith rode down the Nile on the back on a crocodile, her sole protector and fellow warrior of the hunt. Neith was armed with wisdom and creation, the ability to weave truth into any situation by bringing the light of the Full Moon into the darkness of the earth. She was the goddess of the hunt, carrying two quick spears, symbolizing the inner balance of her Masculine and Feminine energies which allowed her to move with stealth speed amongst men, women, gods, goddesses, nature, and the underworld. Neith now embodied the Divine in female form and had the power of creation within her womb."

In a different symbolic handwriting, Pakhet deciphered the following message:

"As our legacies carry on through the generations, females will rise forward with the energies of Divine Wisdom. Neith, as chosen by her soul's Divine right, is one such voluntary soul who is appearing during an era of darkness in the desert. Each Feminine soul who selects this mission will be given a choice that is bigger than herself. She will have multiple opportunities to trust herself and follow her instincts, yet these decisions will not be easy. She is being called to forge a new heart path for the greater good. This collective energy will represent the return of Feminine power as a symbol of humanity's advancement to higher light and a continuation of the earth's natural balancing cycles."

Eight signatures were penned on the bottom of the sheet; she knew one of them was her mother's secret symbol.

On the following sheet, it was explained that her mother's soul role in this lifetime was to birth opposing forces to provide greater strength to one and false power to the other. Both would be loved for their contributions to human evolution, but only one would be open to true growth because her power would come from within. When her mother's soul role had been fulfilled, Ra would call her home through a physical illness, alleviating her of her service. Eight signatures had signed this sheet, too.

Even though they were traditionally an oral culture, a few scribes had decided after one disastrous encounter to mark down their mystical wisdom since they predicted the upcoming fall of their sacred gatherings. Each of the eight signatures had been bestowed with a similar treasure chest of wisdom. Pakhet had received her mother's teachings just in time. Omari must have a similar box. She did not know who held the other six sacred vessels.

Pakhet stared at the messages again, feeling a pride and warmth in her belly. Then she heard laughter approaching in the night, and jolted to look around the river. As she sat on the water's edge, hidden by the grass, a grand ship glided right in front of her. A few shadows sat on the bow as it crept along in darkness; all sailors onboard asleep for the night passage except for the watchers. The boat moved gracefully, as it was pushed forward easily by the flowing stream. Pakhet took this sight as another sign for her own departure, just as Omari had foretold.

She scurried up the embankment, the box clutched to her chest, and raced ahead of the slow moving grand ship. Pakhet arrived, breathless, at her boat's hidden location, and as she quickly pulled the grass coverings off of it, the talking voices grew louder as the ship came in to view again. She set the treasure chest of teachings inside her new floating home, and before untangling the ropes from the boulders, she quickly paused and looked up at the full moon. She spoke aloud firmly to the strong, glowing light:

"I leave my homeland as Pakhet, daughter of a mystical mother and tyrannical father, and as I venture away from this shore on the eve of my eighteenth solstice, I intend to follow the wisdom of nature as my guide and connector to Ra. I am one with my light, and I embrace my dark so my unconscious shadows do not control my destiny. I will now be known as Neith and I am open to the power of this Divine rebirth."

She stepped eagerly onto the boat, allowing it to sink slightly under her weight, and then leaned over to untie all attachments to this life. Waves from the grand ship started to hit the shore, and she rocked with the rhythm, until the boat was untied and floating on its own. She used one of her oars to valiantly push away from the edge.

The men's voices continued upstream as the Nile flowed north to Memphis. She quickly paddled to get behind the boat since it blocked the wind and allowed her to sail in its full protection.

From this vantage point, the land and river looked completely new. Her feet, steady and firm, knew the wood planks would support her. The night wind danced through her hair and a few long strands softly landed on her face. Her posture was strong and straight as she held her own atop the river's natural rhythm. She kept glancing up to the sky and then down to the water's edge, absorbing the new sensations of her oldest friend.

As she glanced to the right, Neith saw torches of light

flaring up around the family compound, but then they slowly disappeared into the night's embrace. On her left, she watched small shadows change with slight movements as the full moon altered their shapes. The men in the grand ship continued to laugh as she stroked forward with gentle ease. She sent a silent blessing to her dear friend Omari, hoping the night had also granted him a safe passage.

When the river current slowed slightly, she set down the oar and tightly secured her mystical box with rope. It held everything she would need for her new life. Whatever may come, whatever lies ahead, she knew her strength would always be found in trusting herself, honoring her instincts and emotions, following the guidance of nature, and remembering that she was always connected to Ra. After the wild life-changing developments of tonight, Neith had more belief in herself than ever before because she had saved herself from every potential disaster. She had everything within her in each situation, and she felt this emerging strength and power deep in her being. No matter what may come, she would always be taken care of when she tuned into what she innately possessed - her intuition, her intelligence, her emotions, her Divine connection.

With that thought, a slight shiver ran down her spine, and she thought she heard her mother's smile in the night air. She looked up at the stars and smiled in return. Then she turned her sights to the wonders of her fresh adventure.

As the moon slowly sank into the deep pockets of darkness right before the dawn, Neith could feel the beginning of her rebirth, of her next heroine's journey. Everything had led her to this place, this time, this emergence into her true Self. She could feel a whole new world opening up to her with every curve and bend of the river. An inner excitement was growing with each forceful stroke.

And as she sailed towards the approaching sunbreak, the river's flow expertly navigating her to a new version of herself, she never saw the protective momma crocodile silently gliding mere inches behind her little boat's waves.

Soul Imprint Healing

Spiritual Independence

When you trust what is best for you, you are opening up to more of your power. We hear this a lot through various spiritual teachings, and yet it is a part of life that we must individually practice for ourselves in order to truly experience it. Spiritual independence is connecting with what is right and true for you, regardless of any external energies, and allowing that perspective to be enough for you. It may make you different than others in your immediate social circle or family, but it also makes you a special expression of Divine energy that contributes to the wide spectrum of spiritual understandings in the world.

Your soul chooses the themes it wishes to heal, transform, and release in this lifetime. This work requires being brave, courageous and self-loving, to step out of any "personalities" and into the higher energies that support spiritual expansion and independence. You may find yourself seeking and asking questions that lead you to wisdom that is perfect for you, even if it is not in mass culture or what is popular at the time.

Just as Omari and Pakhet returned to ancient mystery school teachings, you may connect with any spiritual wisdom that supports navigating lower denser energies, experiences, people, and feelings that is perfectly suitable for you. It does not mean you need to share this information with others, of course, but it will fulfill you. It will provide you with exactly what you need to be a fuller expression of yourself.

Spiritual independence is an acceptance of yourself and your soul's needs that perfectly sustains you. As you honor this part of your journey, you will also step into greater personal power.

Stepping Into Greater Personal Power

The most difficult revelations and life transitions happen so you can step into greater personal power. It will not feel like this at the time. In fact, it will often feel like the exact opposite is occurring and that you are powerless in some way. This perspective is a gift that actually shows you where you need to be stronger in your own energy.

As the night unfolded, Pakhet continually reached deeper into herself for guidance and insights about which actions to take as she was captured and hunted. Her answers were always inside herself even though she felt powerless throughout the night. She trusted herself in the moment and kept looking for her connections to Ra to guide her forward. Pakhet was forced to know herself better and to claim her inner gifts with power. Ultimately, this lead her to a stronger sense of herself and the rebirth of her identity in one lifetime. Pakhet was the modern heroine ahead of her time who bravely claimed the transformation of her life, and stepped into her independent Self as she was guided to take control of her destiny.

We all have situations in our lives that have pushed us further than we believed we could handle. As the popular saying goes, "What doesn't kill you makes you stronger." From a soul perspective, these times of adversity, challenge, and hardship are designed to connect you with more of your power and strength because you are much bigger than you can imagine. You are stronger than you've been led to believe, and your soul wants you to tap into this deeper power. We often see this better in hindsight than when we are going through it, but know that your soul is with you at all times during this temporary experiences of powerlessness. Your soul is guiding you expertly into a new definition of your own power.

One of the ways this experience of powerlessness, and then rebirth, can occur is through family soul contracts.

Family Soul Contracts

Family relationships are always intentional. We need people to play certain roles in our lives so we can grow, heal, and evolve into our true Selves with power and confidence. Family roles are key to this development because they begin at birth and set the stage for what we elected to learn in this lifetime. Our initial subconscious programming and belief systems begin with these relationships.

From a spiritual perspective, family members often have soul contracts with us, and these may not be the loving, kind, or compassionate roles that we expect or crave. We have soul contracts that focus on what we need to learn and how we need to grow in this lifetime, which can be through a variety of hard experiences or challenging dynamics. Pakhet stepped into her own because of her abusive father and brother, and through the spiritual guidance of her mother. These are very different energies, obviously, but all supported her path of becoming self-reliant, wiser, and more trusting of her own messages. Her family soul contracts pushed her forward like nothing else could have done.

Family dynamics are a prime area of soul growth. They establish our feelings of love, connection, value, appreciation, and belonging in the world. Family relationships are our first interactions with other people, and they help us see where we fit in. There is also an element of commonality between all of us because genetically-speaking, we are each required to have two parents, most typically a mother and father, as we begin our lives. From this starting point, we unconsciously learn about Masculine and Feminine roles, and how we interact with both of them. All of these energies can be viewed as part of our family soul contracts that are meant to support our individual growth, and can even push us forward into making huge sweeping changes in our lives.

Rebirthing While In Human Form

With the global rise in consciousness, more options are available to us than ever before because we can connect with higher understandings around how to use our energy. One of these expressions is through the ability to rebirth ourselves while living, meaning, we do not have to die in order to begin again. We have more choices, options, and possibilities for our lives than ever before. Along with resources, education, and global connections, you can choose to change your life in drastic ways that support the truth of who you are now.

In previous incarnations, there were many limitations to these choices for various reasons, such as an inability to travel easily and quickly; daily responsibilities for survival; family or tribal obligations; lack of education; and stereotypical life roles, just to name a few. But as humanity has expanded in global awareness and connections, new possibilities have emerged that allow you to explore, evolve, and transform faster than any other previous time in history.

Rebirthing your self-identity is typically preceded by a Dark Night of the Soul. A Dark Night of the Soul experience is a level of consciousness dying. You are surrendering and allowing old energy to die as a form of reincarnation. It is possible to be consciously aware of yourself dying because you experience extreme grief, emotional depths, deeper parts of yourself, unexplainable loss, and a sense of uncertainty about where your life is going next. This is an elevation of your consciousness in one lifetime where you don't have to die in order to start again; the energy supports your re-birth because there are higher levels of energy available to you now.

In a spiritual sense, you can become fuller in your soul energy in a single incarnation without having to physically die. You now have the ability to rebirth yourself multiple times in one existence. With free will, you can revamp your life based on what is best for your growth and where you want to direct your life. This can happen in any number of ways, of course, and it may occur as something bigger than yourself pushing you further into a new life. Pakhet experienced this rebirth through events that seemed out of her control, and yet her mystical mother knew it was part of her life path to have a grand rebirth as she turned eighteen years old. It was written in her soul mission to become a new version of herself that would guide her further into her true power, which is connected to Awakening Consciousness.

Awakening Consciousness

Awakening Consciousness is the understanding that we are each responsible for our own energy, in every situation, all of the time. As a powerful creator of your life, you are the master of your energy, and everything (yep, *everything*) supports your learning and understanding of your energy. Awakening Consciousness is about actively claiming full power over all aspects of your life, from financial and professional experiences, to the karmic lessons, soul work, and belief systems you as a Soul chose to experience in this lifetime.

Awakening Consciousness is understanding the vastness of yourself as a soul, beyond the restrictions of physical, Ego-Mind, or third dimensional life. You are an eternal being having a temporary experience.

As you connect to Awakening Consciousness, the Bigger Picture becomes evident and you open up to more of your innate soul gifts, talents, and skills, including potential intuition development, psychic abilities, telepathy, channeling, energy work, healing, and other esoteric interests that support you as a soul.

Awakening Consciousness is energized by spiritual understanding, authenticity, exploration, meditation, self-reflection, and soul work. As a result, responsibility, boundaries, discernment, and honoring your authentic path become regular life themes.

With Awakening Consciousness, we learn more about ourselves as beings with eternal soul energy. We examine our unconscious belief systems, energetic patterns, karmic energies, and how we are powerfully creating everything in our lives. We see each other with a loving, detached lens, knowing that every being is on their own soul journey and in human form to learn lessons for soul growth. We detach from the polarity and dualities of Earth Consciousness since every person is viewed as a wise soul intentionally choosing their experiences. Fear-based emotional reactions and intense feelings are non-existent because every person is honored for what they are choosing, conscious or unconscious, and every person is seen as equally powerful. Respect and acceptance dominates.

A high level of responsibility infuses every choice with this energy. There is an understanding that something doesn't happen to you; it happens *for* your growth and learning. Awakening Consciousness asks: *Why did I create this? What is the best and highest understanding of this experience? And how will I powerfully and intentionally use my energy next?*

Combined with Heart Consciousness, this is where mammoth service and gifts to humanity can occur as well as collective evolutions in personal power. Making powerful choices that honor your own energy is a regular guiding intention.

A DESERT BONFIRE
{Style}

HIS CHISELED PROFILE BLENDED seamlessly into the shadows of the muddy mountains, creating an indistinguishable landscape between his hardened face and the edgy terrain. His sharp nose, sculpted forehead, and chin merged into the night and reappeared as dark, jagged hillsides in the distance. His wrinkles were the deep valleys and hidden crevices of the ancient land. She only knew which angles belonged to him when he slowly inhaled the musky sky, creating the only movement against the stoic backdrop, and then calmly exhaled out puffs of stardust. She watched his stubby eyelashes slowly descend, as if they were sweeping the mountain side and wiping away layers of forgotten earth.

She sat silently on the rough red blanket, a foot of dirt separating their dancing shadows that grew and shrank with every flame. She waited for his words, his wisdom, his next breath. A pack of coyotes howled in the distance, somewhere, as if they were leaving messages for the sunrise. The fire was hot enough to burn her toes, so she kept her feet tucked underneath her legs and waited. Waited for this stranger to lead the ceremony. Waited for what she was ready to receive. She simply waited.

He had appeared before her during a walk yesterday afternoon. As she roamed over the low hills and brown shrubs, she had felt the presence of a powerful energy approach from behind. She stopped walking and listened, tilting her chin up to the mahogany hills. A river of chills ran down her spine in the desert heat, and that was when the new presence had surrounded her. It felt loving, wise, and safe; as if an expected friend had finally arrived right on time.

She began walking again with her ears tuned to a higher frequency of messages. She listened above the distant call of the birds and the soft sway of the low bushes.

"You have returned to our ancient land, sister, and we welcome your presence at this time. It is wonderful to connect with you in this shared environment." She could trust this male voice. She smiled with a knowingness.

He continued. "Sister, how can we lovingly guide you forward at this time on your path?"

She halted to survey the distant landscape and pondered the question. It was pivotal yet simple; how could guidance assist her the most right now? The flat clouds slowly rolled above as if the answer was hidden within their soft puffs. Then without saying a spoken word, she responded to the guidance.

"Elder, I am ready to clear more energies from my recent experiences, but I have felt stuck in doing so. There is a spinning in my mind and a continuation of old stories in my head that I wish to finalize, yet I feel that they keep interacting with   me."

"Sister, in your world, there is a timing for all things. The energies you speak of are still moving through you, yet they are also looking for a new place to land. With your conscious awareness, you can direct all energies to their final Divine place through a sacred ritual that loves and honors all."

"I am ready for that guidance, Elder.

"Then we will create your bonfire. Tonight, as you lay down to sleep, we will be in contact to co-create your clearing and elevate your soul energy to a higher level."

Then a wind had breezed by her, twisting up her hair and

ruffling her shirt, as his presence disappeared back into the hills.

She fell asleep that night with the intention of being open to his guidance. Yet as she began to rest into deep sleep, she felt herself being carried away to another time and place when she was only twenty-two-years-old, to an experience she hadn't thought about in years.

Her pointer finger pushed the sticky black intercom button to speak to the distracted jail attendant. In his cramped front post, the six monitors to his left were vacant black-and-white screens, yet managed to capture his full attention as if something could happen at any moment: a fight, a yelling match, a rule-breaking event of some kind.

"I'm here to see Megan." Her voice came over the speaker, taking his attention away from the small black boxes, as his hard brown eyes meet her green eyes.

The guard assessed her keenly. No unexpected visitors just showed up here to meet the detainees.

She spoke again. "I was actually just here yesterday with the women's group speaking about sexual assault prevention..."

"Is she expecting you again today?"

"No, I just..." She didn't even have a known reason for this second visit. "I just wanted to follow-up with her about something we talked about yesterday."

"What's your name, ma'am?"

"Molly McCord. I signed in yesterday, too." He grabbed the visitor log from the previous day and scanned it for her name. Without looking up, he commanded, "ID, please."

"Sure." She passed her driver's license through the metal paper slot. He barely looked at it, and then slid a visitor's form back for her to sign-in again.

"You can speak to her in a private room, but only twenty minutes today." She nodded in return, putting the driver's licenses back in her wallet as he buzzed the first jail door open.

Molly walked into the cramped hallway before he buzzed open a second door for her to pass through. Stale air filled up every corner of the standing space. Harsh lighting from above made it uncomfortable to wait here long. She yanked open the second steel door to the juvenile detention center, then it violently slammed shut behind her. And for the second time in twenty-four hours, she felt a change in her body as the reality of being locked behind these doors and walls sets in.

The guard led her to a small vacant conference room on the left, covered with beige and gray in all directions - beige linoleum, gray table, gray chairs, beige walls. Straight ahead down the hall, Molly saw the open recreation space where girls could watch television, play board games, read, or lounge on older scratchy couches. High windows beamed in natural light, but the bars across the glass reminded you that the only freedom found here was in looking out those rectangles.

She sat down at a sterile conference table, and suddenly wondered what she was going to say to this sixteen-year-old girl. Molly had not told anyone that she was going back to visit Megan today, and she didn't know why she had to return, yet she couldn't get the idea out of her head.

"Hey." Megan walked in, her shoulder-length brown hair looking recently brushed. She carried herself with the careless saunter of any sixteen-year-old at the mall: confident, insecure, and indifferent all wrapped up into a single stride.

"Hey," Molly replied.

She sat down across from Molly and immediately started twisting her fingers together on the table. Her gum smelled like strawberry, but sounded like sporadic fireworks.

"So....I was here yesterday with the women's group talking about sexual assault and answering your questions and all that..."

"Yeah, I remember."

"I was really struck by your story, and I was wondering if you... maybe wanted to talk more about what you've experienced... or what your plans are when you're out of here...or anything..." Molly stared across at Megan's blank face, looking for any sign of interest, and realizing this might be a huge waste of time.

Megan shrugged. "Sure, whatever. I mean, that's cool." Her two index fingers bent together, then straightened, then intertwined.

"So, I remember you sharing that you still have the same boyfriend as before…"

"Yeah, Mike's awesome. We have plans for when I'm outta here." Her gum smacked.

"And I think you said he's the same guy who assaulted you… is that right?"

"Oh yeah, but he's changed now. He's totally different. He has this new job and he's making plans for us to go to California this summer when I'm done with this place. I can tell in his voice that he's different and he really misses me. He's cool."

Molly watched her intently, knowing this version of the story was selective and edited. Megan's eyes darted quickly around the room as she spoke, never landing in one place for long.

Molly let her words sit in the air for a moment. "Have you ever thought of going back to school and graduating? Since you're sixteen, it's actually the perfect time to do that… you aren't that behind other kids…"

"Nah, school is just so boring, ya know? You only sit all day and nobody cares about algebra in the real world. Mike told me I could do better with him since he has a job and can get me one, too." She paused. "How old are you, anyways?"

"I'm twenty-two. Finishing up my senior year in college. I think school is wonderful, actually. Maybe you just need to find a few classes you're interested in."

"I can't wait to be older," Megan said, ignoring the school topic all together.

"Well, you could also stay here and work, get a job at the mall or somewhere. What if you didn't go to California with Mike?" Molly knew this suggestion was a long-shot, but she had to at least say it. In the history of sixteen-year-old girls, she knew it was never one sentence that changed their minds, but perhaps planting a seed was possible.

"This town sucks. I can't stay here in the rain and cold when Mike is going to move to the sun and heat! We're going to have a great time in California. I'll be outta here in only six months, anyways." Her gum smacked again; she fidgeted with her fingernails.

Molly allowed the silence to be their third companion for a moment.

"Besides, the only person who cares about me is Mike and I can't wait to get away from these other bitches. They've had it worse than me, so I'm really lucky to have a plan."

"Why did you get sent here in the first place?"

"I got caught stealing some stuff, and ya know... I made some stupid mistakes." She didn't elaborate further. "And Mike made some bad decisions too, but he apologized and said it would never happen again, so things are going to be good now." She nodded her head to demonstrate her confidence in this information.

Molly took a deep breath. "I just want you to know, Megan, for whatever it's worth, that there are other choices and you don't need to be with someone who has hurt you. Like we talked about in our presentation yesterday, it is very important to be aware of the power dynamics in relationships and to know that the other person shouldn't be trying to control you, in any way."

Megan stared at the table in silence.

"Is Mike threatening you to go to California with him?"

"He says it's the best choice for me, that there is nothing else here for me anyways..."

"Do you feel safe with him?"

"I don't have anyone else in my life, okay?" Her eyes turned hard; her jaw became stiff.

"If you asked for help here, there are people who could assist you when you get out, like counselors and social workers. Other women can help you."

"They're all lame." She shifted in her chair, tossing her hair back.

"Maybe they're lame to you, but they can help you make

other choices. So just think about it, at least, okay?" Molly leaned across the table and stared back at her defiance.

"Sure, whatever." Megan played with two strings of her hair.

"Have you ever thought about what type of job you want to have in life? Like, what interests you?"

"I'm not good at anything really, but I think being a nurse might be cool. My mom was a nurse."

Then the door jolted opened. "Time's up, ladies!" The guard stood in the doorway, holding the door open for their immediate exit. It had only been ten minutes.

"Well thanks for stopping by. Take care." Megan twirled her hair one more time, then quickly left the room before anything else could be said.

Molly walked out of the beige space with colorless thoughts.

Outside on the sidewalk, Molly's head felt heavy and full; like a rain cloud about to release from the sky above. *Did she hear anything I said?* Probably not. *Is she going to change her plans?* Not likely. *Did any new options get through to her?* No way to know. It was just like every other conversation she and her co-facilitators had had with women who had been sexually assaulted.

Over the past year, Molly had heard too many stories from girls in their community who were holding pockets of shame about an experience they thought they were to blame for. They carried the energy of an experience, hid it from everyone, and absorbed it into their sense of self-worth because it was too scary to talk about or admit what happened. They carried the message that they must have done something wrong, or were stupid, or made a bad choice to even be in that situation in the first place.

So Molly and her college peers had been specially trained in community outreach and group facilitation conversations that allowed girls in junior high, middle school, high school, college dorms, and the juvenile detention center to hear facts about sexual assault, acquaintance rape, and choices they could make after an attack. They shared empowering information about consent, safe sexual choices, and healthy power dynamics in relationships. They answered tough questions from hardened girls. They tenderly listened to young voices approach them afterwards and ask, "Do you have a minute? I want to tell you something...." They challenged women to be in their power and be strong enough to recognize unhealthy behaviors in another, yet know that you are not to blame. An attack is not your fault. It was never something you deserved or chose.

As the rain started pounding down, Molly sat in her car in silence and stared back at the juvenile detention center's multiple barred windows. She knew that even if you have no control over another's decisions or choices, you can at least go back and try to build a bridge. You can try to go into the darkest places that someone is hiding in and bring them a torch of light. *You can go back.* You can go in there with them so they are not alone, and hopefully, maybe, you help them see a new path forward.

Hopefully. Ideally. Maybe. Or maybe not.

Because if women can't trust and support one another in their times of deep pain and vulnerability, then who can they turn to in order to feel safe? Right Sisterhood is when we are there for each other with respect, love, connection, and understanding. It is so easy to keep walking forward on our individual paths and not look around to see who we can help or assist along the way. But if we only follow our own path, eventually we end up alone without the connections we need and crave. Right Sisterhood means we reach out and initiate those connections, knowing we can strengthen and support our sisters in ways we cannot even imagine. We see the power each one of us holds and support her in owning her power more fully. This is why we go back.

As she sat in the car, the windshield gradually became covered with drippy rain and she could no longer see anything clearly. Blurry lines and foggy shapes surrounded every window until it all faded into a cloud of mist. Then in her dream state, her consciousness drifted away from that distant time, and the reality of that interaction in the name of modern sisterhood morphed into a completely different experience of ancient sisterhood.

She was sitting in an open clearing in the middle of a dense forest. A bright full moon hung overhead; walls of trees provided safety and privacy in every direction. It was a windless night with a sweet sage smell in the air. She was sitting on a stone bench in a circle with seven other women. Each was wearing a warm cloak in a single color of the rainbow and holding a specific crystal. A fire roared in the middle of the gathering spot, holding space for light in the night. She sensed this was a sacred ceremony of sisterhood. A seasonal ritual that brought them all together from distant lands, tribes, and ancient lineages.

The woman in the red cloak spoke first. "Sisters, there will be a turning of collective energies soon, just as our Elders spoke of. The earth is entering a new cycle of evolution and learning, and this means we will be challenged to grow in new ways. Much of what we know as Truth will be lost and forgotten so humanity will be given an opportunity to experience another energy. We are prepared for this, and yet we know it will deeply alter Right Sisterhood and our experiences of power." A raven flew down from a nearby tree and perched on her shoulder.

Then the woman in the orange cloak began. "We have each been blessed with understanding the ways and truth of Right Sisterhood. We have been blessed with experiencing the ability to reach out to our sisters; to support them and offer them other paths and choices to make when they may feel lost, stuck, or broken. We have embraced the reality that each of us are stronger in some areas, and we can be of great assistance to those who are feeling weak and off-course. We have each seen the beauty of Right Sisterhood in our soul experiences and know its immense beauty."

The woman in the gold cloak took her turn next, twisting a crystal in her soft hands as she spoke. "We are lucky to know that we each contribute to the whole in special ways through mutual collaboration, wisdom, and love. Our experience of Right Sisterhood is based on seeing the power and beauty in one other, knowing that we are each valued and needed for what we bring to global energies. Our communities and tribes have thrived because we have connected to each other from an open-hearted space that invites one another to shine and be her glorious self." She nodded her in head in honor of all in the circle.

"As we know," began the women in the green cloak, "this will be changing with the rising tides of patriarchy that are emerging in the world. Women will be altered by the new roles and examples of power that will start to dominate many cultures. Collaboration, community, and openness will fade as unconscious men begin to assert control, hierarchy, and new demonstrations of power that focus on the one instead of the many. New structures will be put in place that promote survival instead of cooperation; winning and domination will be valued more than peace or unity. Yet it is wise to note that this version of power does not support the truth of Divine Masculine energy, either. For conscious men in their right power and strength also encompass gifts of the Divine Feminine, and they will be forced to suppress their innate heart energy in order to survive in this energy. We will all be learning together."

The woman in the light blue cloak pushed back her blond hair. "Just as we understand that there is a Divine cycles for all things, we know that this phase will bear many fruits and be beneficial as yet another way to raise consciousness about the use of energy. We pledge to trust the intelligence of this grand cycle and believe that it is serving a meaningful purpose, even if we lose faith or abandon trust along the way. The strength of the mind will overshadow the strength of the heart, yet we choose to believe this, too, will be a beneficial teacher for All. We understand that we will each be called to carry the torch of Right Sisterhood, yet it will be more difficult after the rise of patriarchy when women are shown that they must compete, betray, manipulate, or act aggressively to survive in this cycle."

The woman in the indigo cloak brought the palms of her hands together in front of her heart before speaking. "As we gather now in this sacred ritual of Right Sisterhood, may all women be blessed with the tools and wisdom they need within themselves to return to their Divine Feminine Self. May jealously turn to appreciation. May competition turn to collaboration. May power struggles turn to inner strength. May any and all expressions of feeling less worthy or less valued be turned to greater self-acceptance and deeper Love for Self. May all untruths be balanced in the light of Divine Wisdom in the most perfect ways. May every women be guided on her path to see that she is perfect in her unique beauty for the benefit of All."

The woman in the deep violet cloak adjusted her soft sleeves, then turned both of her palms up to the sky. "Our collective wisdom understands that this is a balancing cycle with many great teachings and lessons. As such, we now bless all men and women who participate in this grand cycle as part of their soul mission. We trust that we will be guided through every phase, twist and turn in the most perfect ways for All. We assert that there will also be a shifting back to inner balance for every being. May every soul who participates in this grand cycle also be gifted with greater connection to their own inner Divine Masculine and Divine Feminine energies in the most perfect way for their soul growth. May we all be teachers for one another and light-filled guides of Divine energy."

Finally the woman in the silver cloak spoke, her dark braid hanging over her shoulder and nearly touching her waist. "May we each carry the light of Right Sisterhood in our blood and in our hearts. May we each make a soul commitment to show up in the world as vessels for Feminine strength, love, and compassion when the world needs it most. May we have the courage to individually and collectively support other women as reflections of ourselves, not as competition, nor enemies, nor adversaries on the path. May we each remember that the heart of the planet will bloom with the fullness of creativity, wisdom, and intelligence that we all offer to the whole. And may we be blessed to remember this ancient wisdom when the world needs it most. And so it is."

"And so it is." The other seven women repeated in response.

Then all eight women stood up, reached right and left to hold hands, and hummed a low chant as the Milky Way swayed above their heads and the fire blazed up to their bellies. The sacred ceremony had invoked the intention to remember Right Sisterhood as a gift of service to the world just as the global energies were shifting with the rise of a dominant religion, expanding world connections, and a destruction of ancient traditions. The bonfire lit up their velvet cloaks like brilliant, sparkling gems.

And now here she was. Sitting in front of another roaring bonfire, but this time in a barren desert. The Elder's profile came in and out of view with each galloping flame and smoke-filled wave. An indigo sky blanketed everything, as if it was all tucked in at the foot of the horizon. She closed her eyes to inhale the aromas of this night which reminded her of multiple soul experiences around the power of fire.

Then the Elder spoke. "Begin to see outlines of figures appear all around this fire, sister. Watch as the front row fills up with familiar faces and energy fields. You will know exactly whom is whom."

With her eyes now adjusted to the night, she slowly witnessed soft transparent clouds begin to take shape and come into form around the bonfire's circle. Individual energies arrived from all stages of her life: a childhood mean girl; teenage friends; former best friends; her first love; her first heartbreak; significant relationships; teachers and mentors; co-workers, assistants, colleagues, and bosses; family members of all kinds. She recognized people from her travels, from Paris, from companies, and social circles. They all sat quietly in the circle and embraced the warmth of the bonfire without saying a word. Then as their human forms gradually appeared more solid, she saw all of her animal companions arrive in front of the circle. A lion lazily stretched all four legs as far as they could go. A heron swooped in to perch atop a log. She saw a mirage of a crocodile shape coming in and out of focus. Furry domestic cats and dogs nestled up near the roaring flames and positioned their fuzzy selves at the closest possible point of warmth; a soft collection of paws, tails, and pink noses.

The Elder continued. "All souls in your life are here by choice, both your choice and their choice. Your soul mates are your growth companions, and you will each evolve, ascend, and continue on your soul journeys separately. Your experiences together are meant to support both of you, and all energies, in Divine ways until it is time for each of you to move into another realm of experiences. The soul mates you see here now are present with honor, respect, gratitude, and love for you. Just as you are present for them with those same messages of appreciation."

She slowly glanced around the bonfire to connect with each person's energy individually. She sensed the different levels of consciousness within each beautiful being, and felt a deep reverence for their contributions to her growth. Swells of emotions moved through her as she recalled those significant situations, or words, or life phases, or conversations, or times they had shared together. She saw their soul's light burning bright in the night. She offered a silent *namaste* to each one.

Then she noticed that two important people in her life were not present. "Elder, I have just realized that two individuals are not here. They have both been exceptionally important to me... yet I cannot see nor feel them." A dark cloud of confusion passed through her mind.

"Sister, neither one is here because they are not ready to let go of the energy exchange with you yet. They are each still living in a fixed paradigm of energy with you that is working for them. They are being sustained by this energy exchange and are choosing on a soul level to keep that experience alive within themselves because they are not ready to move forward yet. This occurs with souls who prefer slower timelines. They remain in some energy dynamics longer, and it is a perfectly acceptable choice for their soul growth."

She looked down at her feet, then at her clasped hands, and considered this insight. She could sense that she already knew this information about each of these individuals, so it was not truly a surprise. Hearing this perspective actually allowed her to remain in soft compassion and deeper forgiveness for them and what they had brought to her path. She intentionally honored their Soul choice to not be here with a silent prayer.

He then continued. "Many individuals in your immediate soul group understand the bigger picture of soul growth, and are ready to either let you go, or move forward with you. But some are choosing to remain in other timelines longer because it is not comfortable for them to proceed ahead yet. Just as you wish to release energies, others wish to remain in them. This is their free will, and it is to be honored. You are wise to allow them this choice and to let it be." She nodded in agreement.

"When members of your immediate soul group make this choice to remain in certain energies, it also benefits other soul groups that they will connect with at some point on their journey. Their current choice will be a learning tool for others as they will now interact with new people and have fresh opportunities to grow, if desired. Each of these individuals will continue to be great teachers for other souls. A perfect system is always in place."

As she glanced around the bonfire, she began to see a second row of shapes, and then a third row emerged from the indigo sky. They all slowly transitioned from soft translucent forms, to foggy white, and then finally became clearer depictions of familiar energies. Her energy surged as she recognized all of these beings.

His voice began again. "After your immediate, or primary soul group, in this lifetime, there are other collections of souls that you interact with across all timelines, dimensions of time, and lifetimes. These individuals are also your soul groups, and each one is involved in some form of an energy experience with you. In fact, some of these people are *you* from other lifetimes."

She slowly glanced around the bonfire to witness a collection of characters glowing in the fire light. Marie, Claude, Paul, Josephine, and Naomi sat silently in the second row; Kaimi, Ipo, Maka, Alana, and the whole tribe were gathered to their right. She recognized the crouched posture of the samurai warrior, the elaborate hair masterpiece of his wife, the sweet smile of their son, and the calm focus of the cook. Behind them, she could make out Pakhet's long black hair, the soft energy of her mother, Issa's strong shoulders, and the bald head of Naeem. Then she saw Fred, his older brother, the men from the firm, and all of the characters from the savannah sitting in silence as the fire mesmerized each of them. The Queen's soft silhouette danced in the flames, and she was accompanied by Gwendolyn, Hannah, Sara, the Legal Counselor, and everyone from the palace, creating a spectacle of shapes, heights, and outlines. To the left of this group, she saw the brightly colored cloaks of all women from the Right Sisterhood. These were all members of her soul group and parts of her soul stories. As she looked at each one, she started to recall her roles and interactions with all of them. The lessons, growth, and experiences they had shared in those lifetimes together. No words were spoken; everyone simply embraced the presence of the moment and the roles they were playing in this grand game.

Beyond these recognizable faces, she started to decipher rows upon rows of more people. Stories she had yet to remember; experiences she had yet to recall; places within herself she had yet to visit. It appeared that the ongoing rows of souls faded off into the horizon.

The Elder spoke again. "Every soul here is a spark in your bonfire, just as you are a spark in their bonfires. You have travelled together through many incarnations to support soul growth and the evolution of the collective. Just as you are each a part of the bonfire, you are also the bonfire within a spark, and together, you are the cosmos."

A giant crackle rose up out of the fire at that instant, lighting up all of the faces and blasting up into the stars above their heads. A new warmth encompassed her body.

"Now that All are present, please visualize putting into the fire all of your completed soul contracts, karmic energies, life lessons, healed relationships, and anything else that is done for you at this time. Imagine all of those energies being thrown into this burning pit now."

She inhaled deeply and visualized everything she knew was complete being offered to the flames. Seeing all these faces in front of her made it exceptionally clear how much she had changed, grown, and evolved on her soul path. She was proud to release with love and gratitude what no longer served her.

After two more deep breaths, she had visually tossed it all into the bonfire. "Okay, done."

He nodded once. "We will now begin the healing ritual. I will stop speaking with words and only speak with energy. As you open your eyes to watch the spectacle, you will sense my messages, and as you close your eyes, you will feel the healing occur."

He closed his eyes and began to make a deep, low humming sound in the cave of his chest. She felt the vibration pulse through the air until it connected with her root chakra; strong, alive, expansive. Then with amazement, she watched the whole bonfire turn to a deep red as the flaming tips soared like scarlet spears higher into the night air.

Then the tone of his humming rose to another note. The energy spiraled up to her second chakra as the bonfire started to change to a dark orange hue. She watched the dancing movements, mesmerized by the spectacle, and then glanced around to see each of her soul mates engaged in the same trance. The humming was working within each of their chakra centers, too.

He then changed the tone again as her solar plexus came alive. The ascending energy felt like a burst of sunshine gold streaming out of her belly. The flames continued to blaze wildly like fierce lightning bolts coming out of the ground. As they grew higher, they also started to extend out wider, as if they were flirting with her toes.

His humming changed again to yet another finely tuned note. A lime green began to emerge from the center of the fire, and slowly evolved to a darker emerald hue. The burning blaze felt warmer, closer to her skin, and appeared to rise up above the heads of all those in the circle. Her heart chakra was pulsing and spinning quickly, as if it was in easy rhythm with the bonfire.

The humming changed once again to a fifth distinct sound as he continued to sit with closed eyes and even breathing. She felt a cleansing sensation rise up to her throat chakra. All of the familiar faces and figures were now fully hidden behind the bright blue flames as the fire continued to grow and expand. She only felt open to it; like the warmest possible embrace she could ever receive.

The sixth humming noise began. A tingling vibration entered her third eye chakra, and she felt energy spinning off her wildly. With her eyes open to the night, she watched as rays of indigo light blasted up into the heavens and disappeared into the inky dark sky. The bonfire escalated up, up, up, and she could feel the energetic presence of her soul mates as they collectively cleared energies together.

The Elder began to create yet another distinct sound in his chest, and with this higher octave, she felt a powerful opening in her crown chakra. She watched as the giant roaring bonfire moved and swayed all around her, and then observed in awe how it slowly changed to a gorgeous violet flame.

Like a powerful magnet, the violet flame transmuted everything to love, forgiveness, and completion as it burned through all lower energies and returned them to their original place of Divine essence. With each blazing flame and jolt of violet fire, she felt herself changing at a deep level, as if her DNA was being rewired and her soul's journey was being newly written. The flames roared up on her body and twisted through her hair, yet she was safe and grounded and strong in this experience.

As the fire continued to ebb and flow, up and out, in every direction possible, the Elder once again changed his humming to a final note of purity. Their dancing fire partner turned to amazing bolts of glowing white flames, like streaks of bleach being splattered up onto the night's dark background. The white fire expanded and danced up into the sky, swirling and twirling and mingling with the distant Milky Way stars.

She was speechless with wonder and alive with stardust. Then the milky-white tips of the fire started to splinter and divide, leaving their original flame source behind and becoming separate entities. The specks rose up higher, multiplied, and spread out across the endless abyss. She watched with amazement as the sky slowly began to fill up with freshly made sparkles. All of the energies from the bonfire's flares were creating new stars in the sky. The clearing of her soul missions, life lessons, soul contracts, karma, healed emotions, healed relationships, and all energies she had agreed to participate in were being transmuted back to the heavens as gorgeous flecks of fresh light. The completion of these soul stories was literally creating more light in the galaxy once they had been healed back to their original source of Love.

The sky continued to twinkle brightly as all of her completed energy became a brighter, purer version of Love. Her physical Self felt weightless and beautifully empty as the bonfire's force carried her away. A spiraling sensation surrounded her as she floated hypnotically into a quiet place of beingness. Slowly, the landscape disappeared and a sense of deep peace filled up all of her senses.

The Elder's humming was now distant, and a softness surrounded her in every direction. The space was white, but colorless; a void, but containing everything. Then she heard with more than her ears a familiar presence that she could only describe as God or Spirit. With quiet wonder, she tuned her frequency to the vibration of Love, which was her natural state and expression, but here it felt bigger. Clearer. Stronger.

In this white space, she heard a grand message reverberate through her cells.

"To be a soul in human form at this time is the greatest gift you can offer the cosmos. You have raised your human consciousness high enough to see beyond what can be seen, and to know beyond what can be known. You have used your free will to be more Love and Light in the most intense areas of human life. You have embraced your lessons and soul growth, while remaining in your capacity to see how everyone is playing roles for each other. You are all in these roles together to support all advancements of humanity. Yet your true power is always within yourself and your choices, which can be very complex when guided by your human free will.

"Regardless of any temporary human experiences or significant lifetimes, remember that you are a beautiful soul who has volunteered to be a participant in this grand human journey. You chose to play specific roles to advance your soul and evolve humanity in the highest possible ways. You chose to play in certain energy spectrums in order to master them and to know your power. You chose to have the fullest experiences possible of every energy so you would know the gifts of all sides. And you volunteered to raise those lower energies up to their highest expressions of Love, forgiveness, and peace."

At that moment, she saw in her mind's eye the image of a graceful arm reaching up with an elegant hand, and it began to pluck other stars from the sky. She saw the palm of the hand come alive with fresh energy because every twinkling cluster it now held was encoded with a unique energy ranging from deep fear to intense Love. As the stars were collected in the grand hand, they swirled together to form a highly unique soul mission. A once-in-this-galaxy mosaic of creation. Then she watched as the special, newly-formed bright mass was handed to an eager soul who proudly proclaimed their willingness to experience this special energy and raise all of its vibration to the highest possible expressions of Love as a form of service to the galaxy.

"You often select the soul missions that are needed most for the benefit of all souls. You wisely choose to carry exactly what you can handle, even if you forget your strength and power, because you know that everything is connected and supported in the galaxy. You are an eternal being of energy who is volunteering to use your power for the good of All. Everything you experience is for your soul's growth and the growth of Oneness. And so it is."

The grand energy presence slowly faded away.

Coming out of the trance, she watched the final rays of the enchanting spectacle shift away and the Elder's humming emerge more clearly. Slowly, calmly, gently, her energy field turned softer and lighter, as if she was now landing on a pillow of angel feathers. She felt her breath running through her body again as her awareness came back to the ground. She sat completely still as his humming continued to flow around her body and then fade into the mountains behind her.

Then once the humming completely stopped, she felt her heartbeat in her chest and her pulse in fingertips. She slowly inhaled and exhaled, then her eyes opened to see the glowing bonfire burning brightly in front of her. The rough red blanket had turned up edges, but showed no sign of fire damage. She glanced around the circle. All of the figures were gone except her teacher.

"They are now cleared, cleaned, and healed, too, Sister, just as you elected to do. When one of your soul mates initiates a healing, all of you are connected to the experience and can choose to participate in it. In other timelines, you were attending their bonfires, and you have now disappeared from their experiences, too." He smiled widely. "That is one of the reasons why the fire becomes so big. You are all co-creating it simultaneously. You are all unlimited sparks of the bonfire, and you are all bonfires creating unlimited sparks."

She smiled in wonder. "I feel so different now, Elder, yet also the same. It is too much to put into words..." Her voice trailed off into the desert night.

"You have transmuted all lower energies back to their

original place of Love, Sister. Your human Self has ascended up to a new experience of energies with this healing and clearing. More soul mates will now appear in this paradigm, more soul lessons will emerge, and you will all continue to learn and grow together on your journeys."

She allowed the words to remain present between them. "Thank you, Elder, for everything. You are a wise teacher and I am supremely grateful for this experience."

His profile responded. "You are welcome, Sister. But I must be clear: you are the wise teacher. You have created various teachers on your journey to remind you of your power and lessons, but all of these beings emerged from the same Source. It is one of the human games we play to direct you back to your own knowingness. For I AM not me. I AM you."

And with a wisp of the warm desert wind, she felt his energy glide over her and land within her body, just as the bonfire roared up again higher into the stars. The intensity of the energy alignment required her to close her eyes, but it did not feel foreign or weird. It was comforting and known; a distant piece of the same puzzle finally arriving.

Then the expansive bonfire gradually became a small spark. Fading, softening, and disappearing in front of her. The retracting heat turned her feet cold. A whole galaxy of energy shrank into a spark of infinity. A vacancy of new air widened all around her. She slowly opened her eyes to find herself in a space of the brightest possible white light in every direction; vibrant, pure, clean, clear. A softening spilled over her body as she felt no thoughts in her mind, no questions or inquiries.

She was simply being in the space as it existed.

All nothingness, yet All That Is.

She didn't feel her body, or heart, or breath.

She was simply existing as pure energy.

A participant in the void of white light.

Beingness.

Then a pause occurred.

Followed by a beat of time.

Then a quantity of measurement began.

And she felt herself transition back to the paradigm of time and space.

A buzz went off in the distance. A cat meowed down the hall. A blast of wind hit the window panes.

She woke up in her bed with cold feet, then reached for her cell phone to look at the time. It was only 5 a.m. on another random Tuesday morning. She rolled over and cozied up to her husband's warm back for a few more hours of blessed pillow time. She placed her hands on her womb where the little feet inside her thumped wildly; the baby turning and dancing to its own rhythm. Then she drifted back to sleep sensing in her groggy state that something had changed yet she was not awake enough yet to describe it.

But when she awakens, she will have received new stars from the heavens to guide her forward on her next soul mission.

When she awakens, she will embrace her next inner well of deep power and endless possibilities.

When she awakens, she will step down from the bed and onto the earth with renewed strength and greater poise.

When she awakens, she will move ahead with grace and turn inward for new wisdom.

When she awakens, she will leap to higher heights of her light and dive to deeper depths of her potential.

When she awakens, she will soar with joy

When she awakens, she will answer the call of a new journey to a higher version of her soul's growth.

And so the next soul adventure begins.

Soul Imprint Healing

Accepting Others' Healing Journey

We have had many lifetimes of being saviors for others. We have healed, saved, guided, rescued and led others to safety in other incarnations because the planet needed these types of leaders at the time. Conversely, we have also been the ones who have been saved and rescued, as well, so we know on a soul level the value of such service. Many of us sincerely have the intention to help, guide, and assist others.

In this lifetime, we are honoring each other as powerful creators of our lives. Everyone here is composed of multiple soul stories with many layers of energy. We are all capable of healing these parts of ourselves in the ways that work best for us. It is our responsibility to allow each person to follow their own healing journey and do what is best for them. This is not always easy. It can be very painful to watch loved ones sabotage themselves, or struggle, or continually make difficult life choices when we want better for them. It is often very challenging to stand back as they continually participate in self-destructive tendencies or voyage further down the path of addiction. Try as we might, very little may get through to them or change their choices.

One thing to remember is that you are not more powerful than they are. Your soul is not better, nor wiser, nor more loved than their soul. Even if you feel you have the best answers and know exactly what to do, these are not ultimately your decisions to make because they are also powerful creators. They are just making different choices about their path and what they are here to learn at this time. Do not allow your Ego-Mind to put you on a pedestal or give you a white horse to ride in on so you can save the day. You may have guidance or helpful information for them, but in a spiritual sense, they are equally powerful in their God energy. And they are demonstrating, unconsciously or consciously, how they are choosing to use their power at this time.

There are times when practical choices must be made, such as when criminal, abusive, and highly destructive behavior is enacted. Be sensible and call the authorities as need. Tough love is necessary at times, and of course every situation is different. Do not give up the practical responsibilities just because you also have a spiritual understanding of what is unfolding. It is vital to be grounded and make smart decisions when another is in need of crucial, life-saving help.

Ultimately it is important to see them as a vessel of God energy. Know that God sees them. God has their back and is *right there* during their darker phases, present in every choice they make and direction they go. More than anything, your true power is in accepting their healing journey. They are a soul on a grand adventure of growth who is learning more about themselves in ways that are best for them. Support and love them for what they are choosing to experience. See their light and God presence. Allow them to be powerful in their human Self without carrying lower energies for them. Even though we cannot make choices for another, nor intrude on their free will, we can offer another path by building bridges.

Building Bridges

Building bridges creates openings. We recognize where someone is, and offer to create or guide them on a new path that takes them to a new destination. This is not about rescuing, nor healing, nor doing the work for them because we understand that they are equally powerful and capable of making choices that are best for them. We are not trying to take anything away from where they are now; we are actually trying to add more to what they can do, or be, or discover about themselves. Building bridges is a safe, supportive way of recognizing that you see them for who they truly are, and you also see a higher version of possibilities that awaits them.

We can build bridges for others in multiple ways: through knowledge and facts; through shared intentions and energy; and through actions and commitments. We can show up to support them physically, intellectually, financially, and psychologically. The intention is to be a gateway of possibilities for what they can create with their power and free will. Oftentimes, we do not even see how big we are when life circumstances have pulled us down into a temporary version of smallness that we have come to accept as our only reality. Bridges open you back up to more of You than you can see in the moment.

One of my driving intentions for being a facilitator for sexual assault prevention was to build bridges for other women. To show them a new path that was out of view, or perhaps not even a possibility they knew existed based on where they were currently standing. Trauma, abuse, and feeling like a victim are very real psychological contributions to one's reality. The effects of sexual assault can show up in a myriad of ways and last for a lifetime, especially if one feels alone, depressed, or that the world is a fearful place.

We cannot force anyone to walk across a bridge, but we can encourage, inspire, and share the benefits of what lies on the other side if they decide to make that choice. Going back to visit Megan in the juvenile detention center was my impulsive, and perhaps naive, attempt at trying to open her up to another way to live her life. I have no idea what choice she made or what happened next in her life, but at least it felt right to reach out and try to get through to this lovely young woman, even if she couldn't hear me or see another bridge to cross in her life. And regardless of anything, I had to also remember that God saw her; the Universe saw her; she was not ignored by Spirit. Whatever she chose would take her to the next point of growth on her journey.

Building bridges also pertains to *holding the space* for someone. Holding the space means we energetically hold the intention for a new action or outcome that is best for them. We support them in their free will and choices by providing an energetic gateway to a new space of possibility. We can do this for each other through a shared intention or desired outcome. You may hold the space for your best friend to find her perfect life companion, or for your partner to connect with the best possible job. Holding the space is a conscious way of loving, supporting, and believing in another person's path while also honoring their choices.

When we see and honor each person as a powerful soul, we empower them to do better and infuse them with the light of who they truly are. With this support, we also reinforce the energy of Right Sisterhood and connecting with others in a pure, safe way.

Right Sisterhood

Divine Feminine energy has an innate need to create, share, open, and love. The highest expression of this God energy is found in trusting Self and connecting to the Universal wisdom of the heart. Divine Feminine expressions are based on love for Self that can be extended as love for others since it flows openly and freely through the God energy channel. There is only more to give, experience, and share; there is only more to co-create together. Essentially, Divine Feminine energy feels safe: safe in herself, safe in her connection with God, and safe in her ability to create, express, and love in her life.

When Divine Feminine energies merge, they create Right Sisterhood. Forces come together and multiply the expressions of love, creating, sharing, and opening. A gathering of Divine Feminine energies is a gathering of God energy that is based on love for All with an openness to receive another's wisdom, creativity, intuition, and specialness. Right Sisterhood is based on the abundance in the Universe and how each person is here with a special soul mission to offer the whole. A place of safety is created for all women to be themselves, speak their truth, and honor their individual paths while also being loved for their unique expression of God energy.

Before the rise of formal religions and patriarchy, women knew Right Sisterhood as a soul experience. They knew the sacredness of their sexuality, their emotions, their creativity, their wisdom, and their intuition. They valued all aspects of their womanhood as needed components that contributed to the Universal whole and brought peace and balance to Right Brotherhood. Women were integral aspects of the Divine that were alive in the fullness of their abilities without needing to prove or do anything to demonstrate their worth.

Right Sisterhood does not mean all women will be friends, or relate, or even like each other. That is not realistic to expect. But there is an underlying *respect* that is present for the commonalities that are shared just for being female on the planet. There is a deeper wisdom that speaks louder than the Ego-Mind and allows her to be her; to have her journey, healing, and growth in the ways that are best for her soul. With Right Sisterhood, acceptance, detachment, honor, and respect allow all women to gracefully be themselves.

The truth of Right Sisterhood has diminished and shrunk in patriarchal societies as women became programmed at a young age to compete, stand out, be perfect, and follow gender roles. All of this pervasive messaging established what it meant to be valued, seen, and loved. *You are more loveable if you're perfect, or if you act like a good girl, or follow these rules, or look pretty, or demonstrate that you are the best at something.* She had to prove her worth to be seen, loved, or heard. Not only did this alter relationship roles among genders, it deeply affected how women related to one another, often unconsciously and without deeper questioning as they saw other women as measuring sticks and comparison tools. The need to out-do, or unnecessarily compete, or take down, or destroy another female became stronger and enacted more Shadow Feminine energies than ever before on the planet. Right Sisterhood was lost as hearts closed, survival needs grew, and trust in another's motive evaporated.

Women lost their ability to connect with the truth of themselves and the truth of each other. But now in modern times, we have more ways to bring these authentic connections and Divine expressions of Self back to the forefront of our Selves and in our lives. We have the ability to undo the deeper patriarchal programming and return to the innate ancient wisdom of our souls, which is the understanding that we are all needed, valued, loved and adored as Feminine expressions of God energy.

Sisterhood can also show up as False Sisterhood. This is when the underlying intention or agenda of a community is based on the Ego-Mind's desires to prove, compete, manipulate, or do harm to others. False Sisterhood is based on Shadow Feminine energies, and have all the tell-tale signs of lower expressions, such as gossip, mean-girl antics, bullying, shaming, and so forth. These gatherings of women may start out one way, and then quickly sidetrack to other intentions or outcomes as the truth of the collective energy emerges. False Sisterhood is when you do not feel safe to be yourself, share your truth, or connect with others. It is a clear sign that this group is perhaps not for you.

In truth, Divine Feminine energy is loved just for *being*. She is accepted and cherished just for being a beautiful vessel of creation and openness. Then Right Sisterhood creates community among women of similar vibration, carries these messages of acceptance and respect, and safely affirms her for who she is in her truth and wisdom. Right Sisterhood accepts her heart, her feelings, her brilliance, and her truth with no strings attached and no need for demonstration of her worth. *There is nothing to prove with Right Sisterhood.* She is enough. She is valued. She is loved. She is perfect God energy in Feminine form.

From this space, she is able to also heal all energies back to Love.

Healing All Energies Back to Love

Our individual and collective soul missions involve healing all memories of separation from God across all lifetimes. We work with these separation energies through all areas of lives, and incarnations as a way to actively demonstrate and employ our innate power. When you exist from a place of love for yourself, you change your vibration, frequency and energetic signature to a higher expression.

Healing energies back to love does not mean you will always experience love in your life. There will still be times of fear and anger, hurt and pain. You will feel deeply and have complex emotions at times; you will experience grief, loss, and times of doubt. All of these expressions are built into the human journey and they do not go away as you rise in consciousness. However, you will view, and interact, with these aspects of yourself differently and come to love them for the messages they bring you.

But now you understand that you are the vessel for these energetic expressions and they are all temporarily flowing through you. You are not limited nor defined by them. You are in charge of them because you are a Universal gateway for all energies. You are composed of Divine Masculine and Shadow Masculine energies, as well as Divine Feminine and Shadow Feminine expressions – and more.

You embody Separation Consciousness, Earth Consciousness, Heart Consciousness, Awakening Consciousness, and Cosmic Consciousness simultaneously. You can make choices on the Elevator of the Ego-Mind or jump on to the Spiral to see how everything is supporting your soul growth. You may toss and turn at times between what you want to really do, and what you feel you should do, and all of this is okay to feel because you are a beautiful open container of Universal wisdom, intelligence, and sensations. All of these energies demonstrate how full you are in potential and possibility.

As you raise your consciousness about yourself in this lifetime, you open up to more of your soul's story. You listen to where you are feeling Separation Consciousness and dive into those parts of yourself with courage and consciousness. There is an inner knowingness that what you are feeling is a message to explore more of your lifetimes, to dive into more of your unconscious patterns and belief systems. You start to ask more compelling, investigative questions: *Why did I create this for my soul's growth? What am I learning perfectly because of this experience? How am I connected to God right now even if I do not feel that way?*

Every soul experience will bring you to higher levels of consciousness and a greater connection to God. Until you arrive at that place, keep going. Keep exploring and digging. Keep discovering what makes your spark of the bonfire so Divinely perfect and uniquely needed at this time on the planet. You are an essential ingredient to the Universal whole, and it is through your energetic expression of Self that you contribute to Oneness.

In this lifetime, millions of us volunteered to awaken ourselves by activating higher levels of consciousness on the planet than ever before. As we each do that within ourselves, we effect the collective unity expression and alter the course of humanity's experiences and direction. We are doing this together now. Understanding your soul's bigger story opens doorways for others to do the same and creates gateways of higher knowledge for All.

Claim the vastness of your soul for the benefit of All. Integrate your unique God energy into every aspect of your soul by reminding yourself that you are always connected, valued, loved and cherished. You will be taken away from this perspective at times. You will forget and become locked into your ego at times because that is part of the ride. The human journey is an ongoing dance between separation and connection; ego and Spirit; individuation and unity. We are journeying on a ride of duality and opposition that pushes us to see how far we can go in either direction with our power and free will.

You are all of these expressions temporarily and yet none of them permanently.

And so the soul journey continues.

THE AWAKENING CONSCIOUSNESS SERIES

The Opening:
The Art of Trapeze

I CAN STILL RECALL one of the most memorable meditations I had after returning from Paris. I was in a white bubble of space, a void of crisp, clear nothingness except my physical self, and the air was exceptionally clean. Stillness and calm filled every direction. I could look out into the distance and see the group of people I just left contained in a separate white bubble. From my vantage point, they were covered by a cloudy film that kept them in their space together; united and connected within the same paradigm of energies. One person was turned away from the group looking for me, not sure where to turn, but searching and wondering. A door was right there for them to walk through, and yet they didn't see it, or couldn't see it, or didn't want to walk in that direction. I turned away from their bubble knowing I could not go back, and that they were comfortable where they were in this space. All Was Well.

As the meditation proceeded, I focused on the vastness of

potentials emerging in other directions all around me. I heard that I was meant to be in this alone space for now as it was healing, centering, and clearing me for what was to come. There was no timeline nor expectations. It was simply the place of beingness. It was simply about experiencing a feeling of nothingness that was supremely safe, guarded, and perfect timed.

When I remained in that state, I felt bliss and a knowingness that I was right on track for everything I intended to learn in this lifetime. In fact, I had even made soul-advancing decisions that were being celebrated in the higher realms because I had unknowingly changed the entire trajectory of my life. A significant timeline change had occurred when I returned from Paris.

Timeline Changes

Think of a train chugging along on a track. At some point, it will eventually slow down and pull into a train station and make a complete stop. Everything will shut down and be put on pause as you decide to get off this train and wait for another one; or stay on this train and keep going down the same track. The train station it pulls into brings you to some type of choice point.

Choice points occur on an intentional soul level to ensure you are actively using your free will for your highest and best good. While empowering and inspiring, choice points can also bring up our deepest fears, doubts, pain, and Shadow energies. That train station is not always a pretty place to hang out, which is why many people jump back onto the same train or remain on a familiar track for a long time. Train stations require us to change something within ourselves first before we can catch the next incoming ride. If we don't do the inner work at each choice point, we eventually - and often unconsciously - find ourselves on a very similar train going down the same track because the energy has not significantly shifted. But when we do complete the inner work, we make new choices that connect us with a new timeline, or in this example, we connect with a new train track.

Timeline changes occur when your inner energy dramatically shifts and you no longer want or need what you previously desired. I knew a significant timeline change had occurred in my life when I no longer felt a desire to move back to Paris.

In fact, something I did not write about in *The Art of Trapeze* is that I did attempt to go back to Europe. I became certified to teach English as a second language and had planned on moving back to the continent to teach English while I started to build my life abroad again. But on the last day of my certification program when we were preparing for our graduation ceremony, my energy sunk hard and fast around moving to Europe again. It felt off and different this time; I wasn't excited or motivated like I had been only a few years prior. I felt heavy around everything I had to do to move across the Atlantic again, including flying my cats back *again* and having to look for a place to live *again* and everything that goes with putting roots into a brand new place. I recall sitting in the classroom as this inner knowingness came through so clearly: *this dream is complete for me.* I trusted that message and let Paris be perfect as it was.

And then it was time to focus on the next still-to-be-defined life dream.

These types of big life vision shifts are confirmation of a timeline change because you have changed so much internally that there is no longer a connection to who you were previously and what you previously wanted. On a smaller scale, you can look at every day on the calendar as a timeline change. Every night we retire by pulling into a train station, and every morning we begin again, either on the same track or a new one.

In a quantum sense, every moment is a change of time. In fact, time does not even exist in quantum terms, so we could throw all of this out the window! Yet our human experiences are grounded in time, space, and physicality because this is one of our soul lessons. We are bringing our timeless energy into the experience of time to remember what it means to be limitless within limits. We are remembering what it means to play this crazy game of energy dynamics within the boundaries of physicality and form. We are bringing our soul presence into our everyday life so we can effectively and powerfully grow and experience the bliss of existence.

All of this occurs because you have everything you need now. This moment in time is where we have access to our whole soul story like never before in humanity's existence

Everything You Need Is Here Now

Your current life holds many clues around what you are here to heal. These hints and nudges show up through repetitive lessons, emotions, patterns, and life themes. They also arise through various locations on the map that hold soul experiences for you. When you travel to different places that call to you, it is most likely because you hold a soul memory of another lifetime at that location.

As we raise our consciousness, we begin to see how all parts of our life are related to the vastness of our energy fields. The Universe is way too intelligent to only exist in a state of randomness. And since you are an integral part of Universal intelligence, then you, too, are not moving through life in a blur of randomness. You are an intentional force of energy.

For example, here is an energy that you may relate to. One of my soul contracts in this lifetime is ending relationship energies that were previously unfinished in other lifetimes. I have met many partners from other incarnations where we were meant to work things out this time around. These relationships were not supposed to be permanent or long-lasting; rather, they were about tying up loose ends, completing unfinished energies, becoming conscious of unresolved emotions, and returning to a place of peace and gratitude for what was learned. Of course, it would have been nice to know that at the time or even beforehand! But oh no, we are rarely privy to what we are learning while we are in lesson and we must move through it with authenticity and trust. It was only in hindsight and through spiritual guidance that I came to understand what was going on. Once I knew the theme, it set me free on many levels and evaporated my confusion around these ongoing dynamics.

The same can be said for any other area of life that is important to you. You carry energies from other incarnations that are providing you with deeper consciousness about the lessons and healing.

Once you connect with the understanding that everything you need to know about yourself as a soul is available to you now, you truly step into this incarnation as being your most powerful lifetime.

Your Most Powerful Lifetime

When you regularly see yourself as a huge energy having a temporary human experience, it literally changes your life perception. You open up to the joys of physical existence, the wonders of relationship dynamics, the beautiful messages of your emotional world, and the fun of expressing your creativity, ideas, wisdom, and Self. You see how you are not here for long, so why not make the most of everything and truly enjoy the present moment of now.

But then we have chores to do, bills to pay, misunderstandings to sort out, irksome co-workers to navigate, and unending distractions to daily life. We have responsibilities and duties that take us away from the present moment. We are required to pay attention, show up, suit up, follow through, and get things done; no one can just sit around meditating all day!

Yet despite the list of Real World obligations that we must attend to, we have the ability to bring greater consciousness into the present experiences and infuse them with a loving detachment. We can tap into the power of ourselves moving through another boring Wednesday simply by observing ourselves in a loving way. The big problems and major issues of life can be made smaller when we see the temporariness of everything, including of ourselves.

"Just look at me existing in this human body for a little while as I continue to have energy experiences in time and space! What a ride!"

From this understanding, we also have the capacity to own this lifetime as our most powerful one ever because we have access to higher levels of consciousness than ever before.

Your Unconscious Self and Conscious Self Both Contribute to Oneness

Our unconscious Self experiences something - a relationship, an emotion, a life-changing event - to support the development of our conscious Self. Our conscious Self then has wisdom to offer back to our unconscious Self that can be further used in other areas of life. These two aspects of ourselves work together to support their mutual growth and development when we are tuned in to the dynamic interplay of energies within us.

One common area of life where we can experience the greatest rise in consciousness is through our emotions. In our modern Western culture, we tend to value happiness more than sadness. We want to be laughing more than we want to experience crying, and we tend to push ourselves to that side of the spectrum for various intentions. I do not believe this is healthy, however, since ultimately it takes us away from our authenticity and fullness. Of course we want happy, light, joyful days to define most of our lives, but we must also have the tools to embrace other emotions authentically, too. We are dynamic, multi-layered beings with the capacity to feel and experience everything; why limit ourselves or our truth because crying is ugly or inconvenient at times?

From an energetic sense, there is no more value placed on happiness than on sadness or grieving. All are energy experiences that help you know yourself more and understand your truth in the moment. As I mentioned in *The Art of Trapeze*, e-motion is simply "energy in motion" that is moving through you to be acknowledged, cleared, and released. We feel these emotions in ourselves, of course, but that does not mean we need to embrace them as part of our self-identity. You can have an experience and allow it to move through you without claiming it as a permanent part of yourself.

This is especially true with grief, which is one of the most misunderstood, and yet normal, aspects of the human journey. Grief is normal because it connects with loss, and loss is a guarantee throughout our lives since nothing lasts forever. Grieving is when we release our expectations, feelings, attachments, and experiences to a person or experience. We are grieving the end of a timeline and all of its potentials, actualities, and realities. On a grand scale, we may know this as grieving the end of a dream we have held for ourselves, or the end of a phase of life. We are letting go of what had value to us, and allowing that emptiness can be tough. It is certainly not easy, but that doesn't mean it is negative or bad. It is simply an honest acknowledgement of your truth in that moment.

Consciously experiencing the wide spectrum of emotions inside of us is a beautiful gift of humanness. Taken together, all of these energies support Oneness. As you rise in consciousness, you have more wisdom and higher energy to offer back to the globe. As you share your unconscious Self, you connect with others moving through similar experiences, which also contributes to Oneness and provides gateways to higher understanding. All parts of you contribute to Oneness, so why shut down or deny anything that is truly a gift?

The Eternal Truths

How do you connect with Spirit regularly? Do you meditate, listen, write, or perhaps all of these options and more? Are you making time for this form of receiving in your life?

One of the best gifts I received after returning from Paris was feeling clearer in my energy field with a stronger ability to listen to guidance. As unconscious energies within me were swept away, I felt a new opening to even more answers than ever before. And it was because of this soul growth that I was able to finally hear the Eternal Truths from God energy that brought much comfort, wisdom, and understanding.

"You are ready for this knowledge simply because you requested it. The Eternal Truths are simple, dear one:

"You are always Divinely loved, but others may challenge this truth by attempting to make you feel worthless, powerless, invaluable, unlovable and dismissive of your voice. Every experience of feeling unaccepted or unloved is part of your soul's growth and is the gift of a soul contract. What will you choose for yourself? What voice will you hear the loudest? What serves your highest and best good? And is lack of Love ever true?

"You are always abundant beyond measure, but you will experience lack to allow you the opportunity to connect to the eternal abundance of the Universe again. How can there be any lack in an abundant environment? You can choose abundant thoughts and connect to Universal abundance at any time, and you will be given numerous opportunities to connect to unlimited channels of money, creativity, health, joy, and more. Abundance is natural, but you choose how you want to experience it with your energetic intentions.

"You are always safe, but you will experience deep and irrational fears to allow you the opportunity to create a stronger foundation of safety within yourself. Others will provide you with experiences of betrayal, suspicion, deceit, victimhood, and theft so you will have opportunities to consciously build stronger trust within yourself and to walk in greater faith, if you choose. Or you can connect to victim consciousness and see yourself as less than powerful if you want to have that version of the experience.

"*You are always powerful, but you will buy into the belief that you must own, do, or be certain things to access this power. You will be offered many opportunities to be your true, powerful energy, and it will not be what you expect. Your authentic power doesn't depend on anyone else at all, but you will forget this until you are consciously ready to remember. You will wonder about your career path, creative gifts, intuitive powers, life purpose, and "what to do next" because you will think these are the answers you seek, but only until you reach higher levels of consciousness and all of those questions will shift.*"

"*One of the most joyful aspects of these truths is that they are true for everyone who is ready to connect with them.*"

I remembered my dream-self saying, "Wait, crap, I have to write all of this down!" *Pen, pen, pen.* "Where can I keep this for quick access? I need this information tattooed onto my human body so I don't forget!"

"*Dear heart, forgetting all of this is part of the experience. It is required to forget as another way to demonstrate your Soul's power to choose. You will be given many opportunities to remember all of these truths and connect to your beautiful Soul power again. You are more supported and Loved than you could ever imagine. Or why else would you choose this human adventure?*"

The Deepening:
The Modern Heroine's Journey of Consciousness

You are composed of endless stories. Every lifetime is encoded with the potential to reach new levels of consciousness by embarking on a journey that returns you to your soul's wisdom. Book Two in The Awakening Consciousness Series, *The Modern Heroine's Journey of Consciousness,* reveals a path of spiritual growth and assists with navigating the Call of your Soul. This guidebook was written to help understand the potential road ahead, what typically shows up, and the three main stages of energies you experience as you know yourself better.

For all the mystical talk and mysterious unknowns of the future, spiritual growth is not really an unknown path. In fact, it is very well known and has been studied and researched extensively due to the common elements that most people experience. *The Modern Heroine's Journey of Consciousness* is intended to support your conscious soul growth by equipping you with guidance, perspective, and Universal wisdom.

The Full Consciousness Experience

You are composed of all energies, yet you choose certain ones to work with in every lifetime. This helps your soul focus and grow in intentional ways, while also honoring your free will and choices in every incarnation.

There are currently five dominant types of consciousness present today, co-existing, spreading, retracting. I am specifically identifying these as types of consciousness and not levels because levels implies hierarchy or dominance. Using the word type is highly intentional as a way to move beyond the polarities of good and bad; right and wrong; better and worse.

Each type of consciousness offers a different perspective, understanding, and opportunities for growth. Each type has value in providing information and describing experiences. Each type also allows us to choose what perspective is best for our individual, and collective, growth. The five types of consciousness are:

- **Separation Consciousness:** Everything Happens To Me
- **Earth Consciousness:** What You See Is What You Get
- **Heart Consciousness:** I Am You And You Are Me
- **Awakening Consciousness:** I AM Powerful In All Ways
- **Cosmic Consciousness:** I AM An Eternal Being In An Eternal Universe

As you ascend to higher levels of personal understanding, you see more of the light in every person, experience, and life phase. You see how you have the power to choose your level of consciousness at any time and within any scenario. Your power of choice is always with you, and will constantly open you up to your soul's perspective. Yet this takes ongoing practice with our conscious minds. We must actively bring the energy of conscious awareness to all aspects of our lives and this is how we continually ascend.

We spiral up by owning the full spectrum of energies within you is what makes you strong. We must go into the deeper levels of ourselves to re-emerge with true happiness.

There are many unknown delights, new developments, and unexpected ways the Modern Heroine's journey of consciousness unfolds. It happens on the best timeline for each person and it is uniquely their own soul energy experience based on what they are ready to learn and understand. Each journey occurs according to a person's preferred pace, speed, comfort level, and commitment. However, there are eight defining characteristics of the Modern Heroine's spiritual growth journey:

- **It's solo.** She does it by herself, for herself.
- **It's unknown.** She moves outside of a comfort zone.
- **It tests limits**. She is pushed by multiple external circumstances.
- **It's emotional.** She experiences the full spectrum of her inner world.
- **It's transformational.** She experiences a death, rebirth, and is forever changed.
- **It's risky.** She is required to leap somehow - emotionally, financially, psychologically, mentally, spiritually.
- **It's comprehensive.** She moves through most of the stages of the journey, and experiences the Opening, the Deepening, and the Renewal.
- **It's a permanent and significant change in self-identity.** She becomes more of herself than ever before.

These requirements are ultimately about uniting YOU in physical form with YOU in soul form. Each one asks you to trust more, trust deeper, go further, and step into the Divine knowingness that You as a single entity are, in fact, an unlimited entity of everything. You have everything you need, but have you been pushed or nudged to really own all of yourself? To fully claim all of your power and emotions and heart and dreams? To truly know what it's like to walk with your soul's light in every step?

As spiritual seekers, we can each talk the talk any time we want and spout the "right" language and well-rehearsed quotes. We can each proclaim a version of the truth and say we know what is best, what is right, what is the highest spiritual understanding of an experience. But it's only when you "walk the walk" and get real with yourself by having your own authentic experience that you step into your full light. Only you can do that; only you can have that journey within your own energy field. And it's by Divine nudge that you are ready to begin that journey into full consciousness.

The New Female: Merging Divine Feminine and Divine Masculine Energies Within

She knows when to assert herself and be fierce. And when to go within for softness and nurturing. She knows when it's time to open up to the world and invoke the joys of sisterhood. And when she must voyage ahead on her own with only her Soul's compass guiding the way.

She senses when she is meant to create in her own space. And when it is time to assert herself externally and get things done in the world.

She feels her inner world authentically. And knows when she must rise above and take necessary actions to create her biggest dreams in the Real World.

She is the NEW female who is merging both her Divine Feminine and Divine Masculine energies within to be her own

Modern Heroine.

She is rising in her own consciousness and rising in her power and rising in her voice and rising her energy in the world for the betterment of humanity. And it is time for her to shine brighter with these intentions.

Brave. Tender. Independent. Contributing. Creative. Loving. Leading. Strong. Inspired. Focused.

We are living in the energy of merging gender archetypes into a modern expression of Self that supports and enhances our modern, complex lives. Yet we are each responsible for doing this work internally with grace and confidence.

Merging WITHIN. Emerging OUT.

The NEW Female is her own Modern Heroine and embraces both her Feminine and Masculine energies as vital components to the FULLNESS of who she is.

But where do these energies originate from and how can you transmute any lower expressions back to Love? This is the Renewal stage that is shared in *The Unlimited Sparks of a Bonfire*.

The Renewal:
The Unlimited Sparks of a Bonfire

Present Lifetime

You hold multiple energies from past lives that are very much present right now. They are layers and imprints that create energies of experiences. We know these as stories. Our stories; the stories of our lives.

Within each of the stories in this book, every individual experiences energies that push them further into their soul growth. They are on a journey of consciousness

Energy Waves

When you experience a big wave of intense energy in your life, such as deep grief or unexplained anger or a significant trigger, it is highly likely that you are picking up on that energy wave from your Self in other lifetimes that are happening simultaneously. As a timeless being, you are always connected to all aspects of your Soul's energy in other timelines. Energy waves come in to move something through you with the effects benefiting those other dimensions of times.

For example, when I returned from Paris and was navigating deep grief, the intensity of those emotions were not solely about that one experience. I was processing, feeling, and ultimately releasing emotional imprints from other lifetimes. I was unconsciously picking up on what other versions of myself were going through in other incarnations, and yet the present version of Me had the capabilities and willingness to go deeper into the raw feelings more so than other versions of Me could handle in their respective experiences. Molly in this timeline was co-creating and working with other versions of Molly in other lifetimes (whatever roles those might be) and shifting the energy across all dimensions. That is one of the reasons why this lifetime is so amazing! We are more consciously connected to our power than ever before, and we can do this quantum work. We can access all parts of ourselves with these energy waves that come in.

Clearing potential is highly present with all energy waves. When you fully and consciously go into an energy with the intention of owning it all, you begin to shift the core of the energy at the lowest possible level. It is a bit like diving down to the deepest part of the ocean, seeing what is at the foundation, and then rearranging - or sand blasting, or obliterating - everything that you consciously want to change. But it is only by diving down and seeing it that you can do that; that work cannot be done from the surface level or half-ass attempt.

After I had that brutally honest experience of grief, those core emotions were finished and healed within my energy field. I look back on that time period in my life, and I can lovingly observe myself in that trying space, but I do not relate to that emotional experience anymore. A deep clearing occurred at my core level that was a huge release point of completing those emotions across all lifetimes, all timelines, and all dimensions. The energy wave came through and gifted me with the opportunity to release. Done. Gone. Clear the slates.

You will know this shift has occurred in you because you will feel a neutrality.

The Neutral Point

Everything in the Universe begins from the zero, or non-zero, point of nothingness. Energy is neutral, and in fact it is non-recognizable, until a value is assigned to it. This value can be deciphered through physics, or form, or judgment, or a creation process, or any number of variable sources. Once the energy is determined to "be" something, it continues "being" whatever it is until something else defines it once again. In our human experiences, this is often where the mind comes in to think, label, ponder, describe, or judge it, moving the energy from a neutral point into "something else."

The Universe does not do the same. The Universal Mind is a creator of all potentials and probabilities that can exist in the galaxy, and beyond galaxies. Within this framework, everything is neutral and has value simply for existing. Everything is connected and contributes to the creation and/or experience of everything else. The Universal web of energy, if you will.

This same understanding applies to our human experiences, and yet we forget this because we are shrouded in belief systems, judgments, ideologies, philosophies, and unconsciousness. We have created an experience of free will where all choices are possible and probable, yet they come with attachments of some sort; often judgment is the biggest one.

But when we remove belief systems, judgments, ideologies, philosophies, and unconsciousness, we return to the purity of the neutral point. The place where everything exists as an experience of energy, and therefore it is valuable. It is worthy of simply being an experience.

Now, how easy is it for us to apply this same understanding to our emotions? Oftentimes it is not easy at all. We are conditioned and taught to value happiness more than sadness; to value laughter more than tears; to value the good more than the bad; to value what is "higher" more than what is a "lower" experience. But the Universe does not hold those same judgments, and instead sees the value of all energies. Your soul sees the value of all of your expressions.

When you clear deep energies at a core level, you return to this neutral point. You see how you were having an experience of energy that taught you something valuable. You can then choose to love yourself simply for having that experience of energy. You can remove the judgments or limiting interpretations that your current human self may create, and instead tell yourself that you, as an infinite being, had yet another ride on this crazy-train called life.

Think of every energy experience as a different ride at an amusement park. Some rides we want to go on multiple times and perhaps never get off of, whereas other rides we're all set with one spin on that crazy-maker. But all rides must eventually come to an end, and we will surely have those that we prefer over others. The only energy that will continue on is the experience of ongoing energy. This amusement park does not close, so what will you find yourself experiencing next?

The neutral point is also where you will have the sensation of zero emotional attachment. You will feel a void and view only with the eyes of an observer. Some people are like this innately (perhaps you know a few individuals who seem emotionless), and they are teaching us to look with detachment at all things. There are many gifts in this understanding since there are fewer emotional ties or inner complications to work through. Embodying the neutral point in one's life is a soul choice that may be balancing out other lifetimes where emotional energy was excessive, poorly used, or fully learned and mastered.

And yet life includes the beauty of emotions! Our feeling nature is one of our greatest assets and connects us to each other in limitless ways. Compassion, empathy, forgiveness, and love are each amazing gifts to share and receive. Being in touch with our emotional world allows us to experience the full spectrum of life, and marvel in every color of the rainbow. So there is much to be said for not existing at the neutral point on a regular basis.

To put it into perspective, the neutral point will be most valuable after the experience of a deep emotional trigger. You will value the detached viewpoint after healing an aspect of yourself that previously caused hurt, fear, or pain.

Think of the neutral point as an end goal for anything that deeply hurts, pains, angers, or triggers you. Working honestly with the emotion will heal you. Acknowledging the messages of the emotion will heal you. Owning everything you feel will heal you. Imagine yourself speaking to this emotion as if it is part of your inner child. Listen, comfort, and care for this aspect of yourself.

Most neutral points occur after you experience a timeline change. Often, distance and time are required to truly be detached and complete with something. Although, it is also possible to feel the change instantaneously, too! It simply depends on how deeply the energy is embedded within you. Take a moment and think back to a key defining moment of your life that was challenging, painful, or life-changing. If you have consciously worked with the deeper emotions around that experience, chances are you can view it from the neutral point. It no longer triggers you or causes you that same emotional experience. It is far away, or complete, or seems like another lifetime ago.

The neutral point is a beautiful gift you have given yourself because it has set you free from that emotional energy and has allowed you to grow forward.

And then the journey continues. A new field of energetic possibilities and potentials will present itself to you. Something else will call to your soul.

ABOUT THE AUTHOR

MOLLY McCORD, M.A. IS A bestselling author of eight books, radio show host, and modern consciousness teacher.

Her debut memoir, *The Art of Trapeze: One Woman's Journey of Soaring, Surrendering, and Awakening*, hit #1 in 2 Amazon categories within 3 days. *The Art of Trapeze* is the first book in her Awakening Consciousness Series, followed by *The Modern Heroine's Journey of Consciousness*, in which she integrates Joseph Campbell's hero's journey with spiritual growth. Molly contributed to the bestselling *The Thought That Changed My Life Forever* where she was published alongside such luminaries as Dr. Michael Bernard Beckwith, Dr. Joe Dispenza, and Dr. Bernie Siegel.

Often referred to as a Consciousness Catalyst, Molly's popular website, www.ConsciousCoolChic.com was nominated by Intent.com for Best Spirituality Website in 2011. She hosts a popular weekly radio show attracted over 70,000 downloads in the first year.

Molly has a B.A. in Political Science and Women's Studies, and a Master's degree in International Relations and Diplomacy as a formal channel for understanding Global Consciousness with a Jungian perspective. She is currently an Ambassador for Women for Women International, a non-profit organization which provides education and business training for marginalized women in developing countries.

Molly lives in Seattle, WA with her husband and child.

A CONVERSATION
WITH THE AUTHOR

Molly, how did the stories in this book, *The Unlimited Sparks of a Bonfire*, come to you? Did you have them all outlined at the beginning?

Through the years, I've had many connections with my own past lives, and some of those journeys served as the initial inspirations for these stories. I had no outline nor idea about where the stories would go, and it was wonderful to be open to whatever information flowed through.

As I started writing, the characters and events came to me, like visitors knocking on the front door. Then they each sat down at the kitchen table to tell me their story. I only knew the location of a story at the beginning, then the main character and their name would be introduced, and then their personality, life, and other characters would become clear. I consider every story to be very real, actually, and not a work of fiction at all. To me, everything in these adventures happened!

One pronounced theme in many of the stories is the ongoing use of nature. What does nature mean to you in this book?

It is fascinating how this theme emerged organically because again, it wasn't planned in any way, yet every story was so visceral because of the natural world. I could feel the cold mud on the old man's feet as he sat under the geisha house. The Nile River felt like it was *right there* as I was typing, as if I could hear the water ripples and the sounds of boats passing.

I consider nature one of the central characters because of the universality of it in our lives. It is a common, uniting element for everyone, on some level, and it adds grounding to every story. Plus, nature is such a brilliant teacher that it adds another layer of wisdom to what a story or character is conveying. It was enjoyable to see how the natural world came to the forefront in each tale, and I hope readers felt that, too.

The role of nature is also an interesting layer when linked to _The Awakening_ by Kate Chopin, which you reference at the end of _The Art of Trapeze_. Throughout _Unlimited Sparks_, it seems that some characters have an experience of cleansing and renewal through or connected to a river. Was that an intentional storytelling component?

Not at all. In fact, it wasn't until after writing the story of Marie and Claude in France, and how she emerged from the river, that the correlation clicked for me between her awakening story and Kate Chopin's _The Awakening_. Then I saw how prominent the river was as a cleansing agent across many of the stories. That was an organic development and not something I planned.

I'd consider those unexpected connections to be one of the joys of being a writer; being on the receiving end of whatever the story needs to express in order to come alive and be effective. Every story was a wonderful teacher, and I would sit with each one afterwards to understand it more because the information didn't come from "me" or my brain; it came through from the Universe and it was awesome to be that open channel.

The Modern Heroine's Journey of Consciousness really struck a chord with women about their spiritual journey and growth process. Did that surprise you in any way?

Yes and no, since there is certainly no way to know how a book will connect with people. Being on a spiritual growth path has many phases, and it can be quite lonely at times. You can have deep questions about it, and wonder if you're the only one on the planet feeling these things, and you may not have people in your immediate environment who "get it" because they are not following the call of their soul.

My intention with *Modern Heroine* was to help unite women in a way that honors her individuality and unique Self, but acknowledges the universality of being a modern woman, too. There are times in life when it is vital that we are on our own and understand our multiple layers better, but it helps to know you can "look up" and see others out there that you can wave to, so to speak, as you continue down your path.

And on a personal note, to be perfectly honest, the wonderful feedback from *Modern Heroine* has been affirming for my own path, too, because I have felt very alone at times, and there is nothing like connecting with other women through Right Sisterhood to reestablish a sense of community and connection.

Why did you decide to write your messages as a trilogy instead of compiling them into a single book?

It came down to a lot information that would have been overwhelming in one book, which I actually attempted to do at first. I stalled out while writing the first version of *The Art of Trapeze* because I had much more that I wanted to express in the remaining 20% of the book. I was stuck for months, until I realized it was supposed to be a series – yay for those breakthroughs!

Plus, I think it is engaging and enjoyable for a reader to be with the individual messages of each book; to pace themselves and not feel rushed; and to have their own adventure and actively consider what resonates for them. At least, I hope that is their experience.

The Awakening Consciousness Series is quite an unconventional series because every book is very different from the other two. Could you share with us a bit more about that and your vision for the series?

Yes, all of the variances between these three books are certainly one of the series' most peculiar qualities. One is a memoir, one is a spiritual guide, and one could be classified as fiction. Plus, a different narrative is used between all three books as they switch between first person and third person, and stylistically, each one is unique.

One uniting element in the series, then, would be found in the three-stage journey that unfolds between all three books: The Opening, The Deepening, and The Renewal. These phases are connected with Joseph Campbell's three stages in "the hero's journey" as a way to describe a soul's journey in human form. We have The Opening, which is the present lifetime and how life is being experienced today (*The Art of Trapeze*); then we venture deeper into ourselves, our unconscious energies, and a bigger connection to the journey in The Deepening (*Modern Heroine*); and as we emerge with new wisdom, we renew ourselves with fresh revelations based on a fuller understanding of a soul's experiences (*Unlimited Sparks*).

So with this perspective, my vision was to incorporate multiple storytelling techniques to make the information engaging, personal, adventurous, intellectual, and even unexpected for the reader. I liked being able to innovate and keep it fresh, which is also a timely theme in the world of publishing today.

So what is next for you? Any more books in the works?

I feel like I'm just getting started, to tell you the truth. I've written ten books so far, and I actually have at least four more books in progress, but I'm not sure about their release dates yet as I just became a mom for the first time. This little baby blessing inspires me beyond comprehension at times and I feel fresh creativity pouring in regularly, so I'm just going with the flow and trusting the timing.

One thing I do know is that writing *The Unlimited Sparks of a Bonfire* has opened me up to the joys of writing fiction, which I now prefer. Since the stories and characters just came through me, I feel there is more to tell for these characters. For example, I would love to write a book about Pakhet, or Neith's, next adventures as she sails up the Nile. I intentionally left the stories open to pursue additional possibilities for all of those characters, so we'll see what unfolds. I love writing, and even though I came to it in my thirties, I know it will always be a part of how I inspire and empower people to know themselves better.

I have recently created a variety of online mastery courses to help people on their journey of self-mastery. They can all be found on **www.SpiritualityUniversity.com**.

And I also support other authors and spiritual experts in their business development through mentoring and online classes, too, because it is the perfect time for more people to get out there and share their gifts with the world. Contributing to other people's success is one of the best parts of right now because I really believe we need each other's messages and soul wisdom in order to the make the world a better place. We all rise together!

OTHER BOOKS BY MOLLY McCORD

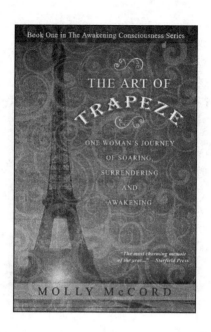

The Art of Trapeze:
One Woman's Journey of Soaring,
Surrendering, and Awakening

Book One
in The Awakening Consciousness Series

Discover Molly's bestselling spiritual memoir that hit #1 in 2
Amazon categories in 3 days!

"*The Art of Trapeze* had me swinging through a swirl of
spirit and sisterhood. An intensely relatable read- down to
earth, charming, humorous, poignant, and infinitely wise - for
those of us on the path of self-discovery and even those who

just want a good story - you will love this book!"
~ Sass Jordan, Juno Award-winning Artist, Canadian Idol Judge, Broadway actress

"An inspiring memoir about a brave go-getter who makes things happen! Molly guides us readers into the power of reemergence as the shining jewels we really are."
~ Rosemary Sneeringer, Literary Editor, Author, TheBookNurturer.com

"Beautifully written, charmingly funny - even hilarious - and remarkably open, honest, and down-to-earth, Ms. McCord has gifted us with a pure example of how life can be such a beautiful, grand adventure..." ~ Starfield Press

On a random Thursday morning, with nothing to lose and only a dream to gain, Molly McCord decides to move to Paris, France to follow the courageous call of her heart. She arrives in a city she has never visited before and where she knows no one, yet she trusts her ability to figure it out because her adventurous life has prepared her for this biggest of leaps. She carries the wisdom of Solitude, Strength, Style, Flexibility, Heart, Endurance, and Grace in her non-matching luggage collection.

Molly's soul-riveting experiences unfold in surprising ways as she discovers the joys and realities of life as a foreigner in France, falls in love with a sexy Turkish man, moves her cats across the Atlantic, enjoys the rare opportunity of working for a U.S. Ambassador, and creates the life of her dreams in less than two years.

Yet when unexpected developments require her to surrender once again, a higher consciousness catches her with a deeper spiritual awakening.

The Art of Trapeze soars with emotional honesty, delightful humor, unexpected wisdom, and inspiring spiritual perspectives around living life to the fullest when nothing is guaranteed except gravity.

The Modern Heroine's Journey of Consciousness

Book Two
in The Awakening Consciousness Series

The book that turned into a viral hit with
over 50,000 shares on Facebook!

The second book in The Awakening Consciousness Series is a must-have guide for any artist, entrepreneur, writer, teacher, or contemporary seeker who is curious about their spiritual journey.

Referencing Joseph Campbell's highly influential "The Hero's Journey," Molly brings groundbreaking wisdom to a modern woman's experiences of spiritual growth.

The Modern Heroine's Journey of Consciousness offers an original exploration through 11 phases of spiritual growth, from answering the Call of her Soul and Opening Up To A

Greater Power, to Surrender, Awakening to Deeper Soul Power, and Mastery of Her Consciousness.

Inspiring, original spiritual concepts include:

- Differences between spirituality and religion
- The five types of consciousness on the planet now
- The Elevator and the Spiral
- Soul Mates, Soul Contracts, Soul Agreements, Soul Groups, Karmic Relationships
- Past life connections to geographic locations
- Surrender and supreme separation from God
- Being conscious in an Unconscious World

And more "a-ha" connections and breakthroughs for conscious living.

The Modern Heroine's Journey of Consciousness brilliantly explains the gifts at every phase of spiritual growth and reveals how the inner journey is an awakening to more of herself.

Your Awakening Self
Connect Deeply With Your True Evolving Soul

MOLLY McCORD

Your Awakening Self:
Connect Deeply With Your True Evolving Soul

Are you feeling new energetic levels in your life? Have you recognized how much you have evolved and grown through this amazing period we are living in? Do you feel a fresh part of yourself emerging and ready to come through?

The spiritual evolution and consciousness expansion will continue on our planet, and it is also a time to celebrate our Selves, our lives, our essences, and our journey as each component has culminated in the experience of NOW.

In "Your Awakening Self: Connect Deeply With Your True Evolving Soul", 26 spiritual topics will open you up further to the innate wisdom of your soul gifts that you are ready to receive now.

As your awakening journey unfolds, new parts of your Self come forth to greet you and this inspiring guide reminds you to stay in your power, integrity, and highest intentions as you greet each day.

Conscious
Messages

Spiritual Wisdom
and Inspirations
for Awakening
Molly McCord

Conscious Messages:
Spiritual Wisdom and Inspirations
for Awakening

A practical, uplifting collection of high-vibrational messages to elevate your energy!

From affirming that Where You Are Is Where You Need to Be and owning your personal truth, to cosmic perspectives on emotional energy, being in alignment with your intentions, and expanding beyond limiting belief systems, these brand new 21 channeled messages provide you with simple, direct perspectives about stepping more fully into your Soul's light.

Inspiring messages include Personal Alignment, Living From Your Heart Space, Making Conscious Changes, Self-Acceptance and Self-Love, and Elevating the Energies of a Catastrophe with a Soul Perspective.

"Conscious Messages" will appeal to anyone who enjoys similar insights from Abraham-Hicks, Sanaya Roman, Duane Packer, Lee Carroll, Steve Rother, and other global leaders in the world of channeling energies for awakening consciousness.

One to keep on your nightstand for joy, clarity, and empowerment!

Conscious Thoughts:
Powerful Affirmations to Connect With Your Soul's Language

This evolutionary guide is a rare combination of modern situations, past life connections, and powerful affirmations that speak to your Soul with high vibrational energy!

Affirmations are conscious thoughts that can be amazingly effective once the root energy is identified. Discover how to heal unconscious patterns, move beyond repetitive lessons, and change your understanding around what is holding you back in life.

Plus, get to the heart of how affirmations work, why they support your spiritual growth, how to use them powerfully, what affirmations do NOT do, and six key tenets for maximum results.

The five short stories with past life connections and healing affirmations include:

- Reclaiming Your Personal Power
- Dealing With Shadow Feminine Energies
- Adult Bullying
- Your Body As Your Ally
- Roadblocks to Creative Expression and A Loving Partnership

Enjoy over 40 original affirmations for Forgiveness, Love, Career, Health, Trust, Creativity, Prosperity, Living Your Best Life, and more!

Caché Paris:
A Guidebook to Discover New Places, Hidden Spaces, and a Favorite Oasis

"Best of the Independent Guides"~ Vine Voice

The secret (and fast) entrance to the Louvre. The fascinating Parisian walk that guides you through centuries of French history in a single afternoon. Strategic advice for beating the crowds at Chateau de Versailles (and what days not to visit!). Three doable, worthwhile day trips from Paris. The best parks and little-known delightful neighborhoods to get lost in as you explore one of the world's favorite cities. And shhhh....probably many new places, hidden spaces, and a favorite oasis that even Rick Steves doesn't know about yet.

Plus, *Caché Paris* reveals more intriguing secrets, including:

• How did exotic animals end up in the middle of Paris?

• Why is the Louvre composed of nine different architectural styles?

• Where can you experience an unexpected (and never busy) bird's eye view of the city?

• Which Parisian park has a grotto, waterfall, and suspension bridge?

• What should you do if you experience a metro strike?

• What select nights of the year are filled with city-wide music, celebration, and dancing in the streets?

With numerous links, resources, and insider's knowledge-based Haute Tips, *Caché Paris* also features French menu cards for translating popular ingredients (especially helpful for those with special dietary needs!); a sample weekly itinerary with unique city highlights; and a variety of activities, adventures, and events so you can create a truly memorable, personable visit to the City of Lights.

This ebook was written specifically for downloading on to your mobile phone, tablet, iPad, or any portable device so you can easily access this information throughout the city – no need to carry a heavy book!

During your Parisian visit, make time for the iconic monuments of the city and indulge in the spectacular cuisine. But then set aside time for creating the iconic moments that you will never forget.

Caché Paris leaves the faux glow-in-the-dark Eiffel Towers behind and introduces you to the real Parisian souvenirs ("to remember") you are ready to experience!

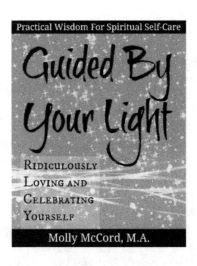

Practical Wisdom For Spiritual Self-Care

Guided By Your Light

RIDICULOUSLY
LOVING AND
CELEBRATING
YOURSELF

Molly McCord, M.A.

Love + Light It Up!
Download the FREE 44-page ebook

Guided By Your Light: Ridiculously Loving and Celebrating Yourself

44-pages of practical wisdom for spiritual self-care, including:

1. It's A Celebration Lifetime!
2. The Journey of Knowing Yourself
3. The Soul Purpose Question
4. Being A High-Vibrational Person
5. Sitting With Your Emotions
6. Return To Sender
7. Accepting Those Who Don't See The Real You
8. Expanding Your Energy Out Into The World
9. Ridiculously Loving Yourself More

Download your copy here at **www.ConsciousSoulGrowth.com**